Christian Values and Economic Life

John C. Bennett

Howard R. Bowen

William Adams Brown, Jr.

G. Bromley Oxnam

Essay Index Reprint Series

BOOKS FOR LIBRARIES PRESS
FREEPORT, NEW YORK

STANDARD BOOK NUMBER:
8369-1559-3

LIBRARY OF CONGRESS CATALOG CARD NUMBER:
71-99624

PRINTED IN THE UNITED STATES OF AMERICA

Contents

Foreword

by Charles P. Taft

Chairman of the Department of the Church and Economic
Life and of its Study Committee

This volume forms part of a larger study of Christian Ethics and Economic Life which was begun in 1949 by the Department of the Church and Economic Life of the Federal Council of the Churches of Christ in America. At the beginning of 1951, the Federal Council was merged with other interdenominational agencies to form the National Council of the Churches of Christ in the United States of America, made up of thirty Protestant and Orthodox church bodies within the United States.

In recent years, religious leaders have recognized that the ethical problems of economic life have become increasingly urgent. The ethics of everyday decisions and practices in economic life, private and public, where we earn our living, are matters also of wide public concern. We need to go behind observed individual acts and group pressures for a deeper understanding of the motives underlying what people do in their economic activities, of how the system fits together, and of how close our preconceived ideas are to reality.

Change is dominant in our national life and perhaps nowhere so much so as in its economic aspects. During the past half-century our ways of life and work have undergone a vast alteration. This change has been accomplished without violence and without great apparent upset, but the tempo of its pace is revolutionary. Certainly if people whose span of life was in the nineteenth century could see what we see in everyday life, they would hardly accept any word but revolution for the process that has brought it about.

This accelerated change demands, for all thoughtful people, an understanding of the effects of this revolution upon ethics and human values. How shall we deal with the dynamism in our economic life so as to preserve and extend the dignity of the individual, respect for the rights of minorities, sensitivity to the public welfare, and free discussion and peaceful persuasion? We cannot rely upon business statistics to measure these intangibles. Judgments of even the best-qualified individuals about actual or impending changes, affected as they are by individual temperament, vested interests, or political partisanship, are equally inadequate if considered separately. The fullest use of all our resources for information and discussion is required for sound progress toward solution of our complex problems.

There is no vital threat to our inherited and cherished values either in the status quo or in change as such. We cannot take ethics into the stratosphere and separate it from practical economic concerns. What is needed is a better understanding both of economic facts and also of those ethical convictions and values which have special significance in the meaning and direction they should give to economic activity.

In many parts of the world we find a fanatic cynicism or a false philosophy in opposition to the foundations upon which Western society is based. What earlier generations took for granted, such as the value and integrity of the individual, the character of government as a tool for service of the people, the capacity of human life for essential decency and justice —these are now challenged with emotional zeal in the name of conflicting assumptions claimed also to be moral.

Here lies the real crisis of the second half of the present century. We must meet this challenge, in so far as it is evil, and clarify in relation to our own institutions the basic ethical affirmations which we support.

The Federal Council of Churches conducted for many

years an educational program on the ethical issues involved in economic life. Many denominational bodies have likewise been active in this field. It has become clear, however, that we need a more careful and realistic investigation of economic life and its relation to spiritual and moral values in a Christian frame of reference. We need to make use of the capacities of social scientists and theologians, in close association with lay persons drawn from many occupations.

Accordingly, as a beginning of such an investigation, a three-year research study was commenced in 1949 under a grant from the Rockefeller Foundation. The Foundation has not sought to exercise any supervisory control over the studies and does not assume responsibility for any of the findings. The results of the study are being presented in six volumes: *Goals of Economic Life*, *The Organizational Revolution*, *Social Responsibilities of the Businessman*, *American Income and Its Use*, *The American Economy—Attitudes and Opinions*, and *Christian Values and Economic Life*. Through a further grant from the same source a second series of studies is now in preparation. These volumes will begin to appear sometime in 1956.

Sincere gratitude is due to the several authors for their devotion and creativity in the writing of these volumes. In all the volumes of this series, the authors have been free to write as they wished and to accept or reject suggestions or criticisms. In the final analysis, each book is the responsibility of the authors.

Others have made valuable contributions to the total study effort of which this volume is an important part. The Reverend Cameron P. Hall, Executive Director of the Department, has given the project his unfailing and effective administrative support. Professor Howard R. Bowen, former Economic Consultant to the Study, made an invaluable contribution in the formulation of the project and aided also in criticism of the

manuscripts. The Reverend A. Dudley Ward served as Director of Studies from the beginning until the fall of 1953. He
carried out with imagination and efficiency his responsibilities
as organizer and coordinator, and gave help also after he had
left for other important work.

A Study Committee of the Department, including both lay
and clerical members and representing a variety of occupations, has reviewed the program of the study at various stages.
Mr. Charles H. Seaver, Editorial Consultant and Secretary
of the Study Committee, has carefully edited the manuscripts
and has been available consistently for counsel.

The National Council of Churches has taken no official
position and assumed no responsibility regarding the content
of any of the volumes. In no sense, therefore, can or should
any statement in this series be regarded as an official declaration of the National Council of Churches or of any of its units.

Preface

by JOHN C. BENNETT

It is the hope of those responsible for this study as a whole that it may provide the most useful materials now available for the formation of a Protestant economic ethic that is relevant to our situation. Roman Catholicism has long had a highly developed economic ethic; from the Protestant standpoint it has erred on the side of offering too many assured answers to ethical questions which cannot be disposed of so conclusively. But within Protestantism we have had little corporate ethical guidance on economic issues, and what we have has been insufficiently related to the wisdom of those who have specialized knowledge of the field. Moreover, Protestantism has been confused because of its own internal conflict between the adherents of a one-sided collectivism on the one hand and a one-sided individualism on the other. This whole study, if it does nothing else, should help to show a way beyond that conflict.

This volume is intended to carry the results of discussion and investigation in the previous five volumes of the series to the point where they can be more readily appropriated by the constituency of the churches that have sponsored the project. It is no substitute for any of the other volumes, but it does attempt to begin to answer the question: What does this study as a whole mean for Christians and churches in the United States? No one can give a full answer who has not taken seriously the material in the other volumes, but the following chapters have been written to be read independently.

It is important to absolve the authors of the other volumes from any responsibility for the judgments expressed in these chapters. Much collaboration between authors lies behind

the study. This collaboration has been most fruitful as it has brought together the representatives of the social sciences, especially economics, and students of theology and Christian ethics. Yet no author has been censored by the others or been prevented by any editorial committee from being true to his own convictions.

It has often been said that the process of collaboration in this study, the interchange of ideas between members of different professions, is as important as the results. That is true; but I think that the results themselves should be seen as a helpful factor in a continuing process both among specialists in the fields represented and within the thinking of the churches. It is hoped that this volume may go far to stimulate the next stage of that process beyond the limited world of the specialists to the wider field of laymen and ministers in the American churches.

Bishop Oxnam, in the first section of this volume, provides what is perhaps not conspicuous enough in the series as a whole: a sense of the Christian moral *imperative* for economic life. He introduces the discussion by emphasizing the social implications of Biblical teachings and by linking our efforts to develop an economic ethic for our time with the creative moments in Christian history in which the same thing has been attempted. He stresses the work of the last two generations which is in a special way the background of this study. Such Christian leaders as Walter Rauschenbusch and the thought and action of many Christian groups and agencies of the Church in the recent past are a part of our heritage. The problems of our time assume a somewhat new form, and we cannot take over unaltered the solutions offered even in this recent past. But there was a powerful and authentically Christian impulse in the Christian social movements of the first half of this century which should not be lost. In the complexity of our problems we are in danger of losing the

sense of urgency that was present in the earlier period, and it is this which Bishop Oxnam brings to us with great force.

Professor Howard Bowen has done something in the second section which is both impossible and necessary! He has summarized the content of the other volumes. (The fifth volume, which has not been published as this volume goes to press, was available in manuscript for Professor Bowen's use.) Professor Bowen has been "economic consultant" for the whole study and has participated in the planning of each of the books he summarizes. In addition he wrote one of the books himself.[1] This summary thus comes from within the project as a whole.

Dr. William Adams Brown, Jr., who has devoted a large part of his professional life as an economist to the problems of foreign trade and the economic side of international relations, has shown the implications for American foreign economic policy of some of the principles which have been developed at many points in the study. He has also, so far as this study is concerned, broken new ground. Though this is touched on in *American Income and Its Use*, nowhere else in the previous volumes has there been any systematic discussion of the ethical problems which America faces as a rich nation in a world that is for the most part economically poor. It is difficult for any nation to be willing to seek economic justice on a world scale at substantial sacrifice to itself, but even if there were no such moral problem, this international dimension of economic ethics would still be baffling.

The final section includes a chapter on economic ethics by Professor Bowen and my own chapters on Christian economic ethics. I am not aware of any important disagreement between Professor Bowen and myself, but he has dealt with

[1] This book, *Social Responsibilities of the Businessman*, has a special significance in relation to the total series. It is the first of a number of books that have been planned as a part of the second series dealing with the social responsibilities of various vocational groups.

the subject as a professional economist and I have tried to present the outlines of a Protestant economic ethic. Why is it necessary to have separate discussions of economic ethics, one by a professional economist and the other by a teacher of Christian theology and ethics? The necessity would be perhaps more obvious if the economist had an ethical view which was itself in sharp contrast with Christian ethics. As it is, I think that Professor Bowen and I start at different points but that we soon meet so far as the ethical norms for economic life are concerned. He starts with the economic realities themselves, and I start with the historic Christian teaching about ethical responsibility.

Christianity does bring to the study of economic life a religious perspective, a sensitive concern for the human consequences of all economic behavior, a spirit of dedication and self-criticism. These may be present in competent discussions of the ethical aspects of economic life by economists who are Christians or who have a similar spirit, but they are likely to be more explicit if Christian ethics is the starting point. Christian ethics involves more searching questions than one usually finds in the discussion of economic problems: questions about the purpose of economic activity, about the effect of our conduct upon *all* of our neighbors, about the distortion of our own judgments and the judgments of the social groups to which we belong by economic interest, about the influence of economic institutions upon the culture as a whole. Yet Christian ethics should prepare Christians to live in the real world which the economist describes. The economist often provides a corrective for misguided idealism because he has learned to watch for the probable effects of economic policies on efficiency and productivity. Also many economists have developed a special sensitivity to the effect of institutional changes upon freedom and flexibility in society.

The Christian should not assume that, as a Christian, he

has any short cut to the solution of economic problems. Instead he should be driven by his faith to work with economists to find the best solutions available. And he should have in view the effects of those solutions that are most likely to be seen by economists as well as those effects that he is best prepared to judge by his understanding of Christian thought. It is with this purpose and in this spirit that economists and theologians in this series address themselves to the same problems.

PART I

The Christian Challenge

G. Bromley Oxnam

1

A Changing Order

"Let the buyer beware" and "To the victor belong the spoils" are slogans that have lost caste. The two-fisted individualist who declared, "The public be damned," is repudiated by the typical representative of contemporary business enterprise and the present-day leader of organized labor. Like the saber-toothed tiger that disappeared in the asphaltum pits at La Brea, the individualist ruled by the law of the jungle is passing from the American scene. Occasionally, to be sure, a "robber baron" emerges and for a brief time pursues his predatory way. But contemporary society looks on a man who seeks to corner the wheat market as a gangster, not a genius; the community is more and more questioning the propriety and the patriotism of pressure groups that seek special privilege from government.

The ruthless men of yesterday who refused to admit the relevance of God to the economic process have been largely succeeded by men of conscience, who regard themselves as responsible leaders of enterprise, subject to moral principle, and required to think in terms of the common good. This does not mean that the battle has been won; but it does mean that the prospects of victory are bright.

This amazing change has been wrought by numerous factors, among them—and perhaps first among them—the preaching of the ethical ideals of religion as proclaimed by the Hebrew prophets and by Jesus. The social principles enunciated by the prophets and manifest in the person and teaching of Jesus were preached with courage by men who believed that God's

3

will must be done on earth. The proclamation of this faith was accompanied by the insistence that competent laymen are charged by the Eternal to discover the concrete means by which the ideals of religion may be translated into the practices of the common life.

SOCIAL IDEALS OF THE CHURCHES

It was on December 4, 1908, that the Federal Council of the Churches of Christ in America adopted "The Social Creed of the Churches." This creed had been formulated a few months earlier by the Committee on the State of the Church, and adopted by the General Conference of the Methodist Episcopal Church meeting at Baltimore. It proclaimed, first, that the churches "must stand for equal rights and complete justice for all men in all stations of life," and further affirmed that the churches must stand "for the most equitable division of the product of industry that can ultimately be devised."

The Social Creed of the Churches was an expression in concrete terms of the principles that had been enunciated by such prophetic preachers and teachers as Josiah Strong, Shailer Matthews, Washington Gladden, and, particularly, Walter Rauschenbusch, whose volume *Christianity and the Social Crisis* published the year before had profoundly influenced the thinking of American churchmen.

Rauschenbusch pointed out that "men are seizing on Jesus as the exponent of their own social convictions. They all claim Him." Rauschenbusch refused to identify Jesus with a particular social reform. He said:

... Jesus was not a social reformer of the modern type. Sociology and political economy were just as far outside of his range of thought as organic chemistry or the geography of America. He saw the evil in the life of men and their sufferings, but he ap-

proached these facts purely from the moral, and not from the economic or historical point of view. He wanted men to live a right life in common, and only in so far as the social questions are moral questions did he deal with them as they confronted him.

And he was more than a teacher of morality. Jesus had learned the greatest and deepest and rarest secret of all—how to live a religious life. When the question of economic wants is solved for the individual and all his outward adjustments are as comfortable as possible, he may still be haunted by the horrible emptiness of his life and feel that existence is a meaningless riddle and delusion. If the question of the distribution of wealth were solved for all society and all lived in average comfort and without urgent anxiety, the question would still be how many would be at peace with their own souls and have that enduring joy and contentment which alone can make the outward things fair and sweet and rise victorious over change. Universal prosperity would not be incompatible with universal *ennui* and *Weltschmerz*. Beyond the question of economic distribution lies the question of moral relations; and beyond the moral relations to men lies the question of the religious communion with that spiritual reality in which we live and move and have our deepest being—with God, the Father of our spirits. Jesus had realized the life of God in the soul of man and the life of man in the love of God. That was the real secret of his life, the wellspring of his purity, his compassion, his unwearied courage, his unquenchable idealism: he knew the Father.

But if he had that greatest of all possessions, the real key to the secret of life, it was his highest social duty to share it and help others to gain what he had. He had to teach men to live as children in the presence of their Father, and no longer as slaves cringing before a despot. He had to show them that the ordinary life of selfishness and hate and anxiety and chafing ambition and covetousness is no life at all, and that they must enter into a new world of love and solidarity and inward contentment. . . .

No comprehension of Jesus is even approximately true which fails to understand that the heart of his heart was religion. No man is a follower of Jesus in the full sense who has not through

him entered into the same life with God. . . . Whoever uncouples the religious and the social life has not understood Jesus.[1]

There were some who saw in the Social Creed a departure from the "simple Gospel"; who did not realize that the propositions of the Social Creed were but the specific expression of principles that lie at the heart of the Christian faith. How can we love our neighbor without considering the questions of poverty, of child labor, "the physical and moral health of the community," and "that degree of leisure for all which is a condition of the highest human life"? How can we share one another's burdens without thinking of "suitable provision for the old age of the workers and for those incapacitated by injury," and "for the protection of the worker from dangerous machinery, occupational disease, injuries, and mortality"? Is it possible to remember the Sabbath day and keep it holy without considering "a release from employment one day in seven"?

The Social Creed was amended in 1912 to include the statement that the churches stood "for the right of employees and employers alike to organize," and subsequently was revised to include "for collective bargaining." Other amendments included the statement that the churches stood "for a new emphasis on the application of Christian principles to the acquisition and use of property."

The so-called "Social Gospel"—a most unfortunate term, since its advocates, like Walter Rauschenbusch, were in no sense abandoning the individual Gospel, but were insisting that a partial Gospel should become a whole Gospel and that the religion of Jesus should become regnant in all the activities of men—became at once a tocsin and a clarion summons.

[1] Walter Rauschenbusch, *Christianity and the Social Crisis*, New York, The Macmillan Company, 1907, pp. 47–8.

A careful scholar, F. Ernest Johnson, in *The Church and Society* declared:

At every point the church is confronted by the issue of method in promoting social change. . . . Devotion to "principles" without regard to specific situations and predictable results is not rugged morality, but obscurantism. In the existing economic situation a struggle is *always going on* between privilege and need, and violence is deeply embedded in the economic structure. There is a pitiable unreality in the average person's attitude toward conflict between social groups. He habitually begins his scrutiny at the point where an outbreak occurs. The deep and silent causes of conflict which lie in unjust social arrangements that make the mass of men dependent upon a few, to their own material and cultural disadvantage—these causes commonly go unrecognized. We have heard much of nonviolent resistance as an ethical method, but there is an evil form of overtly nonviolent resistance by entrenched privilege which can afford to forego aggression. It has no need of violence because it possesses the resources to prevent the working classes by deadly, quiet resistance, from attaining a more abundant life. In the face of such resistance the church cannot justly turn away from a rebellious class or group simply because in desperation it resorts to force. A Christian judgment upon violence must begin with the spiritual violence that begets physical battle. Christianity is deeply and invariably committed to the sense of active good will, but to enjoin its use upon men whom elemental need has forced into unequal struggle, while taking no steps to remove the injustice which has incited them to revolt, is to uphold the hand of the exploiter. The church has sinned abundantly against a considerable part of its own membership in this regard.[2]

It is quite true that the Social Creed was not, at the time of its formulation and proclamation, an expression truly representative of the views of the great body of church members. Dr.

[2] F. Ernest Johnson, *The Church and Society*, New York, The Abingdon Press, 1935, pp. 221–f.

Johnson pointed out that "as an embodiment of rank-and-file conviction" the Creed had "no more validity than the pledges of businessmen to observe the Golden Rule within the existing economic order."[3] It did, rather, express the ethical spirit of the Hebrew prophets and the moral ideals of Jesus.

The leaders of the social movement were early alerted to the danger of relying on mechanics and of assuming that changed externals necessarily meant changes in the character of the individual. The exponents of the Social Gospel were well aware of the necessity for individual redemption; they were evangelists who called for an evangelism that would transform society itself. The opponents of the Social Gospel held fast to a partial Gospel, and failed to see that both individual and social redemption were necessary, if the kingdom of our blessed Lord were to come on the earth.

OUT OF WAR TOWARD PEACE

One of the most striking expressions of the Social Gospel was the publication of the report on the steel strike in 1919, prepared by the Commission on Inquiry of the Inter-Church World Movement. Its chairman was Bishop Francis J. McConnell, and its vice chairman Dr. Daniel A. Poling. These leaders believed that ethical principles must be tested out in concrete situations. The Steel Strike Report dealt with "causative facts—with abiding conditions in the steel industry —and only secondarily with conflicts of policies and their influence on national institutions and modes of thought." It recorded the facts that 69,000 men were working a 12-hour day, according to the testimony of Judge Elbert H. Gary, Chairman of the Finance Committee of the United States Steel Corporation, before a Senate investigating committee; that 70,000 was the number receiving the common labor or

[3] *Ibid.*, p. 217.

lowest rate of pay. The Report states: "This means approximately 350,000 men, women, and children are directly affected by the longest hours or the smallest pay in that part of the industry owned by the United States Steel Corporation, which fixes pay and hours without conference with the labor force. Since the Corporation controls about half the industry, it is therefore a reasonably conservative estimate that the working conditions of three-quarters of a million of the nation's population have their lives determined arbitrarily by the twelve-hour day or the lowest pay in the steel industry."[4]

The Steel Strike Report recommended the adoption of the eight-hour shift on all continuous processes, the limiting of the day to not more than ten hours on duty, with not more than a six-day and a fifty-four-hour week, with at least a minimum comfort wage. It recommended the recognition of the right to join regular craft unions; and further that organized labor exercise democracy and self-control, especially in regard to the calling, conduct, and settlement of strikes. Other recommendations were that the unions be reorganized to share in the responsibility for production and in the control of production processes; scrupulously avoid all advocates of violence; accept all possible proffers of publicity and conciliation; promote Americanization in all possible ways, and insist on an American standard of living for all workingmen; and prepare more adequate technical information for the public in regard to all conditions that bear on the calling and conduct of a strike.[5]

The Report further recommended to the press "that it free itself of the all too well founded charge of bias, favoring capital as against labor, and redeem its power as a promoter of truth and a formulator of public opinion by searching out

[4] New York, Harcourt, Brace, and Howe, Inc., 1920, p. 5.
[5] Ibid., pp. 248–f.

all the facts in regard to industrial questions and publishing them without fear or favor."

The Report pleaded with the pulpit that it "be diligent to discharge its legitimate prophetic role as an advocate of justice, righteousness, and humanity in all such conflicts of human interest as those involved in industrial strife." It condemned unsparingly "those authorities who suspended the right of free speech and peaceful assemblage before, during, and after the steel strike."[6]

The reaction to the Steel Strike Report ran the gamut of vicious charges of Bolshevism among the clergy to an extensive *Analysis of the Inter-Church World Movement's Report on the Steel Strike* by Marshall Olds. As Mr. Olds questioned some factual statements in the Commission's report, so members of the Commission questioned factual statements in the Olds report. But who would justify the twelve-hour day in steel today? Who will deny that the Commission on Inquiry proceeded in both an American and a Christian spirit, and dealt with issues that are properly the concern of religion?

It is unfortunately true that the leadership of American business during that period gave itself too exclusively to problems of production; it did not direct its genius to the solution of social problems. One social problem involved in the twelve-hour day, for instance, was its effect on family life, more than its physical effect on the workers. The genius that proved to be so conspicuously successful in mastering the problems of production would no doubt have been equally successful if it had resolved to give life to the ethical ideals of Jesus, after first kneeling at an altar to pray, "Thy will be done."

Mr. Benjamin F. Fairless, chairman of the Board of the United States Steel Corporation, writes under the heading "Christian Vocation in Steel" in *The Christian Century* of

[6] *Ibid.*, p. 250.

November 11, 1953: "The important thing is that the corporation, by its policies and its conduct of the business, should offer the individual an opportunity for Christian service in the workaday world. In evaluating any industry from this standpoint, it seems to me that there are several basic questions which must be answered. First: Is there regard for the individual?" He also asks, "Does the organization render a service?" These are vital questions. They were raised by the church long ago, because they were central in the concern of Jesus; and it was the raising of these questions by the church that, in large measure, developed the conscience that is manifest in industrial leadership today.

It was but yesterday that a large sector of industry was organized on a civil war basis in its relations with labor. The attempt of labor to organize was met by a determined effort on the part of owners and management to estop organization. They used methods of violence as well as the equally effective weapons of the law, which was more tolerant of violence on the part of management than on the part of strikers. Employers used propaganda, black list, "yellow-dog contract," company housing, company store, espionage, and the *agent provocateur*; and cleverly bought up labor leaders by offering them better jobs and flattering pay. For many years management maintained its advantage in the areas of conflict.

At the turn of the century, when the nation was deeply disturbed by the anthracite coal strike, the National Association of Manufacturers became a leader in an antiunion offensive. A carefully organized campaign of propaganda followed, in which speakers were subsidized, publicity bureaus set up, and vast quantities of literature issued, with the general intent of discrediting labor organizations and of creating a public judgment that they were dangerous and a menace to the republic. Other associations of employers were organized

to oppose unionism, or to deal collectively with national unions, in their various industries.

During these years, under cover or in open outbreaks, there was a sort of civil war in various industries. The violence of management included the kidnaping, beating, and even murdering of union leaders. Vigilante groups were established, and economic pressures of many kinds were used. Labor fought back; and violence of every form is in the record. Racketeers took over some labor organizations, and carried on criminal enterprise, relying on force and fear, intimidation and violence, to compel legitimate enterprises to surrender their rights of property and to submit to gangsters. It is a sordid story; but happily is largely a matter of the past.

The point is that the fighting leader was often a man of force. Management met uncompromising and unreasonable men; at times it had to deal with incompetent men whose ignorance was equaled by their lack of integrity. History warns us that generals are seldom the best arbiters of conflicts in which they have been engaged; so labor leaders trained to lead in battle may not always make good negotiators or wise administrators. When the two-fisted employer squared off against the two-fisted labor leader, the public watched the fight—and paid the bill.

When the industrial life is based on conflict, the unifying force in each contending party is the presence of an enemy. Unfortunately an enemy seldom makes a permanent contribution to unity. When a war is won or lost or the particular industrial disturbance comes to an end, the enemy may disappear, as an enemy; and this unifying force therefore ceases to be. Labor then needed the unifying power of an ideal. Fortunately that unifying power is present today in much of American labor organization. Collective bargaining has introduced the conference table. Leaders pledged to moral ideals, as well as to the proper protection of the interests they repre-

sent, confer as intelligent men, instead of making or threatening war. Basically, the objectives in such conferences are not only the factors that make for industrial peace, for which Mr. Fairless properly pleads, but also the practices that mean industrial justice, for which religion contends. Commonly accepted standards are necessary to harmonious negotiation. Thus we make progress.

2

Forward Steps

THE DETROIT CONFERENCE

Historically, we have witnessed a fundamental change in half a century. Today, in the words of the statement adopted by the 1950 National Study Conference on the Church and Economic Life, drafted by leaders of religion, business, labor, and education, and adopted by that great conference, we hold: "The Gospel is concerned with all the activities of man, individual and social. The Church, as the custodian of 'the sacred and imperishable message of eternal salvation,' is charged with a fourfold duty, as Christians in fellowship confront the economic life. It must be the teacher of the principles of conduct; a voice of judgment; a guardian of moral and spiritual values already won; and the herald of a better day."

It was the writer's privilege to draft the statement adopted by that Conference. The following paragraphs are taken from it:

Christians judge all economic systems by the imperatives of the Christian faith; Christians must not identify any economic order with the Gospel. The Christian Gospel is not to be found in Adam Smith's *Wealth of Nations* nor in Karl Marx's *Kapital*. It is to be found in Matthew, Mark, Luke, and John, and in the Acts of the Apostles, the Epistles of the New Testament, and the vision of St. John in the Revelation. It is to be found in the preaching of the Hebrew prophets, in the lives of saints and martyrs, in the service of the faithful followers of Christ, and in the continuing revelation of God. That faith affirms the supreme worth of persons.

14

Institutions must be tested finally by their contribution to the enrichment of personality.

It is imperative that Christians confronting economic issues first accept Jesus Christ as Lord. He is our Savior. Evangelism is the primary task of the Church, and of first importance is the personal experience of the love of God and of its transforming power in human life. Salvation means not only forgiveness of past sins but a new relationship with God which brings assurance of final victory over everything that comes between man and God.

Christians must demonstrate that God rules, and that men of differing views can be one in the determination to discover His will. Strong men charged with the direction of industry and strong men charged with leadership in labor and agriculture are obligated to bring dedicated minds to difficult problems, and in the mutual sharing of rich experience to reach conclusions designed to create a more brotherly world. In such meetings, whether at national or local level, the technician and the prophet may be heard, and the views of men who carry responsibility considered. Technical competency also is necessary to translate the ethical ideal into the practice of the common life.

The spirit in which Christians approach the complex and baffling problems of contemporary society is of primary importance. Christians who meet to consider the economic life will do well to kneel in devotion before they rise for discussion. Men who bow in repentant spirit at the Table of the Lord make themselves ready to confer with brothers in the Spirit of the Lord. The Communion Table should precede the conference table, because conference with our fellows will be more productive when preceded by communion with our Christ. . . .

Basically, the approach of the churches to the economic order is determined by the Christian conception of the worth of man. Christians believe that man is created by the Eternal and in His image, that every individual is a child of God, a member of one family, a brother. Christians hold that man is a being of infinite worth, of such worth indeed that God out of love sent His Son

that man by faith in Him might be saved. Man is a self-conscious personality, free to choose right and wrong, responsible, immortal. . . .

Christians hold that God's will has been revealed by His Son, and that the Church is summoned to teach the nations whatsoever things Christ commanded us. Economic practices therefore must be judged by ethical criteria. Whenever or wherever practices violate these principles, the Church must voice judgment and call men to the Christian way. The Church must keep before man the vision of the just and brotherly society as revealed in the Christian concept of the Kingdom of God, which we believe to be God's will for society. It is the faith of Christians that Jesus Christ is the Way, the Truth, and the Life. The advances achieved by the processes of reform and regeneration must be continued until at last economic practices are brought into accord with that Way, become expressions of that Truth, and are in keeping with that Life.

The principles Jesus taught are the revelation of God's will. We believe that the Word became flesh and dwelt among us, that God was in Christ, and that in the truth revealed by Him is to be found salvation for man and for society. Thus the Christian does not approach the economic order bound by the dogmatism of communist, socialist, or capitalist. He comes loyal to Christ, . . . resolved to make His way regnant in the economic life. His question, therefore, is not: is it Communist? is it Socialist? is it capitalist? but, is it Christian?

Christians acquainted with the centuries know that the struggle to emancipate the worker is part of the age-long resolve to lift man to the status of brother. Once the work of the world was done by slaves, but a brother in chains was a contradiction in terms. Slavery had to go. Serfdom was likewise brought under the judgment of God. Feudalism with its aristocracy and privilege gave way. The voice of democracy stirred the people to action with its insistence upon the rights of man, its denial of the divine right of kings, and its call for liberty, equality, and fraternity. Into the

midst of this revolutionary surge came the industrial revolution. Handicraft industry was superseded by the factory system. The worker had ceased to be slave or serf. He had become a free man, free to sell his own labor where he himself determined. A mistaken conception was prevalent, that the unrestricted play of self-interest would in the long run mean social well-being. Laborers in factory and on farm, subjected to exploitation, sought to protect their interests by organizing labor unions. These were at first regarded as conspiracies and ruthlessly suppressed. In the course of the years, the right to organize was won, the worker became more powerful; and the democratic principle was introduced into the work life. Meanwhile, ever-widening research, the development of technology, the genius of management, the skill of labor, and a growing sense of social responsibility resulted in amazing advances.

But man is still exploited by his brother. Vast inequalities in wealth and therefore in status, fundamental differences in scales of value, and wide disparities in the possession of power create and maintain class consciousness. Class is a concept too small to unite men for social emancipation. Upon the basis of class, all that can be done is to make one class ready to fight another class. Man needs a larger unifying concept. It is found in the Christian ideal of brotherhood under the Fatherhood of God, and the Christian teaching of the solidarity of the human family.

Time is of the essence. Principles that mean both unity and justice must be applied soon enough to turn man from the battle-field of class conflict to the cooperative avenues of peaceful progress. The fratricidal struggle of class war upon a world scale must be avoided.

The Christian knows that the Kingdom of God cannot be built upon foundations of economic injustice. He refuses to acquiesce in those inequalities that deny equal opportunity. Equality of consideration does not necessarily mean identity of treatment. The American lives in one of the freest lands upon the earth. His pursuit of happiness under the conditions of liberty has enriched life. Significant advances have been made in equalizing opportun-

ity, and further advances are possible and imperative, but when all such socially controllable inequalities have been removed, there will remain sources of conflict that root in the sinfulness and greed of the human heart. The primary task of the Christian therefore continues to be one of evangelism in which the individual accepts Jesus Christ as Lord and Savior, becomes a new man in Christ Jesus, and moves out in co-operation with his fellow Christians to build an economic life more in accord with the will of God as revealed in Christ. The Gospel is not an opiate; it is, when applied, a regenerating force capable of transforming economic relations into a fellowship and the individual into a brother. . . .

Christians must discover a way in which we can reconcile the necessities of technology and the necessities of brotherhood. . . .

The hunger of any man anywhere becomes the concern of Christian men everywhere. . . .

If man is exploited by man, that becomes an issue of graver import to the theistic Christian than to the atheistic Communist. . . .

There is an obligation to inform the people concerning the facts of economic life. . . .

There must be careful study of the results of the control of natural resources by a few, of the ethical standards practiced in some areas of economic life, of the controls exercised by concentrations of economic power over political institutions. . . .

. . . The Church must attack the atheism of orthodox communism, in which faith in God is called superstition, and also such practical atheism as is present in contemporary capitalism, in which God's will is regarded as irrelevant to the economic process, whenever or wherever it appears in the professions, in labor leadership, in farm organizations, in industrial ownership and management. . . .

The Christian must face up to the issues that are involved both in free enterprise and in adequate planning for the common good.

There is a planning that does mean serfdom. There is a planning that does contribute to freedom. The freedom that enables private enterprise itself to plan must be preserved; but the freedom must be maintained that is essential to democratic decisions in which the people, through their government, plan, for example, for public education and health, conservation of natural resources, fiscal and foreign policy, national defense, cooperation in international bodies, as well as control of monopolies and restraint of antisocial individuals and groups. . . .

. . . Out of the fellowship of the Church should come such understanding that men, standing in the shadow of the Cross, will resolve that, in the name of Christ and with the blessing of the Eternal, they will work together to the end that our economic life shall be more worthy of the name Christian.[1]

WHAT KIND OF CHRISTIAN COOPERATION?

The emphasis on the Social Gospel led naturally to the advocacy of cooperative measures designed to protect the community from predatory individualism or corporate irresponsibility, and also to express the Christian spirit in group action. There were those who reached the conclusion that Socialist measures were better designed to carry Christian principles into action than measures that assumed competitive struggle and the so-called "free market." There were others who saw in the cooperative movement opportunities for Christian living that they did not find in hard competition. Still others regarded the profit motive as essentially evil; and in some communions resolutions were passed that castigated the so-called profit motive. There were others who were fearful that with increasing political control of the economic life freedom might be limited, creativity stifled, and the pos-

[1] *The Responsibility of Christians in an Interdependent Economic World,* Department of the Church and Economic Life, The Federal Council of the Churches of Christ in America, New York, pp. 1–9.

sibility of lifting the standard of living reduced; since without the incentives that lie in the profit-making economy it was felt production would not continue to increase. There were attempts to define the term "Christian society," and such basic institutions as property were brought under careful scrutiny. But the fundamental attack was made on self-interest. It was held that neither greed nor fear is a Christian motive, and that as long as self-interest remains the controlling motive in the economic sphere, a brotherly society that will really cohere is impossible.

In the highly significant report of the Committee on the War and Religious Outlook,[2] entitled *The Church and Industrial Reconstruction*, published in 1920, in an attempt to define the society that would emerge if the Christian ideals were realized in fact today, it was declared:

It would be a cooperative social order in which the sacredness of every life was recognized and everyone found opportunity for the fullest self-expression of which he was capable; in which each individual gave himself gladly and wholeheartedly for ends that are socially valuable; in which the impulses to service and to creative action would be stronger than the acquisitive impulses, and all work be seen in terms of its spiritual significance as making possible fullness of life for all men; in which differences of talent and capacity meant proportional responsibilities and ministry to the common good; in which all lesser differences of race, of nation, and of class served to minister to the richness of an all-inclusive brotherhood; in which there hovered over all a sense of the reality of the Christlike God, so that worship inspired service, as service expressed brotherhood.[3]

To those who insisted this was Utopian, the Committee replied: "The Christian answer to the accusation is definite and unmistakable. This ideal can be realized." Of course

---

[2] Indirectly constituted by the Federal Council of Churches.
[3] *The Church and Industrial Reconstruction*, The Committee on the War and the Religious Outlook, New York, Association Press, 1920, pp. 31–f.

perfect realization is Utopian; but does progress toward this ideal involve increasing coercion on the part of the state? Is the planning—that is, the social planning that was envisioned by many who held these views—likely to lead us to serfdom? Neither Mussolini nor Hitler had at that time come to power. The Communists were in control in Russia, but were passing through a revolutionary period, and it was not quite clear whether or not they had abandoned t..e Communist doctrine that the state would wither. It now has become clear that the totalitarian concepts, left or right, do mean the abolition of freedom.

Many, therefore, draw the conclusion that any cooperative or collective endeavor on the part of the people is in effect a movement toward the end of their freedom. Church leadership has refused to accept such extreme views. It is well aware of the fact that there are those who seek to label sound reform as subversive, for no other reason than to discredit the reform proposal and maintain the *status quo.*

Churchmen have sought to make society impregnable to the attacks of the dynamic ideology that derives from Karl Marx; this means that measures calculated to establish justice and extend brotherhood must be conceived and espoused. Churchmen have rejected the sinister attempts made by some reactionaries to condemn service by public corporations and through public endeavors as "creeping Socialism." They recognize that there are services that can be better rendered by the people through their governments than by private enterprise.

THE CHRISTIAN APPROACH

The Christian approaches all these proposals in terms of the common welfare and the long-time effect on personality. Americans possess the best highway system in the world; it

is collectively owned, but most Americans refuse to call it Socialism; they insist that it is American, and that it is good. Similarly, they look on the public school system as the chief bulwark of democracy; they wisely provided for private schools, but have held public funds for the support of public education. Those who would destroy the public school system of today, either by falsely calling it godless or by libelously designating it as Socialist, play into the hands of the Communist. The public school system has reared generation after generation of American youth who believe in the free way of life, who possess the free mind, and who seek the truth that frees. Americans refuse to call this system Socialist, even though it is collectively owned and in large measure democratically managed. Americans say it is American, and it is good. It is Americanism in action.

Most churchmen are of the opinion that the public health service, the lighthouses along our shores, the Coast Guard, the Bureau of Standards, the Reclamation Service, the Departments of Agriculture and of Commerce, the whole National Parks system are American, and they are good. Technically they may be termed collective endeavors; but who would turn the national parks wholly over to private corporations to be run for profit? There are public collective endeavors that are a part of the American way, and they run the gamut from the Patent Office to the Hoover Dam. They are American, and they are good.

It has been found necessary to regulate certain group activities that are clothed with public interest. Thus came the Interstate Commerce Commission, the Securities and Exchange Commission, the regulatory bodies that deal with public power, with radio and television, with aeronautics, and, of course, with traffic. The power to regulate must be scrutinized with the utmost care; eternal vigilance is necessary here as well as in preserving liberty. But to condemn all such regula-

tion in the name of maintaining freedom is a contradiction in terms; regulation is a part of the American system. It is American, and it is good.

There are great endeavors in which the community uses the public corporation, as in the Tennessee Valley Authority and the Port Authority of New York. The American people have revealed an experimental mind, and have used these answers to certain problems because they have refused to be bound by economic dogma. They prefer to apply an ethical principle, and to use the means most likely to promote the common good and to enrich personality; thus they would serve a practical end with regard for justice under the conditions of freedom.

Churchmen generally share the opinion that the experience of the American people has led them to the conclusion that in the overwhelming majority of enterprises, those that we refer to as private or free or individual enterprises will, in the long run, issue in greater productivity, make greater contribution to creativity, call forth initiative with greater dispatch, and make a greater contribution to the maintenance of freedom than any other system that man at present knows. There are of course enterprises that are inevitably monopolies, and so must be either closely regulated by government or publicly operated.

Churchmen have insisted that we come to these issues in terms of religious principle, not in terms of economic dogmatism.

Trotsky's dictum to the effect that the conflict between capitalism and communism will be determined by the relative coefficients of production is rejected by churchmen. Trotsky thought that the system that will produce goods most cheaply will survive. It is true that man must have bread to live at all; but it is also true that he does not live by bread alone. His primary need, beyond the means of subsistence, is less com-

modity than community. The system that will develop community and brotherhood and contribute most to abundant living is the system that will be victorious among competing social philosophies.

A HALF-CENTURY OF CHANGE

Extraordinary changes have occurred within the last half-century. *Laissez-faire* capitalism, in practice (if it ever was practiced), has ceased to be. The theory that labor was a commodity to be bought in the open market, at a price governed wholly by the law of supply and demand, has been rejected; labor now has status in law. The assumption that labor is merely a commodity was of course rejected by religion; and the organization of labor has for all practical purposes ended that theory. Fundamental restrictions have been placed by the community on the use of property; the right of an individual to do what he pleases, even with his own home, is no longer a fact. He may not build a hundred-story building in a community that has determined the height of the skyline. He may not contaminate the streams that flow through his property. He may not cut down a watershed without making proper provision for reforestation. Competition itself has been brought under law; there are laws against, as well as favoring, the restraint of trade. In a word, the assumption that the unrestricted play of self-interest will in the long run work out for the social good has proved to be false.

There has been a fundamental curbing of the capitalism of yesterday; but—what is more important—a new spirit has come to the capitalist himself. This means that the term used to describe the business practices of yesterday cannot be used to describe the business practices of today. It is unfortunate that in using the term "capitalism" one man has in mind the exploitation of the early capitalist period, and another man

has in mind the service motive as well as the profit motive present in the thinking of responsible leaders of enterprise today. The relation of labor to capital has changed. Labor possesses power, philosophy, and strong leadership; the community has limited the rights of private property, and is insisting today on limiting some of the powers of labor. Power can and does corrupt; it will corrupt a labor organization as well as a business organization, a church as well as a state. The democratization of business practice and of labor organization has made remarkable advance; and the community itself has insisted, for its own protection, on certain controls over both labor and management.

Changes have occurred in the thinking of churchmen relative to the profit motive. There were those who condemned it as utterly immoral. But the question of the profit motive is less regarded today as a question of morality than as a question of priority. The late Archbishop of Canterbury, William Temple, once wrote: "The profit motive is not simply evil; it can have its own right place. But that is not the first place, and the harm in the predominance of the profit motive is not merely that it is an expression of selfishness, whether the form it takes is concerned with dividends or wages, but that to put this first may lead to an ordering of economic life which in fact is damaging to the general interest."[4]

It is this point that is missed by many well-meaning industrialists, who, though they believe sincerely in the free-enterprise system, fail to realize that all enterprise is subject to the judgment of the Gospel. The Gospel is not to be judged by economic practices.

Mr. Clifford F. Hood, President of the United States Steel Corporation, addressing the students and faculty of the Western Theological Seminary in Pittsburgh on September 30,

[4] William Temple, "The Church and the Social Crisis," *The Christian Century*, October 7, 1942, p. 1210.

1953, saw clearly the danger that lies in "statism." He said "religion and mundane industrial enterprise stand in common opposition to deification of the state." He sees in the continuing control of atomic energy by the state a basic threat to freedom. (David E. Lilienthal saw the same threat.) Mr. Hood maintains that "our free economic system, built literally and figuratively on private property, is a servant of all the rest of our liberties." He does not see quite so clearly, apparently— or at least does not mention—that religious liberty is antecedent to other liberties. He assumes the fact of God, and admits "a Power higher than ourselves from whom is derived a positive moral code giving our lives meaning and a sense of purpose that cannot be measured in terms of material achievement."

Subordination, however, of the profit motive to the moral code is not so clearly affirmed. It is apparently assumed that there is some law at work that will guarantee that in the long run the play of self-interest will make for social welfare. This was the old *laissez-faire* emphasis. He says, and quite properly: "In our system—and a better one has yet to be proven in practice—an industrial enterprise must make an adequate profit in order to survive; in order to provide the necessities of life for those whom it employs and their families; in order to provide reasonable compensation to hundreds of thousands of individuals who have supplied capital without which jobs cannot be created." He asks, "Is that bad? Is that to be despised?" Of course not. He holds that "our system of enterprise has elevated the material well-being of the people." What is that system? It includes not only capital, management, and labor in industry, but also many other contributing factors, public and private.

Mr. Hood, however, adds a fundamental statement that reflects the opinion of many enlightened businessmen today: "In American industry I know of no one so arrogant or irrever-

ent as to hint that our system of enterprise has any sanction or ordination from above. We merely believe that, as a practical system of supplying men's material needs, yet preserving human dignity from political and economic tyranny, it is the best system man has yet devised. We also believe that it is a system which is still evolving, one in which there is ceaseless effort to make it better, in the quality of offering greater opportunity for personal development, as well as in its purely material aspects."

In the continuing emphasis on stewardship, the Church is making it abundantly clear that all who possess talent or own property are stewards, and that they hold their talents and their property as trustees; they are accountable to God. In this sense, there is no absolute ownership. The Church has full right to point out to those who have pledged themselves to Christ that such a pledge involves the concept of stewardship; and that as trustees Christians are responsible to God and obligated to do His will.

3

What Is Ahead?

The changes of a half-century suggest further change in the half-century to come. It is at this place that clergyman, industrial executive, and labor leader may come together. If the economic order is in process of change, what are the standards of value that we should use to determine its further evolution? What are the ethical principles on which we base judgment? It is here that the Church makes its fundamental contribution: it must be the teacher of the principles of conduct; it is obligated to voice judgment when those principles are violated; it must hold before men the ideal, and thus never pledge itself in perpetuity to less than the ideal. In all economic practice man stands under the judgment of God.

It is here that one must again recall William Temple. He said: "One danger is here, very insidious, which must be warded off. It is that we shall try to make God the means to our ends, the instrument of our plans. That is sheer disaster. We dedicate ourselves to this enterprise in His name, believing it to be His Will, in the hope that through it He may be glorified in drawing the people to that fellowship which is the counterpart of His holy love."[1]

THE RESPONSIBLE SOCIETY

It was at the First Assembly of the World Council of Churches in Amsterdam that the section on "The Church and the Disorder of Society" lifted up the concept of the responsi-

[1] *Ibid.,* p. 1211.

ble society. It declared: "Man is created and called to be a free being, responsible to God and his neighbor. Any tendencies in State and society depriving man of the possibility of acting responsibly are a denial of God's intention for man and His work of salvation. A responsible society is one where freedom is the freedom of men who acknowledge responsibility to justice and public order, and where those who hold political authority or economic power are responsible for its exercise to God and the people whose welfare is affected by it." The report, grounded in the Christian conception of man, declared further: "Man must never be made a mere means for political or economic ends. Man is not made for the State, but the State for man. Man is not made for production, but production for man. For a society to be responsible under modern conditions it is required that the people have freedom to control, to criticise and to change their governments, that power be made responsible by law and tradition, and be distributed as widely as possible through the whole community. It is required that economic justice and provision of equality of opportunity be established for all the members of society."[2]

Delegates to the Assembly of the World Council called on Christians to recognize "the hand of God in the revolt of multitudes against injustice." They held that in this revolt it is injustice that gives communism much of its appeal. They insisted that the Church must recapture "the original Christian solidarity with the world's distressed people." The report stressed the points of conflict between Christianity and atheistic Marxist communism; it indicated the conflicts between Christianity and capitalism. Properly it came to the conclusion: "The greatest contribution that the Church can make to the renewal of society is for it to be renewed in its own life in faith and obedience to its Lord. Such inner renewal

[2] The Christian's responsibility extending beyond national boundaries is treated extensively in Part III of this volume.

includes a clearer grasp of the meaning of the Gospel for the whole life of men. . . . The social influence of the Church must come primarily from its influence upon its members through constant teaching and preaching of Christian truth in ways that illuminate the historical conditions in which men live and the problems which they face."[3] Therefore the World Council said: "We have to ask God to teach us together to say No and to say Yes in truth. No, to all that flouts the love of Christ, to every system, every programme, and every person that treats any man as though he were an irresponsible thing or a means of profit, to the defenders of injustice in the name of order, to those who sow the seeds of war or urge war as inevitable; Yes, to all that conforms to the love of Christ, to all who seek for justice, to the peacemakers, to all who hope, fight, and suffer for the cause of man, to all who—even without knowing it—look for new heavens and a new earth wherein dwelleth righteousness."[4]

FREEDOM AND JUSTICE

The mistaken notion that all forms of collective or cooperative endeavor lead to serfdom has occasioned a demand in some quarters for a return to something like *laissez-faire* capitalism. Strangely enough, this emphasis has been associated with a demand for personal evangelism. There has been an attempt to identify the "simple Gospel" with *laissez faire*. Just as there are those who would deify the state, and declare that to criticize the state is to engage in blasphemy, so there are those who would make the economic order sacrosanct. To make of one voice the hallelujahs of religion and the hurrahs of the state is, in effect, to make the state supreme, to deny

[3] *The Church and the Disorder of Society*, New York, Harper & Brothers, 1948, pp. 200–204.
[4] *Ibid.*, p. 194.

God's relevance thereto, and to become, for all practical purposes, atheist. There was a time when the owners of slaves insisted that slavery was ordained of God; there was a time also when it was held that kings ruled by divine right, and that an order with its nobles and serfs had been established by the Eternal. Those who would identify socialism and Christianity, the cooperatives and Christianity, capitalism and Christianity, make the same mistake that was made by the owners of slaves and the kings and the nobles of yesterday. Historically conditioned political, economic, and social systems will pass. We sing, "Oh where are kings and empires now?" Jesus Christ is the same yesterday today, and forever; the judgments of God endure. "Thou shalt have no other gods before me." A man's final loyalty is to God.

Within the Church is a minority that insists on a return to "free" or unrestricted individualism; and there is a minority that demands the establishment of some form of collectivism. The vast majority, however, hold to the Christian faith, and use it as the standard by which they judge the economic order. In so doing, they come to some of the fundamental issues of our day—the issues of power and of justice. Power must be brought under democratic control—all forms of power, political, economic, ecclesiastical. Justice must be established by the democratic process. Far-seeing men realize that in the free-enterprise system there is the possibility of keeping power under control. There is, of course, a trend toward monopoly, which must be regulated or restrained; but when monopoly is curbed there is a dispersion of power within the capitalist order.

Gustav Stolper in *Foreign Affairs* states:

1. Under capitalism, the businessman makes a miscalculation at his own risk; his mistake in the worst case spells economic ruin for him. The errors of the planning commission are paid for by the community at large.

2. If a hundred thousand businessmen are planning away, each on his own account, the mathematical chances that shrewdness and folly will offset each other to a certain extent are incomparably greater than in a case where the decision as to the economic fate of a nation is entrusted to one central brain.

3 (and most important). Capitalism functions under an objective law made manifest through the market—through prices and interest rates. The dictator, under capitalism, is the consumer. . . . The capitalistic businessman can never escape the dictatorship of the market. . . .

Under planned economy the dictator is not the consumer but the producer—the state—which prescribes how the consumer is to deport himself, what and how much he is to eat, what clothes he is to wear, where he is to live, what manner of life he is to follow. And the moment the socialist state acquires dictatorship over the consumer . . . it also assumes control over technical progress.

Then Professor Stolper declares: "The decisive questions are whether individual freedom can exist apart from private property and freedom of consumption, and how highly one is to prize individual freedom. For even were capitalism incurably affected by all the evils ascribed to it by its opponents, it would still be a blessing to be defended to the last ditch if it were the only thinkable economic system under which individual freedom—freedom not only in the material sphere but freedom of thought, speech, and movement—could be assured, and if a socialistically planned economy precludes such freedom by nature and definition."[5]

Unfortunately churchmen have seen the development of monopoly, the coming of the cartel, and the concentration of economic power. They have seen at the same time the passing of thousands of separate enterprises which had produced what was necessary, had faced rigorous competition, and had

[5] Gustav Stolper, "Politics versus Economics," *Foreign Affairs*, April 1934, pp. 367–8.

needed to improve products in order to sell. Such separate units are necessary, if power is to be kept under control. The people have been fearful that "big business" or "big labor" or other big organized economic groups, if growing bigger, would grow more irresponsible. Thus many have held that capitalism is its own executioner. They have witnessed also an unwillingness, whether of management or labor, in one field of production or another, to pass on the benefits of capitalist production to the consumer.

There have been some endeavors by those who would maintain the so-called free economy to silence its constructive critics. It is necessary to have not only the dispersal of economic power, but also the maintenance of distributed groups, such as church, school, press, radio, sufficiently free to express individual opinion, and to constitute the necessary checks and balances on the power of the state, as well as on the power that develops in monopoly or other economic concentration. There is a danger that free economic units may unite, and in the united economic power become more powerful than the people themselves, whose power lies in a state deriving its powers from the consent of the governed.

If freedom is to be maintained, justice must be established. There are those who, properly interested in maintaining order, fail to understand the necessity of establishing justice. Just as power must be brought under democratic control, so also justice must be established by the democratic process. It is balance that is essential. The older issue of the one and the many is still before us. How do we reconcile liberty and law? Liberty is the principle of change; law is the principle of order.

It is precisely at this place that the Church, enunciating the law of love, brings to mankind the principle of unity; it is here that Christians make their basic contribution: liberty and law are to be reconciled in love.

THE CHRISTIAN VOCATION

"The Christian vocation" is a term of historic interest and of contemporary significance. There is a universal obligation to work; but it is not enough for a Christian to work—he should be engaged in socially useful work; his labor should meet a need. It should contribute to the common good; it should add to the common wealth. This is in keeping with the dictum of the Apostle Paul, "If anyone would not work, neither should he eat."

A Christian cannot divorce work and worship. When a Christian prays, "Not my will but Thine be done," he is actually pledging to the God he worships to express God's will in the place he works. The Christian is concerned with the spirit that is brought to the job as well as with the nature of the job itself. He is also concerned with the work life as a whole—with the spirit that infuses it, the objectives toward which it moves, and the principles around which it is organized.

Work must be seen in terms of its spiritual significance, as making possible fullness of life for all men everywhere. All work that produces the necessary, the useful, the beautiful, the spiritual, is entitled to respect; and in this sense all workers are equal; all are engaged in some socially necessary task. The word "vocation" means "calling." For the Christian, the call is from God. Unfortunately this sacred term has been secularized, and is today associated with occupation, job, chore, hobby; but "vocation" means more than these words can ever mean. The Great Commission of our Blessed Lord applies to the work of every Christian. The Christian worker is a missionary, in the sense that he carries the Gospel, by what he is and by what he does, to all whom he meets; and seeks to transform the industrial order itself, until at last it too is an expression of the Gospel.

The solution to the problem of vocation does not consign us all to the monastery. The Christian must not fear the mine, the mill, the market; his call is not usually to the monk's cell. Spiritual disciplines are requisite to the spiritual life; but telling beads one by one is not to be compared with meeting needs day by day. We must turn back to the Reformation doctrine of the calling of the Christian man. The reformers may have pressed this matter too far; but the Christian man who realizes that work must be done "as unto God" is the man who gives an honest day's work for an honest day's pay. It means also the building of an honest order—honest in the sense that its ruling principles are in harmony with the morality written into the nature of things. Work becomes a calling when it is pledged to purpose, and when the purpose is the will of the Eternal. That purpose was seen in Christ; and it means fullness of life for all, and in such work joy overflows.

In literally thousands of communities throughout the United States, men and women of the Church in many walks of life seek to discover practical measures that will express the Christian ideal in the common life. The Woman's Society of Christian Service in one of the great denominations—a society whose membership is in excess of 1,600,000—spent a year studying "the Christian's vocation." They considered the principle of creative purchase, which, in simple terms, means that when an article is purchased a demand for that article is created, and consequently purchases create more of the commodity that is bought. They asked, "Is a Christian responsible for the results that flow from his purchases? How can a housewife know the conditions of manufacture that lie back of the article she buys?" They considered the attempt to answer the question found in the use of the "union label." They asked, "Where does the church buy? Where do church men and women buy? In the cheapest market or in the fairest market? Where does our duty lie? Do we purchase as cheaply

as possible in order to . . . have more to distribute to retired preachers? Or do we realize that every life is sacred, and that no group should benefit at the expense of another group, and thus express the law of love as we recognize the law of creative purchase?"[6] They raised the question whether it would be possible for the women of the church as a whole to prepare and keep current a buyer's guide in which the simple facts concerning employer-employee relations could be stated, the kinds of plants, and the conditions of work described, the housing of the workers set forth. They considered a fundamental fact, namely, that the purchasing power of more than a million women might be decisive in improving conditions of work across the nation.

Many ministers recognize the fact that they are not called on to face some issues that a worker must face. An expert brick mason may lay a certain number of bricks each day, but because work at high speeds makes heavy physical demands, the number of years in which he may work may therefore be shortened. Or, again, if the pace is too swift, fewer men can handle all the work, and fellow workers may be laid off. The workers therefore may seek to determine the number of bricks that can reasonably be laid in a given day. To some, such attempts appear to be soldiering, or a form of sabotage; to others, they are an expression of brotherhood. Some may press their demands so far that their action becomes in fact a slow-down, and thus exploits management—or, even more, the consumer. There is the very difficult question, too, how far, if at all, is a slow-down justified? More abundant living for all is dependent on increased productivity by all. Sometimes the slow-down becomes a coercive weapon used by unscrupulous labor leaders.

Now a mason has to say yes or no to these practices. If he

---

[6] G. Bromley Oxnam, The Christian's Vocation, Women's Division of Christian Service, The Methodist Church, Cincinnati, 1950, pp. 44 ff.

insists on laying a larger number of bricks he may find himself in trouble with his union; if he refuses to do his best, he may have difficulty with his conscience. A minister is apart from these issues; he can discuss them, but he isn't called upon to act. Yet he may face a similar issue in his own duties. A businessman must make decisions, and his business fails or succeeds because of his decisions. A professor can postpone his opinion until tomorrow, or next year, though his action or inaction may affect the lives of others; but a lawyer who faces an opponent intellectually his equal must make decisions in the courtroom, and cases are won or lost in the light of decision. A surgeon has a life at stake on the operating table.

This points to the necessity of conference and common study under the Christian spirit. Significant contribution is made to the resolving of these issues when men charged with management, men of the labor force, and the clergy meet to discuss and to find a common answer to questions that often lead to conflict. The fact of meeting each other and the spirit that is present are often as important as the tentative solution that may be reached.

The Church and Industrial Relations

The Church becomes increasingly aware of the fact that millions of the American population and therefore millions of church members are related to the labor movement. Millions find in labor opportunity to express ethical idealism. The communist seeks to infiltrate the labor movement, to win it to the ideology of communism.

The bishops of the Methodist Church, in an episcopal address delivered to the General Conference—which is its highest legislative body—asked: "Is there no obligation upon the part of Christianity to carry the religion of Jesus to the workers of the world in such fashion that His teaching so

masters our work life that the worker may himself think of
the Christ as Lord and Master? The Church sends its mission-
aries to the far corners of the earth to lay the foundations of a
Christian world. What of a definite attempt to contribute to
the labor movement of the world a leadership pledged to
Christ?" The bishops sought to answer that question with a
concrete proposal:

Let us suppose that the Methodist Church had definitely
resolved to do this thing under some appropriate commission or
Board and had determined to recruit each year fifty of its finest
youth to contribute to this high end. Let us assume that these
young people have been selected with the greatest care, that they
are persons of undoubted religious experience, of high intellectual
qualifications, of executive ability. The plan would involve rigorous
training in some great university center in which they might be
prepared to become leaders of labor, but qualified likewise to
become efficient operatives in mines, in mills, in factories, on
railroads. Upon graduation, are they to present themselves to the
labor movement with the declaration, Here are your future leaders?
Not at all. They are to go to work, asking nothing for themselves,
with no assumption that because of their superior education they
are to be chosen immediately as the leaders of labor. They must
win their way in terms of their worth. Let them join the union
and rise to such leadership as their talents and service deserve. At
first, this will be leadership upon the local level, subsequently upon
the state level, and, finally, in the national and international
realm. If fifty such persons go into the labor movement each year
for twenty years, out of this thousand will come a leadership of
great power. It must be pointed out that this is no plan to tone
down the demands for social justice. A person who gives himself
to labor, who refuses to accept promotion to the higher paid
managerial position, is a person of conviction. It is the man of
conviction who is loyal to the demand for justice when the individual ruled by expediency falters and fails.

Let Methodism provide specifically for the recruiting of such

young people. Let them be trained in our schools, given the graduate courses necessary for full preparation, then let them go to work. The relation of the Church to them would be one of intimate fellowship, perhaps at the end of five or seven years to provide a year of continuing graduate study or travel. The Church should be frank. It should make the plan perfectly clear to the leaders of labor. It should make it clear that we are not seeking to infiltrate and to control, that we are seeking solely to contribute in terms of character the finest young people we possess, to the end that the ideals that will be regnant in the conduct of labor for the years to come will be Christian ideals. Let it be assumed that our Church will be contributing to the business leadership of the nation men similarly Christian. We are discussing at the moment our contribution to labor. Is it too much to believe that leaders of organized labor and leaders of organized business, both followers of Jesus Christ, may be able to face the economic issues in terms of problem-solving, in terms of Christian brotherhood, and thus enable us to lift our productivity, to respect one another, to avoid the ways of class conflict, and to demonstrate that within freedom we can move to a social order more just, more brotherly than can be established ever upon the basis of battle?[7]

Some church federations have organized inquiry commissions whose purpose is to make careful, scientific study of the facts involved in industrial disputes and make these facts available to the community; a sound public opinion cannot be developed on the basis of partisan reporting.

THE RIGHT TO INCOME

In many communities competent economists, in conference with studious representatives of labor, of business, and of the Church, have considered such fundamental yet such bafflingly difficult questions as the right to income. Why should there

[7] Journal of the 1948 General Conference of the Methodist Church, New York, Methodist Publishing House, pp. 191–3.

be such disparities in income? For instance, teachers generally receive small salaries; lawyers' fees are apt to be large. A professor in a Midwestern university, loved and honored by his students, a man of inspirational personality who made contribution in terms of character of the highest significance, served his university for fifty years. One of his students became a distinguished lawyer; he settled an estate which he said took him about thirty days of working time; and then he received more as his fee for settling that estate than the professor did for fifty years of teaching. A motion picture actress receives a fabulous sum; and the men who discovered insulin give their discovery to the profession. A man inherits a piece of property in the business section of a great city; he does nothing to improve it. Other men build great buildings on opposite corners; they pay heavy taxes on these buildings, but the man who has made no contribution to the community pays taxes on the basis of his unimproved property. These questions are not designed to advocate any particular answer, but to indicate that such issues must be thought through and the practices judged by the religion of Jesus.

There are no easy answers. It is necessary to move forward in terms of the largest possible agreement presently attainable; but Christians never pledge themselves to such practices in perpetuity. They continue to raise the questions and to seek judgment in the light of the Christian ideal. Is it possible to base income on the service rendered? Who determines the value of service? Are the dangers of social control greater than the threats to community that lie in such disparity of reward? When the free mind in the free society plays on problems of this kind, the truth that frees will be discovered.

Unless we stand ready to declare the ethical demands of Jesus invalid, and in effect to condemn His thinking as "perfectionist ethics," the questions must be faced. Perhaps it will be seen that the economic problem is less a matter involving

reform or revolution than a matter of regeneration. It was Jesus Himself who enunciated the doctrine of the new birth. We know that individuals can be reborn. So too, the economic life, the social life, the political life! We are pledged to the proposition that "In the name of Jesus, the world shall be reborn!"

PART II

Findings of the Study

Howard R. Bowen

4

Goals of Economic Life

This book is the sixth in a series of volumes dealing with the ethical aspects of economic life. The preceding five volumes have offered many insights and judgments regarding the basic goals that are, or should be, sought through economic activity. Volume 1 of the series, *Goals of Economic Life*, was concerned primarily with goals. It consisted of a series of essays by noted scholars representing various disciplines, each of whom approached the subject from the vantage-point of his own field. The other volumes, though dealing with specialized topics of ethical significance, were necessarily concerned also with underlying goals. In this chapter we shall draw on all these studies (but primarily Volume 1) in exploring the question: What are the goals (or values, or ends) in terms of which the goodness or badness of economic institutions, policies, and decisions should be judged?

In this and succeeding chapters we shall make frequent footnote references to the five preceding volumes in this series (all of which have been published by Harper & Brothers, New York, in 1953 and 1954). For brevity, these references will be made in abbreviated form as follows:

A. D. Ward (editor), *Goals of Economic Life*, to be cited as *Goals*.

K. E. Boulding, *The Organizational Revolution*, to be cited as *Org. Rev.*

H. R. Bowen, *Social Responsibilities of the Businessman*, to be cited as *Soc. Resp.*

E. E. Hoyt, M. G. Reid, J. L. McConnell, and J. M. Hooks, *American Income and Its Use*, to be cited as *Amer. Income*.

A. D. Ward, S. A. Leavy, and L. Z. Freedman, *The American Economy—Attitudes and Opinions*, A Report of Surveys (in preparation), to be cited as *Am. Ec.*

The goals of economic life are not in any way separable from the goals of *life*. Economic activity is an important part of the totality of human experience. It is partly means to a wide range of ends, but it is also partly an end in itself. Therefore this chapter leads us to that most fundamental of questions: What are the goals or ends of human life itself?

It would be presumptuous to suppose that an authoritative statement of the "true" goals of life could be dashed off in a few pages. The question of the meaning of life is one that has never been answered except tentatively and incompletely, even by the world's greatest thinkers and teachers; the mystery of life is never fully revealed to finite man. His view of the goals of life is therefore always indistinct. His perspective, moreover, is conditioned by his particular experiences and his culture;[1] therefore the goals as seen by any one person or group are always relative to his (their) time and place in history.[2] "Both the needs of individuals and the imperatives of social existence are much the same everywhere, and there are numerous thematic [or basic] values which can be recognized in all cultures."[3] Moreover, the similarity of the ethical creeds of various societies widely separated in time and place suggests that there are at least some general underlying principles for the guidance of human conduct. Professor T. M. Greene

---

[1] *Goals*, pp. 162–3, 209, 228, 246, 259, 306, 344–5, 359, 398. The goals of life may be distorted by the culture. A good society is one in which "right goals are generally accepted and in which the institutions favor the attainment of these goals." Cf. Reinhold Niebuhr, *An Interpretation of Christian Ethics*, Harper & Brothers, New York, 1935, p. 182.

[2] *Goals*, pp. 7, 9, 11, 19, 88, 308–9, 378, 382, 393, 440.

[3] *Goals*, p. 308. See also *Org. Rev.*, pp. 66–7.

suggests that the goals of life are universal and objective. He says that "what man responds to in his multiple evaluations, insofar as they are realistically oriented, is an integral part of his ultimate environment and not merely a fiction of his individual or collective creative imagination. Objective values are as real as any other major aspect of his world, as discoverable by man, and, as far as human experience indicates, as orderly and coercive."[4] Yet Professor Greene is careful to show "that all human evaluations have been, are, and must be finite and fallible," and that they "are inevitably 'conditioned' both psychologically and socially."[5] Therefore, he argues, an experimental and tentative approach to all human problems is required.[6] In any event, the following discussion of goals is offered not as a dogmatic prescription but as a general point of view from which to consider the relation of economic activity to the attainment of fundamental human goals.

CHRISTIAN LOVE

The primary and overarching aim of life is Christian love— by which is meant the love of God and of the neighbor. Implicit in this ideal of love is that the fulfillment of one's life is achieved through others.[7] All other goals are subordinate to this one. Only as we strive toward the ideal of love does life take on ultimate purpose or meaning; and it is only as the individual becomes imbued with this ideal that he finds significance in his daily experiences. Indeed, it is only within this frame of reference that goals become possible in any significant sense. Without the seeking for love, and the pattern of motives

[4] *Goals*, pp. 377-8.
[5] *Ibid.*, p. 382.
[6] *Ibid.*, p. 393.
[7] *Goals*, pp. 25-6, 362, 438-42. Cf. H. Richard Niebuhr, *Christ and Culture*, Harper & Brothers, New York, 1951, pp. 11-29.

which that implies,[8] subordinate goals prove to be empty, and life turns out to be purposeless floundering. Thus the several goals presented below are all to be regarded as subordinate to, or as applications of, the overarching ideal of love.

Love of neighbor should be broadly inclusive. One of the most frequently recurrent themes in this series of books is the need for wider inclusiveness in our concept of the neighbor. This need derives from that extreme interdependence which characterizes modern society. Our actions often affect distant human beings whom we never actually know or see, and our concern for others must encompass all those whose lives we affect.[9] Love of neighbor, therefore, must not be limited to immediate persons or to members of some in-group to which we happen to belong, but should embrace all of humanity. Albert Schweitzer in his concept "reverence for life" even suggests that this love should extend to all living things.

It is clearly more difficult to be concerned about persons remote from us than about persons whom we know and see in our families, our work places, and our neighborhoods. As Professor Niebuhr has said, "The wider the communities, whether national or international, the less they can count on organic, subrational, and submoral forces of cohesion and the more they must depend upon man's conscious sense of responsibility for the welfare of others than those who are peculiarly his own."[10]

Economic activity creates extensive and complex relations of interdependence among persons, and involves an amazing variety of human relationships. Therefore love of neighbor

[8] Group belonging and cooperation have been found by modern psychology to be highly effective motives. Competition, self-interest, and profit are by no means always more powerful as motives than cooperation or group loyalty. Goals, pp. 300–4, 329, 337–8, 345–7.

[9] Goals, pp. 15, 359–61, 449–50; Org. Rev., pp. 10–12; Soc. Resp., pp. 122–3; Amer. Income, pp. 44 ff.

[10] Goals, p. 449; see also pp. 14–15, 25, 89–90, 140, 173, 346, 359–61; Soc. Resp., pp. 122–3; Amer. Income, pp. 11, 57.

should have a prominent place in economic motivation. The doctrine of love implies in this context that each individual should be concerned about the effects of his actions on the welfare of others—including not only those persons with whom he comes into personal contact but also those whom he never sees or knows. Frequently the ideal of love with reference to economic affairs is expressed by the terms "stewardship" or "social responsibility."[11] It applies with special force to those persons whose positions of power give them great influence over the lives of others; for example, businessmen, labor leaders, farm leaders, and public officials. But it applies as well to less powerful individuals. Even the humblest of us occupies a position of some influence in the complex network of economic relationships. Each of us performs tasks on which others depend; each is engaged in activities which must be coordinated with those of others; and each experiences face-to-face contacts with others in his daily life as worker and as consumer.

But, in this imperfect world, we cannot rely solely on love, or on the sense of responsibility to others, to guide the conduct of individuals in their economic roles. Individual human beings, even with the noblest of intentions, do not always know what is good for others; and, in any case, individuals cannot be relied on to act consistently from selfless motives. It is all too easy for individuals to see their own interests more clearly than the interests of others.[12] Hence, in the practical world, individual actions must be guided by competition, informal social controls, and law. When possible, self-interest must be harnessed to the social interest; and in so far as this is not possible, self-interest must be controlled.[13] Yet love remains as the ultimate ideal. It must be employed so far as prac-

[11] *Soc. Resp.*, pp. 3–6, 12–13, 28–30.
[12] *Goals*, pp. 173, 410, 441–2; *Soc. Resp.*, pp. 34–5, 115–7.
[13] *Goals*, pp. 13, 15, 174–6, 359, 412, 441–6; *Soc. Resp.*, pp. 115–21.

ticable not only as a motive for individual conduct but as a guiding principle underlying our social controls. Without the spirit of love and the mutual concern and cooperation that it implies, the conditions for community and economy would be lacking, and social life would be utterly intolerable.[14]

Eleven Subordinate Goals

Though the ideal of love is the over-arching goal of life and of economic life, there are other subordinate goals of great importance.

1. *Survival and Physical Well-being (Productivity)*. Each individual should have access to the conditions necessary for health, safety, comfort, and reasonable longevity. This implies that he should have opportunity to achieve satisfaction of the physiological needs of food, sleep, and minimal physical comfort. He should be protected from hunger, extremes of heat and cold, unusual hazards, physical pain, back-breaking or nerve-racking labor, and cumulative fatigue.[15]

The known conditions of survival and physical comfort have for most peoples been relatively easy to achieve. Apparently most societies have ordinarily enjoyed a surplus of productive power over and above that required for mere creature need. They have had "luxuries," leisure, aesthetic enjoyment, or costly religious rites.[16] And in advanced industrial societies this surplus has been so great that the attainment of creature needs has become a relatively minor (though essential) objective. The question arises, therefore, as to how much surplus income people should have in addition to the goods required for survival and minimal physical comfort. Just how

[14] *Goals*, pp. 41, 141, 284.
[15] *Goals*, pp. 45–7, 186–7, 264, 362.
[16] *Goals*, pp. 85, 87–8, 322–3, 332–3. Sometimes, of course, they have maintained these "extras" even at the sacrifice of the minimal needs for survival.

great this surplus of goods should be is, of course, a moot question. Each society, or class within society, defines for itself, in terms of its dominant value system and in terms of the available productive power, that amount of income it regards as the social minimum. And this concept changes, for any society, through time. For example, the amount of income that is regarded in modern America as the indispensable minimum for "health and decency" would seem like fabulous riches to a frontier homesteader, a medieval serf, or a Chinese coolie.[17]

An impressive feature of the several volumes in this series is the absence of asceticism or of denial of the things of this world. There is general agreement on the desirability of a high level of consumption, and there is frequent reference to poverty as an evil that is "crippling to human personality."[18] The consensus was aptly expressed by Professor Boulding: "But even if the chief end of man is to know God and enjoy Him forever, the enjoyment of goods is surely not inconsistent with enjoyment of good, and God is better served by a race whose capacities are not stinted by inadequate food, shelter, education, or health."[19]

While a high level of consumption (and requisite productivity and progress) may be approved, yet over-preoccupation with material objects, luxuries, and comfort must be criticized as a widespread evil and a constant temptation. And the exalting of goods as symbols of status and as sources of power must be sharply condemned.[20] As Professor Niebuhr has suggested, there is a materialism both of poverty and of wealth.[21]

The goal of *survival and physical well-being* is, of course,

[17] Amer. Income, pp. xii, 213.
[18] Goals, pp. 72–4, 398–9, 418, 455–6, 459; Soc. Resp., p. 37; Amer. Income, pp. 137, 202.
[19] Goals, p. 72.
[20] Amer. Income, pp. 23 ff; Goals, pp. 73–4. Conspicuous consumption is found even in primitive societies, Goals, p. 331.
[21] Goals, p. 425. See also Goals, pp. 73–4, 420; Amer. Income, pp. 3–12.

achieved pre-eminently through economic activity. The goods and services to sustain life, to give physical comfort, and to provide a high level of consumption are the direct result of production. The corresponding economic goal, therefore, is *productivity* or *efficiency*.[22] And if we look forward to future improvements in the amount of these goods and services, a related goal is *progress*.[23] But physical well-being and the level of living are related not alone to the quantity (and quality) of goods and services, but also to the conditions under which these goods are produced, and to the amount of leisure. Hence, another economic objective is safe, healthful, and pleasant working conditions and adequate leisure.[24]

2. *Fellowship.* Each individual should have a variety of satisfying human relationships. He needs intimate affection and a place in a family circle. He needs to be accepted and respected by his neighbors and colleagues—to have a sense of belonging, of friendship, and of sociability. He should participate in political and economic decisions affecting his welfare, and should have opportunity for joining in cooperative endeavors, both in his work and in his other activities.[25]

Economic life affords an abundance and a variety of human relationships. People are thrown together in the work place, the union hall, the Farm Bureau meeting, the annual "convention," the government "conference," the market place, etc. Sometimes the relationship is that of members of a team, and sometimes it is that of competitors, negotiators, salesmen, or buyers. This great variety of relationships offers abundant opportunity for fellowship. It can offer the individual a sense of belonging, of participation in matters affecting him, of friendship, of sociability, and of cooperative endeavor. At the same time, economic life also affects the family, the com-

[22] *Soc. Resp.*, pp. 8–9.
[23] *Goals*, pp. 52–83, 362, 370, 416.
[24] *Soc. Resp.*, pp. 46–7, 110–15, 208–11.
[25] *Goals*, pp. 25–6, 334; *Soc. Resp.*, pp. 41–3.

munity, and the social activities of individuals. For example, night work, extended travel, employment of women and children, and the demands of business on the time and energies of executives, have obvious effects on family and community life. The formation of economic classes, and conflicts among these classes, may divide the community and even set brother against brother. Clearly, economic life is influential in determining the range and quality of human relationships. Therefore one of the goals of economic life is *fellowship*.

3. *Dignity and Humility.* Each individual should have the opportunity to earn a position in society of dignity and self-respect. This follows from the basic concept of the dignity of man and the essential worth of the human individual.[26] But this goal should not be inflated into a passion for prestige or power of the kind that places one individual over others—and thereby places the others below him.[27] Prestige and power are in fact widespread human ambitions and powerful motives—as was so clearly recognized in Ecclesiastes. Yet the quest of prestige and power is obviously contrary to the law of love and of justice, and is an expression of man's sinful tendency to place himself above others. Nevertheless, in organized society it is necessary that some men be given power over others, and it is probably inevitable that some will be accorded more prestige than others. The laws of love and justice dictate that such power should be exercised responsibly as a trust in the interests of all, or that it should be brought under social control, and that such prestige should be worn with true humility.[28]

In modern society the status of most people is linked closely with their occupations and incomes.[29] When one inquires

[26] *Goals*, pp. 116, 352–5, 362.
[27] *Goals*, pp. 84–117, 319–20, 333, 411, 446–7.
[28] *Soc. Resp.*, pp. 34–5; *Goals*, pp. 47, 73, 129–30, 145, 189, 263–4, 291.
[29] *Goals*, pp. 84-117.

about a person, the answer is likely to be in terms of his economic position; for example, "He is a farmer," or "He owns the corner drugstore," or "She is the wife of the vice president of the First National Bank," or "She is the widow of a salesman and she lost all her money in the depression." One's economic position therefore is important in determining his social status, and one of the goals of economic life is to create social attitudes that will give all persons opportunity for positions of dignity[30]—yet when they reach positions of power and prestige that they will conduct themselves responsibly and humbly.

Social status is achieved not only through production but also through consumption. The use of goods and services often serves as a symbol of prestige. Dignity and humility are thus objectives of consumption, just as they are of production.

4. *Enlightenment.* The individual should have opportunity to learn about the world in which he lives. He should be able to satisfy his intellectual curiosity, and to acquire the skills and knowledge for intelligent citizenship, efficient work, and informed living.[31]

Work may afford many opportunities for enlargement of the human mind. It can offer intellectual experience and contact with many aspects of the world. It can challenge the individual to enlarge his perspective, and can stimulate him to exercise his powers of imagination and reason. On the other hand, some kinds and conditions of work can be narrowing and intellectually stifling. Similarly, consumption, or the use of goods and services, offers many opportunities for enlargement of the mind. A goal of economic life—in both its productive and consumptive aspects—is *enlightenment.*

5. *Aesthetic Enjoyment.* The individual should have the opportunity to appreciate aesthetic values in art, nature, ritual,

[30] *Goals,* p. 119.
[31] *Goals,* p. 262.

and personal relations. Many aesthetic values are attainable through both production and consumption. Work may be conducted in ugly or beautiful surroundings. Human relationships in economic life may be conducted with refinement or crudity of manner. Products may be designed with regard for their beauty, or they may be crassly utilitarian. Consumption may be directed toward the realization of aesthetic values, or may lead to vulgarity. A goal of economic life is *aesthetic enjoyment*.

6. *Creativity*. The individual should be able to express his personality through creative activities. He should be able to identify himself with the results of his own activity, and to take pride in his achievements, whether they be intellectual, aesthetic, political, or other.[32]

Work and consumption abound in opportunities for creative expression of the individual personality; on the other hand, they may stifle the inclination of men to create. One of the goals of economic life is to extend and enlarge the possibilities for creativity.[33]

7. *New Experience*. An important goal of life is suggested by the words variability, spontaneity, whimsy, novelty, excitement, fun, sport, holiday, striving against odds, solving problems, innovation, invention, etc. Each individual should have opportunity for new experience. It would be a dreary and monotonous world if established routines were repeated endlessly without variation. Human beings need to break established patterns, to find new ways, to act irrationally at times, to overcome boredom. They need problems to solve, obstacles to meet, new worlds to conquer, new ideas to think about.[34] One of the great social problems is to provide constructive and peaceful ways of attaining this legitimate goal. If men's restless

[32] *Goals*, pp. 109, 116–7, 362, 370, 422.
[33] *Goals*, p. 68.
[34] *Goals*, pp. 211, 264.

energies and innovating tendencies are not drained off in useful or harmless channels, they will be diverted to destructive purposes. The importance of new experience as a goal is enhanced by the fact that it is probably a condition of progress. Though change and progress are not necessarily the same thing, progress is impossible without change.[35]

Both production and consumption offer abundant opportunities for variety, spontaneity, innovation, and problem-solving. In work, this is found in invention, competition, risk-taking, adjustment to changing conditions. It is more likely to be the preserve of managerial groups than of rank and file workers. In fact, much ordinary work is plagued with monotony, and lacks the relief and stimulus that come with change. Doubtless many workers achieve new experience by changing jobs, and from this point of view labor turnover may not be an unmixed evil. Consumption also affords many opportunities for new experience. For example, this may be the underlying function of the changes in fashion, and the seeking for novelty and excitement that is so characteristic of modern consumer behavior. In any case, new experience is one of the goals of economic life.

8. *Security*. Each individual should have assurance that the objective conditions necessary for attainment of the above goals will be reasonably accessible to him. This implies that he should be able to live in an orderly and peaceful society with reasonably settled institutions and consistent behavior patterns.[36] This also implies that he should be able to live in a society in which people can count on one another. Individuals must be expected to keep their word, to tell the truth, to follow lawful or accepted rules of conduct, and to abstain from unlawful or unethical coercion of others.[37]

[35] *Goals*, pp. 60, 264.
[36] *Soc. Resp.*, p. 9. Order might have been set out as a separate goal rather than subsumed under *security*.
[37] *Ibid.*, pp. 11, 12.

As a goal of *economic* life, security refers to the degree of assurance that one's income and one's economic position as producer and consumer may be maintained in the future. This is achieved partly through general economic stability or absence of wide fluctuations in economic activity, partly through social insurance against the contingencies of life, and partly through the maintenance of orderly and consistent behavior patterns in economic relationships. This last implies freedom from arbitrary and unpredictable changes in the "rules of the game," and the conduct of economic relationships in an atmosphere of mutual trust.

9. *Freedom.* Freedom, which is the opportunity to pursue one's goals without restraint, is rated high as a value by the contributors to the five preceding volumes in this series.[38] Indeed, a fundamental tenet of Christian doctrine is that man is endowed with freedom of choice, and that he has substantial power to direct his own life when he is free of external restraints. This power includes the ability to make wrong choices as well as right ones.[39] Among the important freedoms is freedom to select and rank the goals to be sought, as well as to select the means. In practice, both the goals and the means tend to be culturally determined, yet in a free society variability among individuals is permitted; it is not required that every person pursue the same ends by the same methods. That is why, in describing the above-listed goals, each was referred to as an opportunity or a right, rather than something which must be forced on the individual regardless of his own valuations. A corollary of freedom is the right to be different. Perhaps the most important freedom, because it is the essential condition of all other freedoms, is freedom of thought and speech.[40]

[38] *Goals*, pp. 11, 48–9, 109, 116, 125, 192, 204–30, 264, 292, 309, 321, 415, 448–9.
[39] *Ibid.*, p. 125.
[40] *Goals*, pp. 192, 209, 292.

But freedom, like the other goals, can be overdone. The freedom of one individual may be at the expense of the freedom or other objectives of other individuals. Moreover, excessive freedom places on the individual an onerous burden of decision-making. Just as habit is a useful device to free us from recurrent decision-making, so culture patterns are useful in providing guides to conduct that may be followed without the necessity of decision-making.[41] Freedom, therefore, must be reserved for those actions where it counts.

In the economic sphere, freedom takes several forms: freedom of enterprise, freedom of consumer choice, freedom of occupational and job choice, freedom of investment, freedom of property, freedom of market-price determination, and freedom of organization. In so far as the government is an economic decision-maker, the freedoms implied in political democracy are also economic freedoms. All these freedoms are available, in greater or lesser degree, within the "free enterprise system" or "capitalism." Hence, many of the authors of the five books in this series, all of whom attach great importance to freedom, expressed themselves as generally favorable to capitalism on the ground that it is conducive to freedom.[42] This was in no sense a blanket endorsement of *laissez-faire* capitalism, however, as all of them recognized that freedom entails the assumption of responsibilities more far-reaching than men are prepared to undertake, and therefore that informal and formal social controls are also necessary.[43] Yet because of the high valuation placed on freedom and the skepticism regarding political power, most would lean toward economic freedom in preference to economic controls when the net advantages of the two policies were in approximate balance.[44]

[41] *Goals*, pp. 48–9.
[42] *Goals*, pp. 24–7, 50, 177, 191–3, 219–23, 226, 264–5, 357, 433–7.
[43] *Goals*, pp. 38, 49, 50, 145, 157–61, 191–3, 199–202, 224, 230, 237, 427, 437, 447.
[44] *Goals*, pp. 182, 231–47, 250, 258, 261, 268–70, 363, 437, 444, 446.

10. *Justice.* The Christian law of love does not imply neglect of the self. The individual is asked "to love thy neighbor as thyself." He is enjoined to be as concerned about others as he is about himself—neither more nor less. Moreover, while friendship is a legitimate relationship, the individual is to be as much concerned, basically, with the welfare of one neighbor as with that of another; all men are of equal worth. Thus, a corollary of the law of love is the principle of *justice.* It implies that all men are entitled to be treated equally, and to have access to equal opportunities.[45] But perfect and all-inclusive love cannot be expected of finite and sinful men. Men are, in fact, inclined to favor their own interests (or the interests of groups with which they identify.) In this imperfect world, therefore, justice requires compromise among the conflicting claims of self-centered individuals, and machinery for effecting these compromises.

In economic life, justice is a crucial issue especially with reference to the distribution of opportunity for personal development and for economic advancement, and with reference to distribution of income.[46] Justice requires broad diffusion of opportunity among all persons, regardless of class, race, family connections, religion, sex, age, political opinion, or physical appearance. It also requires equity in the distribution of income. Justice refers not alone to the equitable treatment of persons living at any one time, but also to the equitable treatment of persons living at different times. Thus, justice involves concern for the interests of future generations, with reference to size of population, use of natural resources, capital accumulation, and advancement of technical knowledge.[47] It is sometimes assumed that if productivity is great enough, the problem of economic justice will become less urgent, because then even the poorest individuals will have an

[45] *Goals,* pp. 438, 449.
[46] *Goals,* pp. 154–5, 418, 422.
[47] *Goals,* pp. 47, 162–4, 168–71.

adequate *absolute* amount of income for minimal "comfort and decency." The riches of some will not then be acquired at the expense of bare necessities for others. But the assumption that justice is thereby satisfied is false, because people are vitally concerned about *differences* even when the absolute amount of income is large and poverty is not an issue.[48]

11. *Personality.* The preceding goals were stated in terms of the kinds of life experiences we wish people to have. These goals can be translated into the kinds of persons we wish them to be. Goals can then be regarded as qualities of human personality; accordingly, a desirable personality would be defined as one that is favorably conditioned toward the various goals.[49]

There is one important and subtle difference, however, between goals viewed as life experiences and goals viewed as qualities of human personality. The former refers to objective conditions as viewed by an observer; the latter to the subjective attitudes of the individual toward these conditions. For example, an individual may have a high level of living and yet feel impoverished; he may have a rich variety of human relationships and yet feel lonely; he may have a position of dignity and even prestige and yet feel inferior; he may be enlightened and feel ignorant; he may have access to beauty and yet feel starved for aesthetic satisfaction; he may have richly varied experiences and yet feel bored; he may be secure and yet feel insecure;[50] he may be free yet feel enslaved; and so on.

All of this implies that one of the goals is adjustment of the individual to the conditions of life. Complete adjustment in the sense of passive acquiescence is not what is wanted; the goal is a creative tension between satisfaction and dissatisfaction that enables the individual to accept and to participate

48 *Goals,* p. 457.
49 *Goals,* pp. 24, 116.
50 On emotional aspects of security, see *Amer. Income,* pp. 289–90.

in his world and yet motivates him to strive toward its improvement.[51]

Economic life exerts a profound influence on the human personality. It may lead to satisfaction or to frustration, to adjustment or to mental disorder.[52] It may bring into play the noblest or the basest motives.[53] "It can truly be said to make the men and women who work in it, no less truly than the commodities it turns out for the market."[54]

RELATIONSHIPS AMONG THE GOALS

A list of goals like the preceding is inevitably arbitrary. The list might have contained more than eleven items, or fewer. The several goals might have been classified, described, or weighted differently. The purpose of this list, however, was to present a point of view and not a definitive catalog. Its purpose was to show specifically how the fundamental goals of life are partly attainable through economic activity. But a listing of goals is likely to be artificial even for this purpose, because, by setting out each goal separately, we tend to obscure their essential relationships. These relationships are so numerous and so complex that it may be positively misleading to consider any one of the goals in isolation from the others. The several goals can be most usefully regarded as elements of a *Gestalt*, or complex pattern, not as a list of separate, independent items.

The several goals are sometimes *competitive*, in the sense that the greater attainment of one may be secured only at the sacrifice of others; and they are sometimes *complementary*, in the sense that the greater attainment of some may con-

[51] *Goals*, p. 362.
[52] *Am. Ec.*
[53] *Goals*, p. 418.
[54] J. M. Clark, *Social Control of Business*, 1st ed., University of Chicago Press, Chicago, 1926, p. 47.

tribute to the realization of others.[55] In some cases, the same pair of goals may be in some respects competitive and in other respects complementary.

The competitiveness of the several goals is due partly to the fact that life is finite. The more of a person's life (time, energy, thought) that is devoted to one goal, the less will be left over for another. For example, if an individual pursues fellowship, he may have less time, energy, and thought available for creativity, or enlightenment, or new experience, or security. The competitiveness of the several goals is also due to the fact that the greater attainment of a goal by one individual may be at the expense of the attainment of that goal (or other goals) by other individuals. Whenever the attainment of a goal requires scarce means, the use of those means by one individual may deny their use by other individuals. Thus, the freedom of one individual to pursue his goals (for example, high level of consumption, prestige, new experience) may be a denial of the freedom of other individuals to pursue these goals. It is for this reason that freedom is never an absolute right, but one that must be tempered by justice and ultimately by responsibility and love. As Professor Niebuhr has said, "the law of love is the final law of human freedom."[56]

The complementary relationships among the goals is due partly to the fact that the attainment of one may enhance the general welfare of the individual and thus increase his ability to attain others. For example, a high level of consumption may increase the ability of individuals to be creative, or to achieve freedom, or to enjoy fellowship. On the other hand, creativity, freedom, and fellowship may increase the productivity of individuals and thus raise their level of consumption.[57] Similarly, the attainment of goals by some persons often enhances the welfare of other persons; indeed, the

[55] Goals, pp. 229–30, 233–4, 294.
[56] Goals, p. 449.
[57] Goals, pp. 80, 152–3, 225–7, 282, 288.

world is in most respects better for each of us when our contemporaries are able to achieve fulfillment than when their lives are stunted and miserable.

Because of the complex interdependence among these goals, no one of them can be regarded as an absolute; the pursuit of each must be guided in part by its effect on the attainment of the others. The object is to achieve a good life, viewed as a whole, not to maximize some arbitrary sum of discrete parts viewed separately. This interdependence means that the several goals are often in conflict. The most difficult moral problems, therefore, involve choosing among conflicting alternatives—the giving up some one value in order to get more of another. And many of the moral errors we are prone to commit are due to our placing excessive weight on some goals and neglecting others. A high level of consumption, for example, is an entirely legitimate goal, yet preoccupation with this objective as an end in itself can warp a life. Similarly, excessive concern with any single goal, such as justice or security or freedom or new experience or dignity, to the exclusion of other goals, is certain to produce unbalanced lives and a distorted social order. What we seek is something analogous to the biological conception of *homeostasis*, or the general well-being of the total organism.[58]

The network of relationships among the goals is so complex that a formula for the good life is utterly unfeasible—at least in our present state of knowledge.[59]

Life must continue to be what it has always been—an art

[58] *Goals*, pp. 9, 277–304, 309, 380, 420. Compare also the psychological "field theory," *Goals*, pp. 340–3, 347–64.

[59] Professor F. H. Knight has said: "There can be no mathematical formula for maximum performance in connection with such values as victory or vengeance, beauty, morality, adventure, love, sport, conversation, family life, social success, or most of the things that people really care about." "Economic Science in Recent Discussion," *American Economic Review*, June 1934, p. 238. On the other hand, Professor Boulding observes: "It is by no means absurd to suppose that an empirical 'moral function' could be constructed giving at least a statistical approximation, within a definite range of error, to a moral consensus." *Org. Rev.*, p. 14.

in which we strive to achieve a reasonably harmonious balance among our several goals so that life in its totality may be as good as we can make it within our various and limited moral perspectives.[60] Moreover, there is no presumption that the same pattern of values fits all individuals. We are endowed with different temperaments, different capacities, and different life experiences. We find fulfillment in different ways. We therefore tend to weight the various goals differently, and to appraise the means differently. The ultimate significance of freedom is that we are permitted to work out the pattern of our lives, guided by very broad general principles, according to our particular characteristics and insights. One of the by-products of freedom, therefore, is an infinite variety of human action, as each individual attempts to solve life's problems. Perhaps this variety of human experience is itself one of the ends of life. And one of the necessary conditions of human freedom is that we show tolerance toward the differing solutions reached by other persons.[61]

Since the goals of life are also the goals of economic life, it follows that the same complex interdependence of goals exists in our economic activity. There are competitive relationships, for example, between economic freedom and economic security. There may be complementary relationships in the economic sphere between enlightenment and personal adjustment, between fellowship and new experience, or between creativity and productivity. In the ordering of a good economic life, therefore, these relationships must be continuously considered. No one of the goals may be regarded as an absolute, to be considered in isolation from the others. For example, it is a mistake to regard productivity as the only goal of economic life—as we in twentieth-century America are so prone to do. We must be prepared to make difficult

[60] *Goals,* pp. 229–30.
[61] *Goals,* pp. 448–9.

choices when the greater attainment of one goal can be had only at the expense of another; and we must be prepared to increase the attainment of some goals when these contribute also to the attainment of others.

It is fashionable nowadays to emphasize the competitive relationships among various pairs of goals. We are told repeatedly that security and distributive justice stand in the way of productivity and freedom. This is doubtless true; and perhaps one of the evils of our day is the excessive preoccupation with the more static goals of security and distributive justice at the expense of the more venturesome goals of productivity and freedom. Yet even here the relationship is not *solely* competitive. Security and justice, at least up to a point, are also conditions of productivity and freedom. The problem, as in all questions involving choice among multiple goals, is to achieve a "good" balance—to give no single goal more weight than it deserves.

The Range of Ethical Issues in Economic Life

Economic life consists of a myriad of decisions and actions pertaining to the use of those scarce means of production that we know as labor, land, and capital. These decisions and actions are made by persons ranging from the most humble to the most powerful; and they are made by persons acting sometimes individually and sometimes in groups—such as families, corporations, labor unions, clubs, and governments. A housewife making up her shopping list, a worker carrying out his daily tasks, a youth selecting his vocation, a man of wealth choosing an investment, a businessman deciding on a new product, a labor union negotiating a new wage contract, a legislature deliberating on a tax bill, a diplomat arranging a trade treaty, or a political leader formulating a new plan for

regulation of an industry—these and many other such decisions and actions make up the totality of economic life.

Each decision or action presents both an ethical and a technical aspect, and each may be evaluated according to both ethical and technical criteria. Ethical criteria are invoked when we ask: Is this decision or action directed toward desirable ends? We then judge it in terms of its intended effect in realizing valued goals of economic life—goals like those described in this chapter. Is it designed to enhance, for example, productivity, security, freedom, justice? Technical criteria are applied when we ask: Is this decision or action appropriate to the end in view? We then judge it in terms of its likely effect in achieving the goal toward which it is directed. For an action to be good, it must be justified by more than good intentions; it must also be appropriate to its end, otherwise it may be no better and perhaps even worse than an action that is frankly directed toward evil ends. To do good in this world requires more than good will; it requires also knowledge of the consequences of actions. And this is a stiff requirement in the field of human affairs, because our knowledge of consequences is so often imperfect and unreliable.

Despite the shortcomings of our technical knowledge, we often fall into the bad habit of treating economic issues as though they were exclusively technical questions. We often regard the ends as so self-evident that they need not detain us, and we assume that we can proceed directly to the technical question of how the given ends may be most efficiently realized. We often fall into the delusion of treating a great variety of economic issues as though the single end of economic life were to maximize the value[62] of the national income, and our economic policy often becomes merely the formulation of techniques to achieve this one end. It is, of course, entirely appropriate to concentrate on technique

[62] This refers to money value in dollars of constant purchasing power.

when the ends are given; but concern with technique should never blind us to the fact that the selection of goals is also a problem requiring our best thought and most sensitive valuations. Most important economic decisions and actions are freighted with ethical significance, and must be judged partly by reference to the goals toward which they are oriented.

5

Major Economic Problems

Chapter 4 was a review of ideas concerning the goals of economic life, which had been considered in the five preceding volumes in this series. In this chapter we shall continue to draw on the earlier volumes by summarizing briefly the main conclusions reached on the following subjects: organized groups in economic life, social responsibilities of the businessman, wealth and the good life, distribution of income and levels of consumption, the support of dependents, economic values and problems of the common man, and psychoneurosis and economic life.

Organized Groups in Economic Life

Professor Kenneth E. Boulding, in his study, *The Organizational Revolution*, explored the implications of the great rise in the number, size, and power of organizations during the past century. Though his study was concerned with organizations of all kinds and types, his major emphasis was on economic organizations whose purpose is the economic advancement or protection of their members. Leading examples are labor unions, farm organizations, and business organizations including corporations, trade associations, and cooperatives. Professor Boulding also included the national state as an economic organization, and dealt with it in both its communist and social-democratic forms. He pointed out that the rise of organizations has modified our economic system, and requires

rethinking of our principles and standards of public policy and private morality to fit the changed conditions.

Organizations arise in response to the needs, desires, and ambitions of individuals. Among these are the need for identification with something larger and more significant than one's own pleasures and pains, the need for status which organizations can symbolize and formalize, and the need or desire for whatever material benefits or protections the organizations can give. But the "organizational revolution" of the past century is attributed by Professor Boulding primarily to improved techniques of organization that have resulted chiefly from the rapid advances in communication.

The economic effects of organizations on the allocation of resources and on the distribution of income, he believes, have probably been less than is commonly supposed. In so far as organizations make possible the specialization and division of labor and other economies of scale, they are favorable to productivity. But there are many possibilities for achieving these ends through the spontaneous operation of the market that do not require conscious and formal organization. Organizations have tended to make wages and prices less flexible (more stable) than they would otherwise have been; they may have introduced a bias toward inflation; and they have introduced collective negotiations and rivalry among large power blocs in place of the more automatic, impersonal, and atomistic transactions of the market. They have probably had a relatively small effect on the distribution of income.

From the point of view of ethical motivation, organized groups may have produced a real gain, in that they have widened the area of the individual's concern for others. A person who is part of an organization becomes involved in the welfare of all members of the group. He is motivated to make sacrifices for others that he might otherwise not be willing to make. At the same time, his concern for others tends

to stop at the boundaries of his in-group, and the very fact of his membership in an organization may lead him to hostility toward other groups. An effect of organizations is to divide society into mutually hostile groups. One of the dilemmas of modern society is to achieve wider fellowship without sacrificing the inner fellowship of organized groups.

The rise of organizations and of the power they represent also raises issues concerning the relationships between organizations and their members, and suggests the overwhelming importance of internal democracy in the conduct of organized groups. There are also important ethical dilemmas for members when the organizations to which they belong are directed toward evil ends or become corrupt.

The ultimate in organized power is totalitarianism. Because of this danger, it is desirable to prevent excessive concentrations of organized power. Professor Boulding concludes that a "polylithic" society, with numerous organizations and with ample scope for competition through the impersonal market, is a desirable and urgent goal.

SOCIAL RESPONSIBILITIES OF BUSINESSMEN

The study of the social responsibilities of businessmen[1] examines the frequently asserted proposition that the voluntary assumption of social responsibility by businessmen is, or might be, a practicable means toward ameliorating economic problems and attaining greater social welfare. It is shown that the businessman occupies a strategic position in American life. The degree of influence and power that the businessman exercises over the lives of others, near and far, places upon him the moral responsibility to recognize the social implications of his decisions and to consider the social interest—along with his private interest—in arriving at these

[1] *Soc. Resp.*

decisions. His duty is to ask himself how the decisions he makes in the ongoing operation of his business relate to social goals, and how he might advance the attainment of these goals by appropriate modification of his decisions.

Frequently it is argued that businessmen need consider only their private interests, and that competition will prevent unfavorable consequences of the pursuit of this self-interest. This is the traditional theory of *laissez faire*. Although it is true that the private interest and the social interest are often in harmony (or could be made compatible), yet in fact they are not always in harmony. It has always been necessary, therefore, to place controls over businessmen in the form of law and custom, and to require businessmen to assume responsibility voluntarily to carry on their affairs in ways that are socially desirable. This was true even in the heyday of *laissez faire*, and is even more true in this latter day of advanced technology, giant enterprise, minute specialization, and interdependence. To the extent that businessmen are able voluntarily to adapt their behavior to social requirements, the need for social control in one form or another is by so much diminished.

Businessmen, however, as the study shows, are not the only ones who are called upon to assume social obligations. The same kind of responsibility is to be expected of workers and their unions, farmers and their organizations, cooperatives, trade associations, professional workers, and even consumers. But because of the strategic position and power of businessmen, the onus on them is particularly heavy.

Many leading businessmen have demonstrated, by both word and deed, that they are sensitive to the social obligations of their calling, and are searching for ways to harmonize the social interest with their own private interest. Many businessmen think of themselves as trustees mediating among the in-

terests of stockholders, workers, suppliers, customers, their local communities, and the general public.

The fact that businessmen are increasingly concerned about their social responsibilities is explained in several ways. First, businessmen have been forced to be so because they have been operating in a climate of opinion in which increased public regulation, and even public ownership, have been considered ever-present threats, and because they have been confronted with the relentless pressure of a determined labor movement. Second, businessmen have been persuaded to consider their social responsibilities because, as members of society, they have come to share the evolving standards of the society as to what business ought to be like and how it ought to be operated. Third, as a result of the separation of ownership and control in the large corporation, management has become increasingly professionalized, and more broadly representative of various interests and points of view.

The doctrine of social responsibility is frequently subject to criticism on the ground that competition would prevent businessmen from assuming costly social obligations, or that the added burden of cost would reduce productive efficiency. It is true that costs would sometimes be increased. It is true also that these costs might be shifted to consumers in the form of higher prices. It does not follow, however, that social consequences of production should be ignored. The welfare of the people can be raised not only by increasing the flow of final goods but also by improving the conditions under which these goods are produced. Moreover, in a progressive society competition will not necessarily prevent some of the progress from occurring in the form of improved conditions of production.

The doctrine of social responsibility is also often criticized on the ground that businessmen are too incorrigibly wedded to the profit motive to consider voluntarily their social re-

sponsibilities. But the author finds that businessmen have many motives, of which profit is but one—though of course a powerful one. And businessmen recognize that even their profits, in the long run, will depend on their contribution to social welfare. Hence, the concept of social responsibility merges with the long-run interests of businessmen.

If the doctrine of social responsibility is to become a more significant force in shaping the decisions and actions of businessmen, the attitudes of businessmen must become more attuned to social needs, and the attitude of the public must become more insistent in its demand for good social performance from business. In achieving both of these conditions, religious groups have an important task. But in our desire to increase the social responsiveness of business, let us not impose burdens heavier than can be borne, or make demands that strain the capacity of men to serve the interests of others. In particular, unreasonable attacks on profit and the profit system should be avoided. Moreover, when businessmen are asked to follow certain lines of behavior, it is important that the prescriptions be technically valid in the sense that they will actually contribute toward the end desired.

Several changes in business organization and practice might help in advancing the concept of social responsibility as a force in business management. For example, public members might be included in boards of directors; representatives of the public interest might be given positions in management; business firms might be subjected to periodic appraisals of their social performance—a kind of social audit; business managers might be more broadly educated; business operations might be subjected to greater publicity; and more attention might be given to research in the social aspects of business decisions.

A major proposal, emanating from many sources including the Roman Catholic Church, is for broader participation in

business and economic decisions. To this end, industry councils, and national economic councils, are often proposed. In Western Europe several experiments along this line have been undertaken.

The principal conclusions of the study are: (1) that the problem of identifying and formulating the social responsibilities of businessmen is an extremely complex matter that goes to the very root of our basic social and economic philosophy; (2) that, though it is easy to assert that businessmen should assume certain responsibilities, deeper analysis often shows that there are strict limits to the range and extent of the responsibilities they can reasonably be expected to assume; (3) that much careful study, research, and ethical analysis will be required before we shall be able to formulate the social responsibilities of business in a form that will be concrete and widely acceptable; (4) that in this study various points of view and various kinds of technical competency must be effectively represented; (5) that the economic problems of our society—problems such as instability, insecurity, injustice, and lack of work satisfaction—cannot be solved merely by turning the responsibility over to business. Businessmen—and other groups as well—can contribute by assuming those responsibilities that they can reasonably bear. Part of the job rests with other groups, and part of it must be undertaken by government. One of the great needs of our society, therefore, is to achieve cooperative and mutual relationships among groups, and between government and groups, such that urgent social purposes can be effectively defined and carried out. In this, businessmen have an important constructive role to play—a role that includes both leadership and cooperation.

WEALTH AND THE GOOD LIFE

The study of wealth and the good life by Professor Elizabeth E. Hoyt is a critique of the content of American consump-

tion.[2] Our consumption practices are subjected to critical examination and suggestions for improvement are offered.

Among the aspirations of the American people, no other is so universally proclaimed as a *high level of consumption*. By this is meant an abundance of the goods and services that flow from the labor, natural resources, and capital so richly supplied on this continent.

For individuals, this aspiration is in the form of a desire to secure for one's self and one's family more of material goods and services. For the nation as a whole, this aspiration is in the form of a myriad of public policies designed, or rationalized, to raise still higher a level of consumption that already surpasses anything in recorded history. Politicians announce that their programs are directed toward a higher level of consumption. Businessmen boast of the productivity of the free enterprise system. And almost everyone accepts as axiomatic that the road to human welfare lies in the direction of ever-increasing quantities of goods and services.

A *high level of consumption* is given so lofty a place among the values of the American people that pride in their country and their culture is commonly expressed in terms of the great supply of material things this nation affords. And perhaps the most widely-respected members of modern American society are the scientists, inventors, engineers, and business organizers who provide the technological base on which the high level of consumption rests.

One might expect, says Professor Hoyt, that this devoted concern for ever larger quantities of material things would be matched by an equally zealous concern for the uses to which these things are to be put. Unhappily, one finds that this is not so. Instead, there is a kind of naïve view that if only more production could be piled on top of an already bounteous supply, something good would come of it all. Few are those who ask: What are we getting out of all this production? Do

[2] *Amer. Income*, pp. 3-77.

our wealth and income add up to anything important in terms of values that lie close to the center and the meaning of life? How might the uses to which we devote our riches be improved? These are questions that tax our capacity to look inward, and so we turn on our television sets and ignore them.

In short, we are content to consider consumption as an end in itself rather than as a means to the good life. We are content with the belief that whatever things individuals choose to buy, under the pressure and compulsions they face in our materialistic culture, are the things that are *prima facie* worth producing. We leave largely by default the question of how the use of our abundant goods and services may contribute toward, or detract from, the attainment of more fundamental human goals. How much of our energy and attention is given to increasing the flow of goods and services—any goods and services! And how little is given to the problem of what things are worth producing, and how these might be used for the fuller attainment of higher human purposes!

When questions are raised regarding the use of our abundant material things, there is no implication that abundance is *per se* undesirable. The technology that makes this abundance possible is itself neutral; it has possibilities for both good and ill. This we have seen most dramatically in the case of atomic energy; but it applies as well to all material things and powers emanating from technology. Food may be used to nourish the body, or it may be used to destroy the body through overindulgence. Television may be used to enlarge men's minds and spirits and to bring them into sympathetic communication with other lives, or it may be an instrument of banality and degradation. One can go through the whole list of material goods and services and find that each is capable of either use or misuse. As Professor Hoyt suggests, most of us, in our more thoughtful moments, know that these things are true; yet in our actions we proceed in the sublime con-

fidence that more and more goods will somehow automatically yield a counterpart in greater human well-being.

Technology has the power to provide the goods necessary for more people to live with health and strength; it can be used to ease our traditional back-bending burdens; it can be used to conserve our time and energy from menial tasks so that we can devote ourselves to more important things; it can be used to help us achieve a variety of intellectual, aesthetic, and spiritual values. In short, technology can be the instrument for achieving human purposes of the highest order.

On the other hand—we sometimes see this less clearly—technology and its fruits can be used for unworthy ends, and can contribute to the debasement of men. But perhaps more important, men become so fascinated by technology and its products that these things actually absorb men's lives and divert them from higher values. Thus, caught up in a kind of materialistic rat race, men neglect the intellectual, aesthetic, spiritual, and humanitarian aspects of their lives. The root of the problem is that we have the power to produce more material things than we know how to use wisely. The surplus tends to be used up in the perpetual multiplication of gadgets —a process that is stimulated by invidious motives and high-pressure selling. Our desire to keep up appearances, to follow fashion, to maintain social status, distracts us from pursuing the deeper values of life. Most of us, unhappily, are relatively helpless to resist the embrace of technology, because the pattern of consumption and of life that it dictates becomes part of the cultural milieu. It can be resisted only by those few who dare nonconformity.

When we ask the positive question of how our productive powers *ought* to be used, Professor Hoyt points out that we immediately face problems of the deepest import. There are no ready-made formulas to guide us. For example, with reference to any object of consumer expenditure, there is great

difficulty in deciding just what is necessary to physical, psychical, and spiritual welfare, as distinguished from what is conventional or what is required for "keeping up."

Even for such a fundamental human need as nutrition, those minimal requirements that on the basis of scientific evidence may be called necessities cannot be rigorously prescribed. Such knowledge as we have indicates that the minimal requirements could be met with a diet far less costly than that now customary in the United States. Provision of food above this minimum can be justified only on psychical, aesthetic, or other grounds. The minimal physical requirements for clothing and housing are probably even more difficult to ascertain with scientific precision, and the essential minimum is even smaller, in relation to American consumption practice, than in the case of food.

When we turn to objects of expenditure like education, aesthetics, recreation, religion, or even children, the minimal requirements must be expressed mostly in terms of the psychical, emotional, or spiritual needs of men rather than in terms of physical requirements. Thus it is clear that science is of little help to us except in defining the minimal conditions of life, physical strength and health, and perhaps the minimal conditions of mental health (though the latter is so enmeshed in the culture as almost to defy any definition independent of culture).

Of one thing we can be reasonably sure: that the productive power of our technological society greatly exceeds the requirements for sustaining life and meeting the minimal needs of human beings. The question is: How shall the surplus be used? Shall it be used to provide an endless round of gadgets, of excitement, of self-indulgence, of novelty for its own sake, of emulation, of self-defeating efforts to surpass one's neighbors and excite their envy, of conformity with senseless conventions, of noise, and of superficiality? Shall we continue to

be so enthralled by technology and its works that our time and energy become dissipated in pursuit of its illusory rewards? Most important of all, shall we continue to allow a large share of the surplus to be destroyed in recurrent wars?

Professor Hoyt's answer to these rhetorical questions is clearly negative. There are two alternatives. One would be to reduce our production, and to renounce many of the things technology makes possible for us. This would seem both impracticable and undesirable, in view of the poverty and scarcity that confront most of the world's people. The other alternative is to find ways of utilizing the surplus that will contribute more fully (1) to our own development as human beings, and (2) to the needs of the larger world community of which we are a part and toward which we have responsibilities.

What we require is a philosophy of consumption or of the use of material wealth. There is no ready-made formula for this. The problem is one that people, individually and collectively, must work out for themselves. Certain general principles may, however, be tentatively advanced.

First, with respect to our own consumption, there can be little doubt that the range of choices is too restricted. Our culture opens up a wealth of possibilities for using material things for excitement, self-indulgence, emulation, etc.; but it does not correspondingly, or so fully, present to individuals the possibilities of using wealth for the attainment of intellectual, aesthetic, and spiritual goals. The advantages of a new refrigerator are more obvious than the benefits of a new truth, a new friend, an aesthetic experience, or tranquility. We need to develop more fully the possibilities of new types of consumption, in which the satisfactions and achievements to be gained are more deeply humane and satisfying than those to be found in the acquisition and display of physical things. Our problem is to achieve a more harmonious balance between the material and spiritual aspects of consumption.

Second, there is little doubt that our culture does not present to people the possibilities of *sharing* with others so clearly as it does the possibilities of using things for ourselves. There are enormous potentialities in the use of our productivity for the purpose of extending our contacts with other peoples, of developing our understanding of them, of learning from them, and of sharing our substance with them. The author suggests that to achieve this enlargement of our human relationships, and this sharing with others, requires the application of imagination and skill far beyond what we have known. It calls for no less than the use of our technology and the wealth it provides to carry out the commandment of *love*—a love that extends to our neighbors both at home and abroad. It requires an outward-looking and outward-sharing point of view in the use of our wealth—in place of the acquisitive, emulative attitude that is the disease of American society today.

DISTRIBUTION OF INCOME
AND LEVELS OF CONSUMPTION

The study of the distribution of income in America, by Professor Margaret G. Reid, assembles and interprets known facts about the division of our national income among households, and about levels of consumption.[3]

As Professor Reid shows, available data regarding incomes of the American people are very inadequate for the purposes to which they are often put. She warns against the many misinterpretations that arise from their uninformed use. In her study she tries to draw only warranted inferences from these data.

Per capita income in the United States far exceeds that in any other country. Apart from temporary declines in several

[3] Amer. Income, pp. 81–220.

depressions, U.S. per capita income, in terms of dollars of constant purchasing power, has been increasing steadily, and there is good reason to suppose that important increases will continue.

The predominant source of family income in the United States is the wages and salaries of workers. Therefore a study of the labor force, and of changes in its composition, depicts the changing sources of family income. The major changes in the labor force during the first half of the century were: (1) a decline in the percentage of young people (though this trend was at least temporarily reversed during World War II); (2) a decline in the percentage of old people in the labor force, much of which may be involuntary; (3) a marked increase in the percentage of married women in the labor force.

The percentage of married women carrying on gainful work is relatively low when there are young children in the family and when the husband is present in the family and earning a fairly good income; it is relatively high when the husband's earnings are small and when the children are of school age or there are no children. There is considerable uncertainty about sound social policy concerning the gainful employment of married women—particularly of mothers.

Differences in income among various types of families have apparently narrowed in some important respects within the past fifteen years. The percentage increase in per capita income had been greater in those states with low incomes than in those with high incomes. The per capita and per family incomes of non-white members of the population have increased more rapidly than those of whites. The income in low-paid occupations has increased relatively more than the income of high-paid occupations. Moreover, there has been some shrinkage in the percentage of total workers in the low-paid occupations. There is a marked association between incomes and years of schooling completed. It is possible that

the decrease in the percentage of persons with limited schooling may have contributed to the narrowing of the gap between the low-paid and high-paid occupations.

The annual income of farm families has increased more rapidly than that of non-farm families. On the question of the present income status of farm families as compared with non-farm families, careful examination of the data suggests that, when regional, racial, and other factors are taken into account, the real income of farm families is about as high as that of urban families, and perhaps a little higher than that of rural non-farm families. In so far as the difference between the farm and non-farm groups is due to regional and racial factors, a question is raised about the merits of our present farm policy that largely ignores the basic problem.

The great majority of families are dependent on one earner. Where there are additional earners, family incomes tend to be raised—but in many cases not greatly, because the additional earner is often a child or wife with a part-time job.

Great differences occur in income through the lifetime of individuals, and the family income cycle is chiefly determined by the life cycle of male earnings. This cycle starts out in youth at a low level of earnings, rises to a peak in middle life, and falls off again in old age. The resulting family income cycle is not closely related to family needs as measured by number of dependents.

About 7 per cent of all families have no earners, and these usually have very low incomes. In this group are many families with children and aged persons. There are many indications that children tend to be heavily concentrated in families with relatively low incomes.

Data on the distribution of income among households by amount of income are not well suited to measuring the degree of inequality or poverty; such data show a high degree of inequality. If measures of real economic welfare, as distinct from

money income, were available, the inequality would be found to be considerably less than the crude statistics now show. A large part of the lower income groups is made up of unrelated individuals (not members of families), of families with no earners, and of farmers whose real income is probably substantially higher than recorded money income. There is also some highly tentative evidence that incomes are becoming more nearly equal (though the data are very inadequate for this type of measurement). But after all these explanations of differences in income distribution have been made, there is no doubt that considerable poverty exists in the United States today—though probably not much among families who have full-time workers in the labor force.

THE SUPPORT OF DEPENDENTS

This study, by Professor Joseph L. McConnell and Miss Janet Hooks, is primarily an investigation of the American family in relation to the care of dependent individuals.[4]

The process of transition, over the past several centuries, from a pastoral-agricultural to an industrial society has been accompanied by profound changes in our social institutions and attitudes. Among these changes, none has been more significant than the metamorphosis in the structure of the family, and in our attitude toward familial relationships and responsibilities. These changes have given rise to important social problems concerning the support of dependent persons, to which we are still searching for solutions, though in the past several decades enormous progress has been made.

In all societies the source of income, or the means of livelihood, is production. One of the fundamental characteristics of human beings is that during a large fraction of their lives they are not able to produce enough to live on; or, more

[4] Amer. Income, pp. 223–291.

accurately, the market value of their productive contribution is not sufficient to command the necessary income for self-support. This is true in childhood, during periods of illness (mental or physical), and during old age. One of the major functions of the family, during all historic times, has been to provide reliable methods of assuring the support of those persons who are not able to support themselves. Thus a function of the family has been to nurture children, to care for the sick and the incompetent, and to provide for the aged.

Various societies have evolved different means of accomplishing these ends; that is, different family structures and different concepts of responsibility for the support of dependents. One of the most ancient is the *clan* family, which consists of a large group of persons related by blood or marriage, and which makes systematic provision for the support of all its dependent members. Another is the *stem* family, in which the lineage is transmitted through the eldest son, who becomes head of the household and assumes responsibility for the support and care of members of the family who become dependent. This type of family has been historically common in Western Europe, Japan, and elsewhere. In some respects, the early American frontier family was similar to the stem family.

For our present purposes, the important element in these earlier family forms was that they provided systematic methods of caring for the children and other members of the family who became for any reason dependent. And reinforcing these practices were strong attitudes regarding the responsibility of the family toward its dependent members. These attitudes persist to this day, and influence our thinking on the question of the care of dependents, even after the structure of the family and the means of discharging these responsibilities have undergone revolutionary changes.

For a variety of reasons associated with the transition from

agricultural to industrial life, the authors find that the American family has evolved into an almost purely *conjugal* unit, consisting of a husband, a wife, and their children. This is a small isolated unit, having few close ties, either on an economic or affectional basis, with other family groups or individuals with whom it is related by blood or marriage. Though one may be friendly with uncles, cousins, nephews, grandparents, and other relatives outside the immediate circle of the conjugal family, the relationships are not typically those of mutual economic dependence or even of close affectional relationships. The conjugal family is a very close-knit, self-centered, independent, exclusive, and isolated group.

The conjugal family is a reasonably efficient instrument for nurturing children during their dependency—as long as the family remains intact and the breadwinner is reliable. But, because of its structure and its isolation, it is not an efficient device for the care of its own when the family is broken by death, divorce, or desertion; when the breadwinner becomes ill or dies; or when the breadwinner becomes aged. It is sometimes not efficient even when the family is intact and the breadwinner in his productive years, if the number of children is large. In all these cases, if the conjugal family is expected to assume the responsibilities the clan family was once so well suited to discharge, it will be found inadequate to the task.

This is not to argue that we should return to the clan system; that system had many disadvantages from the point of view of our modern individualistic attitudes, and from the point of view of the successful functioning of an industrial economy. Nor does this suggest that the family should have no responsibility for the security of its own members. But it does suggest that we must seek new solutions to the problem of dependency, and that we must not persist in placing a

greater burden on the conjugal family than it is well suited to carry.

Already our attitudes on this question have changed, as indicated by the enactment of social insurance and by the great popularity of private pension plans. But more remains to be done if we are to achieve adequate security for dependents, and are at the same time to retain the isolated conjugal family.

There are four principal classes of dependents to be considered: (1) those who are members of families broken by death, divorce, or estrangement; (2) those in families in which the breadwinner is ill or incompetent; (3) children who are members of large families; (4) the aged. In each of these cases the economic problem is closely related to psychological problems that emerge from conditions of insecurity, neglect, lack of affection, etc.

In the case of the widows and children of broken families, beginnings have been made through social security legislation to provide aid to dependent children. We are groping toward provision for families in which the breadwinner becomes ill, though little progress has yet been made. Many European countries and Canada have experimented with family allowances to assist those families with large numbers of children. Old age and survivors' insurance, old age assistance, and other public and private pension plans are designed to alleviate the economic problems of old age. It can hardly be said, however, that we have effected an adequate adjustment to the problem of support for dependents that has resulted from industrialism and the changing nature of the family. We still have a great deal of thinking ahead on the basic ethical issue of the extent to which responsibility should be assumed by the family and the extent to which it should be met by social devices.

ECONOMIC VALUES AND PROBLEMS
OF THE COMMON MAN

This study, reported by A. Dudley Ward, was carried out with the facilities of the National Opinion Research Center.[5] It was designed to explore the values that people seek through economic life and the problems they face in their daily economic activities. The study was concerned especially with values and problems relating to work, security, and housing. Data for the study were obtained from interviews with a cross-sectional sample of individuals living in Chicago, Rockford, and adjacent areas. Additional data and a wealth of illustrative detail were derived from the deliberations of 30 discussion groups—located in many parts of the country— which agreed to consider relevant questions and to report to Mr. Ward the results of their deliberations.

A summary of an ambitious empirical study such as this is unlikely to do justice to the rich variety of the informative data presented; only the high spots can be touched on. The interested reader is urged to consult the study itself to obtain a more rounded picture of the values of the American people as there presented.

Perhaps the major emphasis in the study was on *work*. Evidence gathered indicated the obvious—that people work primarily for the things money will buy and for the security their jobs afford. But many regard work not merely as a meal ticket, but as itself an important source of values. Most individuals feel that work contributes to personality and to the fullness of life. This belief was evident in the expressed attitudes of people toward their own jobs; but was indicated even more revealingly in their attitudes toward marginal workers. For example, they believe that work in moderation is "good" for high school students. Similarly, they believe that

[5] *Am. Ec.*

old people should continue to work at an appropriate pace as long as they are physically able. And they approve of the employment of married women when their work does not interfere unduly with the care of children and the functioning of the home.

Not only do people value work for its own sake, but also as a means by which they are able to contribute something to the welfare of their fellow men. Most individuals are able to verbalize readily and explicitly about the value to society of their own jobs. Often this may be rationalization; nevertheless it indicates that people are concerned to contribute something to society through their work.

The evidence from this study indicates that people on the whole are reasonably satisfied with their jobs; indeed, it is remarkable how few were the complaints. This condition is doubtless a reflection of the high level of employment in 1951 when the data were gathered. At that time people were enjoying high wages, and were fortified by the freedom and security that go with the ability to change jobs at will. Some respondents referred to the inadequacy of their earnings; some thought there should be more opportunity to get ahead; some complained of inconvenient hours, physical or nervous strain, monotony, etc. Yet the overwhelming impression one gleans from the study is that most people are reasonably satisfied with their work.

One of the most frequent assumptions made by critics of modern industrial society is that work is destructive of human personality. It is frequently asserted that the minute specialization of modern industrial technology results in monotony, lack of interest in work, inability of the individual worker to appreciate the social significance of his job, and failure to fulfill the creative urge. A careful effort was made to test the validity of this assumption. It was found, through a wide variety of questions bearing both directly and indirectly on the point,

that only a very small proportion of workers share these views of the social critics. Few workers indicated that their jobs are monotonous or lack interest; most had a strong sense of the importance of what they do. Sometimes this importance was expressed in terms of the significance of their work to society, and sometimes in terms of the significance of their tasks to the team of workers (or the firm) of which they are a part. Few indicated that their jobs did not make full use of their talents and capacities. Altogether, the expressed attitudes of the respondents in this study lend little support to the assumption that modern workers are robots whose work involves deadly monotony and destruction of personality.[6]

Social critics also frequently assume that modern work is baneful because of the impersonal human relations on the job. Here again the evidence of the study tends to belie the critics. It was found that one of the most important values people find in their work is the human associations it offers. These associations are with fellow workers, customers, sellers, etc. What people miss most keenly when they do not work is these associations; and what determines whether they like or dislike their jobs is the quality of the human relations involved. Work is anything but impersonal; it is personal, and it provides one of the most important opportunities for satisfying human associations. Indeed, because modern work offers opportunities for satisfying human relations and teamwork, the monotony and boredom postulated by so many social critics is not actually experienced by many workers. In this respect, this study confirms the findings of modern industrial sociology on the importance of informal groups in the work place.

A second part of the study dealt with personal security and

[6] The social critic may properly reply that his assertion is still true—that people have been so deadened by industrial work that they are incapable of realizing their plight. This study, of course, only reports the expressed attitudes of people.

insecurity. Few respondents were preoccupied with fears of unemployment; the data were collected in 1951 after ten years of virtually uninterrupted full employment. Neither were people greatly concerned with fears of economic want in old age. No doubt this reflected the widespread availability of public and private pension arrangements. The overwhelming number of causes of economic insecurity was fears of ill health. The evidence on this was so striking that one is tempted to conclude that inadequate provision for the costs of medical care, and—more important—inadequate provision against loss of income from sickness, accident, or death of the breadwinner, are the greatest sources of insecurity in this country today.

On the whole, the respondents feel that provision for security against contingencies is and should be primarily an individual responsibility. When they think of security, they think of a job, of an income, of money in the bank, of capital assets; they do not think of security in terms of political arrangements. They do not oppose social security, but question the extension of social security on the ground that it might undermine individual initiative and incentive. The study provides little support for the thesis, sometimes advanced, that people are inclined to turn to the government to solve all their problems. Doubtless, to be sure, the feeling of self-reliance and of individual responsibility conveyed by the respondents is as much an expression of long-continued prosperity as of basic attitudes. Yet from this study one gains the distinct impression that the haunting fears engendered by the great depression of the 1930s have been pretty largely allayed, and—at least at the time this study was made—people were facing the future with remarkable assurance.[7] This was apparently true

[7] Of great importance to economists is the strong indication that the influence of the Great Depression on the attitudes of people, an influence that seemed to linger throughout World War II and after, has largely disappeared.

of all classes—manual workers, middle class, salaried persons, and independent businessmen.

Perhaps the most striking feature of the study was the unmistakable interest of the respondents in home ownership; home ownership is one of their leading values. They feel that it is good for them as individuals, and that widespread home ownership is good for the country. They value home ownership partly because they think of it as representing solid family life, good neighborhoods, good environments for children, good citizenship, and social stability. But—perhaps even more important—they regard home ownership as a practicable avenue to personal security. Paying off the mortgage debt is considered a stimulus to steady saving and getting ahead. And when a substantial equity has been attained, the owned home is thought of as a roof over one's head in adversity and old age. At the same time, a majority of the respondents indicated some degree of dissatisfaction with present housing, and either hoped or dreamed of securing better housing (or living arrangements) in the future. The high degree of reported dissatisfaction with present housing may have been due to the fact that much of the interviewing was done in Chicago and vicinity, where housing problems have been acute. Whether similar results would have been obtained in other areas is unknown.

Psychoneurosis and Economic Life

Dr. Stanley A. Leavy and Dr. Lawrence Z. Freedman, psychiatrists in the Yale University School of Medicine, undertook to explore relationships between the problems faced by individuals in their economic life and psychoneurosis.[8] The basic question considered was: What are the effects of the activities and changes of economic life on emotional illness or

[8] Am. Ec.

health? In general, this question was considered with respect to *neurosis* as distinguished from a more serious mental disorder called a *psychosis*. This limitation was made partly because neurotic experience is more closely similar to "normal" behavior, and partly because neurosis is more likely to be attributable to environmental causes than is psychosis. The procedure of the study included a survey of the not-too-extensive literature of the field, and an analysis of the histories of 500 patients. The study proceeded from the assumption that the primary forces leading to neurosis, apart from constitutional factors, are the identifications, fantasies, disappointments, deprivations, and indulgences occurring during the early life of the individual, and the protective mechanisms developed in response to these early experiences. But all the experiences of both early and adult life (including economic life) are of importance in affecting or modifying the tendencies determined in early life.

Economic life is related to emotional health in three ways. First, it exerts important influences on the social environment of childhood. It may produce in the family an atmosphere of anxiety, insecurity, and fear. Poverty may lead to deprivation and humiliation. Overcrowding may have important effects on the formation of ideals. The demands of work may prevent parents from giving sufficient attention to children or may require the prolonged absence of parents. The values, attitudes, and ideals of the child may be conditioned by early economic experiences, which may sensitize him to economic variations.

Second, economic experiences after childhood may cause emotional illness when there is predisposition to it. The problems and strains of economic life—unemployment, failure to achieve "success," and conflicts of values—may precipitate it. There are striking correlations between economic experience and some kinds of emotional disorder.

Third, economic life may be the theater for the expression of neurotic behavior. It provides an "arena for the enactment of competitive struggles which have been going on in one guise or another since childhood." Fears, guilt, and frustration may be expressed in economic terms—for example, in terms of money or jobs.

Studies of emotional illness during an economic depression indicate that poverty, insecurity, or loss of status may be significant causes, in the sense that marginal cases may be pushed over the threshold toward illness. Loss of job is often interpreted by the individual as loss of love or social disapproval, and leads to a sense of guilt. The unreliability of the economic environment may lead to a withdrawal from the attempt to master the environment. On the other hand, the study disclosed few cases in which emotional illness was related to the *type* of work done by the patient.

Work is an important aspect of the life of the individual. It is a source of self-respect, and a means of achieving a sense of belonging and personal worth. Ability to work is one of the criteria of emotional health in our society; illness usually results in a deterioration of the ability to work, which then becomes a sign of illness. Many patients seek help only when illness interferes with their work. Sometimes, however, work provides a partially sublimated expression of neurotic needs; for example, it may provide a screen of acceptability for compulsive overactivity.

Economic life sets up competitive goals, which, by their very competitiveness, cannot be attained by all individuals. "The goal of success is imposed without regard for the fact that the possibilities of its attainment are limited, and furthermore, that the activities necessary for success are by no means necessarily consonant with the recognized virtues of our culture." The failures and the moral ambiguities resulting from the goal of "success" are sources of frustration and conflict. At

the same time, seeking money by competitive effort is gratifying to the destructive needs of the individual; our society, by placing a high value on competitive effort, automatically places a high value on destructive impulses.

The study concludes with the generalization that economic life is a significant determinant of neurosis. "What persons do to earn a living, what kinds of experiences they have had as a result of their parents' problems of earning, what kind of economic mores of the community have been imposed upon them—such things constitute definable elements in the development of neurosis."

PART III

Some International Implications of Christian Economic Ethics

William Adams Brown, Jr.

6

Introduction

The main purpose of some other chapters of this volume is to summarize and appraise the conclusions reached in the earlier volumes of this series. Two of these volumes—*The Goals of Economic Life* and *The Organizational Revolution*—deal with broad intellectual and historical problems, but to a considerable extent they consider these problems as they apply to American experience. The other three—*Social Responsibilities of the Businessman, American Income and Its Use,* and *The American Economy—Attitudes and Opinions*—deal mainly, though not exclusively, with domestic aspects of the American scene. Yet many of the domestic issues raised in all five are of international concern. Until these issues have been analyzed, the technical and moral dilemmas that confront the United States in its international relations cannot be fully understood. This is one of the reasons why the international aspects of this inquiry have been reserved for separate treatment. Another reason is the extraordinary importance of the ethical issues raised by the dominant position now occupied by the United States in the world economy.

It is a major premise of the discussion of moral and ethical problems in this volume that the most fundamental issues of economic life are basically ethical. In the treatment here given of the international aspects of these problems this premise is strictly adhered to. It is rooted in Christian conviction, and implicit in the very nature of the whole inquiry. Since Christian principles assign supreme importance to the individual, the most significant questions that can be asked about the

operation of any economic system concern its effects on the quality of human personality. Any inquiry into the question whether our economic system is or can be made consistent with Christian principles must turn on profoundly ethical issues.

At any given time individuals are to a certain extent prisoners of the economic system under which they live. The ethical problems that confront them must be met within a given institutional framework. This is implied in the use of the term "our" economic system, and confirmed by the analysis of problems drawn from contemporary American economic life. Our economic system, however, is neither static nor American; it is dynamic and international. For want of a better term it has been called "present-day" or "welfare" capitalism; but this terminology is far from satisfactory. Though it suggests that our system is somehow different from the *laissez-faire* capitalism of the past, it does scant justice to the nature of this transformation, and gives no indication of the boundaries within which this system predominates.

The transformation of nineteenth-century capitalism to a stage where a new name for it has had to be found has been proceeding at a different pace and has taken different forms in different countries. In no country has it been due to the blind operation of economic forces; in all it has been the result of individual, group, or collective action in response to new problems brought about by a changing economic environment. This response has had a moral and ethical as well as an economic basis. It cannot be fully understood except in terms of the motivations, inner drives and necessities, and social and humanitarian impulses that have moved individuals in their daily economic life and in their collective actions in matters of social, political, and economic policy.

The social, economic, and political policies that have helped to create "present-day" capitalism have been so diverse in

different parts of the world that it is difficult, if not impossible, to define with any precision the boundaries of "our" economic system. Some of the distinctive characteristics of our system are found in all countries in which capitalistic methods of production are highly developed and a substantial share of the direction of economic life is left to individuals and private groups, but which nevertheless assign major economic responsibilities to government; for example, responsibilities for maintaining economic stability, preventing large-scale unemployment, or providing certain basic forms of social security. Yet such countries may differ widely on such vital matters as their faith in and use of economic planning, their selection of industries and services for public ownership, or their use of taxation to promote a more equitable distribution of property and income. What makes them part of our economic system is that they are *mixed* economies. In all such economies the ethical problems of economic life are similar—though of course not identical—to the American problems analyzed by other authors of this volume.

The departures from *laissez-faire* capitalism which led to "present-day" capitalism have in many ways complicated the international economic relations of the countries that are clearly part of our economic system. It is a truism that the economic interdependence of nations makes it impossible for any such country, least of all the United States, to find satisfactory solutions of its own economic problems in disregard of what is happening elsewhere.

In any country that has a substantial foreign trade or is a substantial exporter or importer of capital, the long chain of transactions that must be completed, if the advantages of extreme division of labor are to be preserved, includes many international transactions. If the international transactions are interrupted, distorted, or unbalanced, the domestic flow of payments and settlements will be disturbed. Many transactions

inside the country that on their face appear to have no relation to foreign trade or investment will be affected. Fluctuations in foreign trade and investment also influence the volume
of money in circulation and hence the stability of prices, and,
if very great, may contribute to inflation or deflation.

Every country, moreover, that is dependent on imports for
the satisfaction of basic needs and the improvement of its
standard of living must devote a sufficient proportion of its
resources to the production of the amount and kind of goods
and services required to pay for its imports. If for any reason
(inflation is one of the most common) it does not do so, such
a country is living beyond its means, and its international accounts get out of order. It comes under pressure to decrease
production for home consumption, and at the same time to
increase production for export by reducing the amount of
money and credit in circulation or by other means. In other
words, the country must submit to some measure of what
economists call "external discipline." This limits to some
degree its freedom to choose among various possible ways of
allocating its material and human resources to various branches
of production. It may—and often does—temporarily interfere with programs for full employment at satisfactory wages,
and with agricultural policies designed to assure agricultural
producers of what is deemed to be an equitable share in the
national income. It may reduce the amount of domestic
resources that would otherwise be considered as properly allo-
cated to carry the economic burden of various social welfare
enterprises.

External discipline (that is, pressure to adjust the domestic economy so that it will fit into an existing or developing international system of trade and payments) is often
resisted by the use of extensive economic controls. Such controls have been both defended and attacked on technical
economic grounds, but the debate has at bottom been con-

cerned with ethical problems. Are the controls essential to preserve the "welfare" state in a given country? Are they merely a means of shifting the economic difficulties of one country onto the shoulders of others? Do they destroy the benefits that can accrue from taking full advantage of the international division of labor, and thus work against, rather than in favor of, economic welfare?

Whenever the economic interdependence of nations sets in motion currents of trade or investment that upset or disturb the economy of any country or deeply affect the welfare of segments of its population, a moral as well as a technical economic dilemma has to be faced. Solutions of internal problems that appear not only to be reasonable and equitable, but also to provide necessary safeguards against the recurrence of social injustice, may and frequently do have international effects that are defensible neither on economic nor on moral grounds.

These difficulties are all compounded by the impact of "our" economic system on countries whose traditions, customs, religious and philosophical beliefs, and economic organization are alien to the dynamic spirit of capitalism in any form. This impact, in fact, has been so great that even the broad definition of "our" system used above does not do justice to its international character. The fields of study that have been drawn upon in Volume I of this series to show the trends of modern scientific thought as they relate to the goals of economic life are as international as freedom of thought itself. They know no international boundaries except those recently drawn by totalitarian dictatorship. The organizational revolution described in Volume II not only has been in progress for many years in all so-called Western capitalist countries, but is today taking hold at an accelerating rate in many underdeveloped countries, especially in the Far East. Many countries have suddenly and without adequate prepara-

tion been brought face to face with the ethical problems of "welfare" capitalism. The proper role of government—the most inclusive of all organizations—has, except in totalitarian states where it is all-embracing, become a major issue in the consideration of problems of economic development.

From a Christian point of view, the assertion that the most important problems of economic life are basically ethical has universal validity. This conviction is, however, by no means a monopoly of countries that call themselves Christian—quite the contrary. Nowhere is concern over the effects of the prevailing economic system on the quality of human life deeper than in non-Christian countries whose economies are being transformed by the influence of our economic system. The free flow of ideas and technical knowledge, the flow of trade and investment, and the demonstrated capacity of our system to provide the material basis for higher standards of living, all combine to make this influence extremely powerful. Serious ethical problems are raised when these forces threaten to undermine the moral and religious basis of another and different social order. One need look no farther than India for a classic example. The interaction of different economic systems is today producing ethical problems that are new both for countries in which "our" economic system prevails and for those in which it does not.

7

America's International Economic Responsibilities

The United States today occupies a position of great power at a time when the world is divided into two opposing camps—the free world facing the totalitarian world. The whole of Asia, Africa, and the Middle East is in a ferment. For the most part countries in these areas have little inclination to become involved in a conflict among great powers; but they cannot escape from the consequences of this struggle either economically or politically. In the realm of thought, feeling, and aspiration, people in these parts of the world are moved partly by a sense of past wrongs, but mainly by a fixed determination to pursue an independent course in which they will be masters of their own fate. In all so-called underdeveloped countries economic development has become a consuming ambition. In Europe many nations not yet fully recovered from the economic effects of the last war are now being called on to carry new burdens of rearmament. It is a matter of transcendent importance how, in such a world, the economic power of the United States is being or will be used.

There are many ways in which a country may be said to "use" its economic power. The image that is perhaps most frequently called up when the use of economic power is discussed in these times is its purposeful employment by a strong nation to impose its will on weaker countries, to secure international agreement on policies and arrangements it deems advantageous to itself, and generally to strengthen its diplomatic

arm. Since economic power includes economic potential for war, the "use" that is at present most likely to obscure all others in the minds of many people is its employment by both sides to gain superior strategic or tactical positions in the "cold war" between the free and the communist worlds. From the point of view of this inquiry, however, it would be seriously misleading to attach exclusive or even primary importance to these particular aspects of present-day international economic diplomacy.

The use of economic power as a weapon to achieve national objectives cannot be condemned out of hand as "power politics," unless these objectives are formulated and imposed unilaterally on other countries with little or no regard to their legitimate interests and views. There is no need to be ashamed of "dollar diplomacy," for example, if the objectives of that diplomacy are constructive and morally desirable, and are pursued in a spirit of international cooperation and good will. There are, in fact, many situations in which the failure of a strong nation to exert its economic power to achieve definite foreign policy objectives can be condemned on ethical grounds as strongly as outright abuse of that power. The ethical issues involved in the use of American economic power as an instrument of foreign policy can, therefore, be dealt with fruitfully only as they emerge from the pursuit by the United States of specific foreign policy objectives. These in turn cannot be judged from an ethical standpoint unless full account is taken of their role in the functioning of our domestic economy and of their impact on the internal economies of other countries.[1]

In the present posture of international affairs any action that the American government may take in the field of foreign economic policy will directly or indirectly affect the economic lives of many individual Americans or groups of Americans,

[1] This problem is discussed further in Chapter 8.

7

America's International Economic Responsibilities

The United States today occupies a position of great power at a time when the world is divided into two opposing camps—the free world facing the totalitarian world. The whole of Asia, Africa, and the Middle East is in a ferment. For the most part countries in these areas have little inclination to become involved in a conflict among great powers; but they cannot escape from the consequences of this struggle either economically or politically. In the realm of thought, feeling, and aspiration, people in these parts of the world are moved partly by a sense of past wrongs, but mainly by a fixed determination to pursue an independent course in which they will be masters of their own fate. In all so-called underdeveloped countries economic development has become a consuming ambition. In Europe many nations not yet fully recovered from the economic effects of the last war are now being called on to carry new burdens of rearmament. It is a matter of transcendent importance how, in such a world, the economic power of the United States is being or will be used.

There are many ways in which a country may be said to "use" its economic power. The image that is perhaps most frequently called up when the use of economic power is discussed in these times is its purposeful employment by a strong nation to impose its will on weaker countries, to secure international agreement on policies and arrangements it deems advantageous to itself, and generally to strengthen its diplomatic

arm. Since economic power includes economic potential for war, the "use" that is at present most likely to obscure all others in the minds of many people is its employment by both sides to gain superior strategic or tactical positions in the "cold war" between the free and the communist worlds. From the point of view of this inquiry, however, it would be seriously misleading to attach exclusive or even primary importance to these particular aspects of present-day international economic diplomacy.

The use of economic power as a weapon to achieve national objectives cannot be condemned out of hand as "power politics," unless these objectives are formulated and imposed unilaterally on other countries with little or no regard to their legitimate interests and views. There is no need to be ashamed of "dollar diplomacy," for example, if the objectives of that diplomacy are constructive and morally desirable, and are pursued in a spirit of international cooperation and good will. There are, in fact, many situations in which the failure of a strong nation to exert its economic power to achieve definite foreign policy objectives can be condemned on ethical grounds as strongly as outright abuse of that power. The ethical issues involved in the use of American economic power as an instrument of foreign policy can, therefore, be dealt with fruitfully only as they emerge from the pursuit by the United States of specific foreign policy objectives. These in turn cannot be judged from an ethical standpoint unless full account is taken of their role in the functioning of our domestic economy and of their impact on the internal economies of other countries.[1]

In the present posture of international affairs any action that the American government may take in the field of foreign economic policy will directly or indirectly affect the economic lives of many individual Americans or groups of Americans,

[1] This problem is discussed further in Chapter 8.

their private interests, and their responsibilities as citizens. At the same time, the manner in which the United States conducts its domestic economic affairs will directly or indirectly affect the economic lives of individuals and groups in many other countries. They, as well as the American people, must take the consequences of our failure to maintain high and stable levels of economic activity in this country, to use our natural resources wisely, or to maintain a social system free of class struggle, prolonged labor-management disputes, and alternating periods of boom and depression. Such failures, if they occur, cannot be reconciled with the external as well as the domestic responsibility that rests jointly on the American people and their government for a wise use of America's great economic resources and productive capacity.

The ethical issues treated elsewhere in this book were concerned mainly with the actions of persons either singly or in groups, when confronted with the choices, perplexities, burdens, and responsibilities of economic life. These burdens and responsibilities do not stop at the water's edge; and the manner in which they are carried is extremely relevant to the question whether the use of American economic power in the world today is or can be made consistent with Christian principles.

INDIVIDUAL RESPONSIBILITY AND NATIONAL RESPONSIBILITY[2]

The individual American is a citizen of a country rich in resources, fortunate in location, endowed with great economic, military, and political power, and dedicated to concepts of individual liberty and religious freedom. Whether he recognizes it or not, this imposes on him a certain measure of international responsibility, which has to be met in the day-to-day

[2] The author is indebted to Dr. Reinhold Niebuhr for helpful criticism and valuable suggestions in the writing of this section.

conduct of private business, in financial and professional dealings, and in all contacts with individuals and groups in the
rest of the world.

It goes without saying that a sense of Christian responsibility
requires the individual American to base his dealings with
foreigners, as with his fellow citizens, on considerations of
mutual advantage, and to refrain from all forms of exploitation. It is equally a truism that Christian love requires him
to respond to the call of human need beyond our borders.
From a Christian point of view his international responsibility
extends far beyond this. In a world of many cultures, of many
different religious insights, and of intensely felt national
and racial loyalties, it includes as a major element the things
of the spirit. Tolerance, fair dealing, cooperation in good
works, sincerity, and a spirit of accommodation in negotiations do not by themselves fully discharge this responsibility.
There must be in addition an inward attitude of respect for
the beliefs and loyalties of foreigners, especially those who see
in the penetration of our economic system a threat to their
cherished values. Given this respect, a willingness to learn
from them and an appreciation of what they can and
do contribute to the enrichment of our personal and national
life follow almost automatically. This implies neither weakness nor subservience; far from involving a compromise with
basic Christian principles, it is a true expression of them.

The development of such an attitude on the part of the
citizens of a country in the position of the United States today,
whether they be in business or in the professions, in the service
of the church or of the state, is a prerequisite for good and cooperative international relations in that part of the world not shut
off from normal international intercourse by impenetrable
barriers of self-imposed isolation. It is also a safeguard against
a fatalistic acceptance of these barriers as permanent. No
dictator, however powerful, can permanently and completely

destroy the bonds of common humanity and of genuine mutual interest that exist among all peoples, on whichever side of the Iron Curtain they may be. It is part of the Christian approach to international relations to proclaim the continued existence of these bonds, and to prepare for the day when the artificial separation that now prevails within the human race can be brought to an end.

Every factor, therefore, that influences the role played by the United States in the conduct of international trade, the flow of international investment, and the settlement of international indebtedness has a direct bearing on the question of how American economic power is being or can be used in the world today. The complexity of the issues often leads individuals to feel helpless, and powerless to deal with them directly. Even granting the importance of the imponderables that have just been referred to, such persons may take the view that the fundamental issues of international economic life are basically economic and not basically ethical. Though this view has already been rejected in the opening statements of this Part, the reasons for rejecting it may be helpfully reformulated somewhat as follows.

In any country whose economy has passed beyond the rudimentary stage, the various segments of the population cooperate to increase the total production available for consumption under a system of division of labor. The division of labor as a form of cooperation provides a community of interest that binds together the different segments of the population. At the same time the division of labor and the separation of economic functions that make increased production possible create conflicts of economic interest that permeate the whole economy of any advanced country. Many ethical problems faced by individuals and groups have their roots in this dual relationship, and many partial solutions of these problems have been worked out without taking adequate

account of the overriding interests of the whole community as opposed to those of one or another of its parts.

It is not different in the world economy and the community of nations. The solution of such problems in one important country always affects the economic life of others. This is the basic justification for asserting that no clear and definite line can be drawn between the ethical issues that arise from the attempt to apply Christian principles in the conduct of our internal affairs and those that arise from the attempt to apply them in our international affairs. A distinction has nevertheless to be drawn between the responsibilities of individuals and groups in reconciling their economic conduct with Christian principles, and the corresponding responsibilities that rest on government in the international field.

In a world of sovereign states in all stages of economic development and varying degrees of economic power, conflicts of economic interest tend to be magnified; and community of economic interest tends to be honored more often in the breach than in the observance. In some important ways the transformation of "our" system into one of "present-day" or "welfare" capitalism has tended to counteract these tendencies, and to bring the theme of community of interest in international relations strongly to the front. But, as has been noted, this change has in some ways also had the opposite effect. Concern for the welfare of their own citizens has often in recent times led very enlightened governments to take measures difficult to reconcile with the welfare of other countries and the general interests of the community of nations. The question of how far the general conclusions reached in Parts I and II can be applied to relations among sovereign states must be faced squarely.

It has sometimes been questioned whether one can speak of applying Christian principles to international conduct. This question is raised because the Christian ethic makes love the

norm of all relationships, and sacrificial love is undoubtedly the highest and purest form. But this norm seems not to be applicable to the actions of governments. A private individual may sacrifice his own interests for the sake of his fellow man; but when he does so he does not compel others to share this sacrifice with him. Yet those entrusted with governmental authority are not in this position. If as a result of their decisions a nation is called on to make sacrifices, even for a higher and more inclusive good, the burden falls on the whole community. A distinction has therefore to be drawn between the ethics of individual life and collective life. This does not, however, totally invalidate Christian principles of conduct in the life of nations. In the collective life of man, as well as in the individual life, we must regard a vast system of mutual relations as the basic datum of ethics. The nation as well as the individual must recognize its responsibilities in this system of mutual relations.

There can be no doubt that heavy responsibilities of this kind rest on the United States as a sovereign state, because of its unique position of economic power. It is sometimes assumed that the discharge of these responsibilities requires the United States to serve interests broader than its own. This view was eloquently stated, for example, in a speech by Secretary of State Acheson on June 29, 1951, before a group of magazine and book publishers: "We will continue to be accepted as the leader only if the other countries believe that the pattern of responsibility within which we operate is a responsibility to interests broader than our own."[3]

This assumption requires careful scrutiny when it is applied to the policies and actions of a sovereign state. Those who urge the Government of the United States to serve interests broader than those of the American people put it in a false position. The benevolent intentions of the government of a

[3] *Department of State Bulletin*, Vol. XXV, No. 630, p. 128.

sovereign state presuming to act for interests broader than its own will not be taken at face value; and such a government is open to charges of hypocrisy brought by other countries. The reason for this is not far to seek. When the people of the United States elect a President and Congress, they entrust to them one primary responsibility—to safeguard and promote the welfare, prosperity, and security of the United States. By the nature of their office they must act in the American interest. They are not and could not be entrusted by the American electorate with responsibility for the welfare of other countries. The welfare of other countries, therefore, cannot be a primary objective of their policies and action; though it can be a very important objective if it is accepted and pursued because it serves the primary one—the welfare of the United States. As far as the government of a sovereign state is concerned, the key to action, including action that promotes the welfare of other countries, is service to its own people.

The National Interest

Consequently the important problem in international relations is to find the points of concurrence between the interests of the nation and the wider good. In the contemporary case the wider good would be the whole democratic civilization embodied in the alliance of free nations. It may seem that since self-sacrifice is excluded this wider good must be defined in terms of "wise self-interest." That is, our responsibilities to other nations must be seen from the standpoint of the national interest. But it must be immediately apparent that if the wider interest is looked at too consistently from the standpoint of the national interest, the national interest will be narrowed to the point where the broader interests really involved in the long-run national interest will be excluded. It is important, therefore, to distinguish between the use of ir-

responsible self-interest as a guide to the actions of the state, and the conception of the national interest that exists in the minds and hearts of its people. A state cannot sacrifice its national interest; but its people—particularly a people informed by Christian ideals—must have a concern for interests other than their own. The statesmen who formulate and conduct foreign policy must have among their motives a genuine concern for the welfare of other countries, if they are to respond effectively to the expression of such concern on the part of their own people, and to give the type of leadership that is called for in a country aspiring to Christian ideals. The men and women recruited to carry out the policy—for example, technicians working in technical assistance programs—must be the kind of people who really care about the welfare of the countries to which they go, if the policy is to be effective.

This concern is the force that prevents the national interest from being so narrow as to come in conflict with wider interests. It establishes a counterweight to a nation's self-interest, which, when expressed in really consistent terms, must set the nation against its allies and friends. In a day when America is called on to be the leader of a vast alliance of free nations, it is particularly important that the moral and religious discipline of our people should operate to prevent the concept of national interest from being too narrow. This must be emphasized, even though it is recognized that the foreign policy of a nation cannot absolutely transcend the national interest.

There are many people who think that the primary obligation of sovereign governments to serve the national interest is a defect in the system of sovereign states so basic that the only remedy is the disappearance of that system. They believe that this system is obsolete, especially in Europe; and they look for the solution of many of our international problems

by a progressive, if not an immediate, surrender of sovereignty. The basic similarity that is emphasized above—between ethical problems arising in the functioning of our economic system within a single country and ethical problems involved in its international functioning—suggests that surrender of sovereignty may not by itself provide or force satisfactory solutions. Many problems we now call international would merely become interregional or domestic, without much change in their character. Some would undoubtedly be more satisfactorily dealt with in a larger political framework than under our present system, but only after a painful period of adjustment. This advantage, moreover, might have to be purchased by the loss of ethical and moral values that are conserved by the institution of the national state.

In any case the United States is, and is likely long to remain, a sovereign state. Its government will continue to use the national interest as the touchstone of its policies. The protecting and safeguarding of that interest will continue to call for the creation, maintenance, and defense of that kind of world order in which a set of values acceptable to the American people will be recognized and respected. The quality of American leadership in contributing to a better economic and political world order will depend in the last analysis on what these values are. A genuine concern for the larger welfare should be among the guiding motives of Christian people— though they should not claim any monopoly of such concern. The deeper and more widespread this concern is, the easier it will be for the government of the United States to provide enlightened, and even Christian, leadership in world affairs.

The American government will continue to promote the general interests of the world community, because only by so doing can it adequately serve the long-run national interest. What can and should be asked of it is that it broaden and elevate its concept of America's national interest. In many

ways it has already done this during the past fifteen years. It has come to identify the national interest of the United States more and more with some of the national interests of other countries, and with the fulfillment of some of their aspirations. Many of its policies have shown an increasing awareness of the community of interest that exists among nations, as it does among individuals and groups. Acting as a sovereign government, it has committed this country to the promotion of free and democratic institutions, to the defense of free nations threatened by aggression, to the building up of collective security, and to the achievement of a just and durable peace. It has committed this country to the principles of the United Nations, including the settlement of international disputes by peaceful means, participation in collective action when breaches of the peace take place, and joint and separate action in cooperation with the United Nations to promote higher standards of living, full employment, and conditions of social and economic progress throughout the world.

In the Declaration of Philadelphia adopted by the International Labor Organization in 1944, the American government accepted the thesis that all national policies and measures —in particular those of an economic character—shall be accepted only in so far as they may be held to promote and not to hinder "the attainment of conditions in which all human beings may pursue and preserve both their material well-being and spiritual development in conditions of freedom and dignity, of economic security and equal opportunity."

By accepting membership in the Food and Agriculture Organization of the United Nations, the United States pledged itself in 1945 to promote the common welfare by furthering separate and collective action for the purpose of raising levels of nutrition and standards of living, securing improvements in the efficiency of production of all food and agricultural products, and bettering the conditions of rural populations.

By its membership in the International Monetary Fund the United States pledged itself in the same year to promote exchange stability and maintain orderly exchange arrangements, to assist in the establishment of a multilateral system of payments in respect of currency transactions, to facilitate the expansion and balanced growth of international trade, and to contribute thereby to the maintenance of high levels of employment and real income and to the development of the productive resources of all the members of the Fund as primary objectives of economic policy.

By its membership in the International Bank for Reconstruction and Development it also pledged itself to assist in the reconstruction and development of the territories of the members by facilitating the investment of capital for productive purposes, to promote private investment, and thereby to assist in raising productivity, standards of living, and conditions of labor.

If it had accepted the Charter of the International Trade Organization, in whose negotiation it took the initiative, and which was signed by the representatives of 53 countries in 1948, these commitments would have been extended to include cooperative action for the reduction of trade barriers, the furthering of access on equal terms to productive facilities, and the promotion of mutual understanding, consultation, and cooperation in the solution of problems relating to international trade in the fields of employment, economic development, commercial policy, business practices, and commodity policy. Though this charter was rejected, many of its commitments are contained in other international documents.

This is but a partial list. It omits, for example, the economic commitments in the Atlantic Charter and the Atlantic Pact. In addition, President Truman, in announcing his famous Point IV program, gave expression to a new sense of international responsibility for the living standards of less fortunate

people. This was the first time that any government had made the economic development of other countries a major feature of its own foreign policy.

It is a Christian responsibility to determine whether these and other similar commitments and pronouncements are an adequate expression of the Christian spirit as applied to international economic relations. There is some ground for believing that, though the United States Government regards membership in the international organizations it has joined as a firm commitment, it has not really accepted their statements of objective as basic to its own policy and action. It is therefore an additional Christian responsibility to decide whether these commitments are being lived up to in the practical application of United States economic policy, and to consider the means whereby the inevitable gap between profession and performance, and between the ideal and the attainable, can be diminished.

Policies of economic collaboration, mutual aid, and cooperative effort to attain mutual security cannot be carried beyond a certain point unless the American people, whose fortunes and interests are affected by them in innumerable ways, not only recognize that they are in the national interest but accept their inevitable consequences. If the state is to carry out its responsibilities to promote the national interest broadly interpreted, its people must realize how greatly the possibility of a responsible course of action in one area of economic life is dependent on what is being done in other areas. They must understand how the ethical problems described elsewhere in this volume are related to the discharge of international responsibilities. Finally, as in all complex situations, they must boldly confront the hard choices, often involving the sacrifice of the lesser to the greater good, that have to be made if lip service to improve international economic relations is to be replaced by constructive action.

FIVE AREAS OF UNITED STATES RESPONSIBILITY

In the chaotic and divided world of today the enlargement of the area in which America's national interest can be identified with that of the world community is a task calling for the solution of an appalling number of difficulties and dilemmas. Four things, however, are clear. If the United States is to act responsibly in the world community the government must follow policies that will (1) prevent the American economy from becoming a disrupting force in the world economy; (2) diminish, if not eliminate, economic maladjustments responsible for the long-continued dependence of other countries on American assistance; (3) contribute to the economic as well as the military strength of the free world; (4) contribute to the solution of the long-range economic problems of underdeveloped countries. Our government must in addition, when the occasion calls for it, be a channel through which the instinctive response of the American people to the call of human need can be made effective.

8

The American Economy

If there is one lesson that has been driven home by the march of events during the past thirty years it is that the international repercussions of the fluctuations in the level of American economic activity impose a grave responsibility on the United States.

In the interwar years these fluctuations were frequent and violent. World War I was followed by an inflation that culminated in a sharp depression in 1920-21. The recovery from this depression was marked by the excesses and delusions of the so-called "new era." Then followed the disaster of the Great Depression. A partial recovery in 1933-37 was followed by a very sharp if short depression in 1938.

This experience was largely responsible for a revolution in public thinking in the United States on the problem of economic stability. The passage of the Employment Act of 1946 recorded the determination of the American people never again to go through the experience of a great depression. The numerous commitments in the United Nations Charter and other international documents dealing with efforts to promote full employment and higher standards of living in the world would not have been acceptable to them unless this basic change of attitude had taken place. The American economy was provided with a number of so-called "built-in" safeguards against depression—notably the social security system and the agricultural price-support system. With some difficulty an understanding was reached between the Treasury and the Federal Reserve System that laid the basis for mone-

tary policies conducive to the prevention of inflation and deflation, without allowing disorderly conditions to prevail in the government bond market. Not only government, but also labor and management, showed much greater readiness to take contracyclical action when required.

For these and other reasons the recent American conversion from war to peace was accomplished with surprisingly little unemployment, and nothing resembling the 1920-21 crisis. Prior to the latter part of 1953 there was only one recession, that of 1949. From the American point of view this was only a mild inventory readjustment. Inflation was the danger most feared. Following the communist invasion of South Korea there was a temporary but violent inflationary price boom, due mainly to expectations of increased public stockpiling and to private inventory accumulation of raw materials expected to become scarce.

The existence of inflationary pressures in the economy led the National Council of Churches to circulate to the churches for study a statement pointing out that the problem of inflation raises grave ethical and moral as well as economic issues. The broad concern of Christians in the stabilization problem was expressed at the beginning of this statement as follows:

Whenever there are general forces at work that create substantial and arbitrary changes in the distribution of income between different groups and occupations in our society, imposing hardships on some, while giving temporary advantages to others irrespective of their past or present contributions to the community, grave moral issues arise to which Christians cannot be indifferent.

Inflation is such a force. . . . [It impairs] and may even destroy the value of past savings and the incentives for future effort, and it undermines safeguards against social injustice painstakingly built up in the past. Christians cannot remain silent when our

society is exposed to this danger, any more than they can remain silent when economic depression and stagnation deprive great numbers of people of opportunities for work and self-support.

The failure of our society to prevent major economic fluctuations has confronted church people with moral and ethical issues arising out of successive periods of deflation and inflation. Since the great depression of the 1930s many barriers have been erected in our society against a recurrence of the evils of deflation. Since the war, however, . . . the major threat to American stability has been inflation. . . . Inflationary forces continue to operate. If not mastered they will produce a reaction and a threat of mass unemployment. Our bulwarks against deflation will then be severely tested.[1]

At the time of writing there is a general feeling of confidence in the United States that these bulwarks will stand fast, and that the country is secure against major depressions. This confidence, unfortunately, is not shared by other countries, whose exports to the United States are quickly affected by any major decline in the level of American economic activity. They are fully aware that the vaunted built-in stabilizers have not yet been tested. The haunting fear that the United States may again lead the world into a repetition of the 1930 experience has not been banished by the good works and the good intentions of the United States since the end of the Second World War. The experience of the 1930s is therefore still pertinent to a discussion of the international responsibilities of the United States nearly a quarter of a century later.

THE LESSON OF THE GREAT DEPRESSION

Before World War II the United States had already achieved a dominant position in the world economy. It had

[1] *Christian Responsibility toward Some Ethical Problems in Inflation,* National Council of Churches, 1952.

become the first exporting nation, and second only to Britain as an importer. In the period before the Great Depression the national income of the United States was in terms of dollars nearly half that of the whole world. The United States consumed almost two-fifths of the world's production of raw materials and foodstuffs, and was responsible for 46 per cent of the industrial production of the world. The United States played a dominant role in the determination of the prices of major products vitally important to the economies of other countries. In addition, it had replaced Great Britain as the chief source of international loan capital. The concentration of such a large proportion of the economic power of the world in the United States meant that variations in American economic activity had profound effects on the economic stability and welfare of the rest of the world.

Despite the American depression of 1920-21 there does not appear to have been in the 1920s anything inherent in the structure of the international balance of payments of the United States that would have made a sound balance-of-payments position impossible. But in the 1930s other countries were faced with the problem of adjusting their economies to a precipitous decline in the amount of dollars provided by American merchandise imports and American capital exports.

United States merchandise imports fell from $4,463 million in 1929 to $1,347 million in 1932, and did not regain their 1929 value until 1937. In 1938 they again fell off sharply.[2] The difficulties of other countries in adjusting to these violent fluctuations in imports were aggravated, first by a radical reduction (in 1929) and then by a reversal (in 1930) of the outward flow of American capital. In the 1920s the net outward flow had averaged about $750 million annually, but

[2] Except in 1938 these variations followed closely changes in the national income of the United States. Merchandise exports fell from $5,347 million in 1929 to $1,667 million in 1932. They rose slowly to a peak in 1937, but did not regain their 1929 level before the end of the decade.

from 1930 to 1938 there was a net capital inflow totaling about $2.4 billion.[3]

These figures dramatize to a high degree the true measure of international responsibility borne by the United States for keeping its own house in order. If the United States had been able to follow postwar financial and other policies adequate to provide a reasonably high level of employment, and, in addition, had been able to play the part of a steady and responsible international lender, the world supply of dollars would have been much higher. It may not be an exaggeration to suppose that the whole economic history of the world, and even its political history, might have been changed.

It is not necessary to labor the point further, that if the United States should allow its economy to suffer another major depression it would be failing disastrously in the discharge of its international responsibilities. Nor is it appropriate to repeat here the analysis of the grave ethical issues involved in any sustained effort to stabilize the American economy. This analysis has been already given in other volumes in this series, and in the statements circulated by the National Council of Churches. Attention must rather be drawn to a number of unresolved and perplexing problems that have risen since 1945, while the United States was making a maximum effort to provide leadership in the restoration of an expanding and stable world economy.

[3] From 1919 to 1930 American foreign investment was only slightly less than $1 billion per annum, but there was an inflow of foreign capital of about $240 million annually. From 1931 to the end of the decade there was a continuing liquidation, with a net disinvestment of American holdings abroad. The United States, however, continued to attract foreign capital. Of the 1930-38 capital inflow about one-third was disinvestment of foreign assets by Americans, and the rest net long-term investment by foreigners in the United States.

INTERNATIONAL RESPONSES TO AMERICAN
READJUSTMENTS—A CHAIN REACTION

One of these problems is the impact that even moderate economic adjustments, such as are almost inseparable from the functioning of a highly productive and dynamic economy like that of the United States, have on other countries. That this is a real and important problem was, to the surprise of many people, made clear by the serious impact abroad of the 1949 inventory recession in the United States. The force of this impact is partly to be explained by the fact that economic recovery in Europe was not then so fully completed as it was during the subsequent recession of 1953, and partly by the fact that the economic predominance of the United States was at that time even greater than it had been during the 1930s. With only 6 per cent of the world's population, the United States was producing about half of the world's manufactured goods. In 1949 American imports were 15 per cent of world imports; and the percentage of the exports of the Philippines, Cuba, Brazil, Chile, Canada, Venezuela, Uruguay, Malaya, and Japan bought by the United States ranged from 72 per cent to 22 per cent. At the same time Europe and its associated currency areas were not able to secure from nondollar areas a supply of foodstuffs and raw material sufficient to cover the increased needs created by their own rapid industrial expansion, and were compelled to depend much more than formerly on imports from the United States, Canada, and other Western Hemisphere countries.[4] Sustained dollar earnings were more than ever essential to their welfare.

---

[4] A Trade and Tariff Policy in the National Interest, prepared by the Public Advisory Board for Mutual Security, Washington, February 1953 (the Bell Report), p. 11. Central America (except British possessions), Venezuela, Colombia, Ecuador, and Bolivia are in the "dollar area."

With the development of the 1949 recession a steady improvement in the dollar position of the rest of the world was brought temporarily to an end. The dollar receipts of the countries participating in the European Recovery Program declined by $500 to $600 million on an annual basis. The exports of these countries as a whole fell about 30 per cent—in some cases as much as 60 per cent. A special report to the Organization for European Economic Cooperation (OEEC) by its chairman and secretary drew from this the pessimistic conclusion that, despite the improvement of the preceding two years, the dollar problem of Europe was not on its way to solution.

One result of the impact of the American inventory recession on other countries was to intensify their efforts to find more effective ways of earning or saving dollars. A fresh impetus was given, for example, to the endeavors by the British Government to restrict the dollar expenditures of Great Britain and the countries associated with it in the monetary system known as the sterling area, by reducing the share of American oil companies in sterling and other markets.[5] These restrictions were defended on the ground that they were "dollar saving" and therefore in accord with the action recommended to Great Britain by the United States. This argument, however, was never accepted by the American companies; and there is no question that Great Britain was anxious to strengthen by all available means its position in this major industry, irrespective of the problem of economizing on dollar expenditures. The United States Government protested, and retaliatory measures were considered, including even the ter-

[5] The measures taken were: (1) stipulations in bilateral trade agreements outside the sterling area (Egypt, Sweden, Brazil, Argentina, and other countries) to accept a larger share of sterling oil; (2) restrictions on payments by other countries into American accounts, including the accounts of American oil companies; (3) the partial substitution of sterling for dollar oil in the sterling area, made possible by increased production by British companies.

mination of American assistance until the situation was corrected. In the meantime strenuous efforts were being made within the United States by part of the petroleum industry, supported by the coal producers, to impose drastic import restrictions on foreign oil.

This whole conflict gradually resolved itself by an expansion of the market at the end of the American recession, though none of the fundamental issues were solved. For a time British measures to restrict American access to sterling markets for oil, and American pressure to restrict British access to the American markets, went hand in hand. Nothing could better illustrate the kind of economic warfare situation that may develop whenever the American economy gets even slightly out of gear. Nor could anything more clearly underline the fact that solutions of the economic problems confronting the Western world can be found most easily through the expansion of effective demand in all major countries, chief among them the United States.

This example of the "dollar oil crisis" has been cited to illustrate how dependent are all hopes of cooperative and relatively unrestricted international economic relations on the avoidance of economic depression in the United States. More intricate and perplexing questions are raised when internal adjustments appear to be forced on other countries because of the way in which the American economy is functioning.

Pressures for such adjustments may arise from many causes, of which a decline in American import demand as the result of a general recession in the United States is only one. Another is failure to check inflationary forces in other countries while the United States is pursuing the path of financial rectitude in this respect. This second one has often been associated in the postwar years with the creation and maintenance of the welfare state. In both cases the foreign

country may be placed in balance-of-payments difficulties—
that is, in a position where it cannot cover its current foreign
obligations without diminishing its imports or increasing its
exports.[6] In some way this situation has to be corrected. It
has seemed to many thoughtful people in other countries
that it should be corrected by exchange controls and trade
restrictions and discriminations, because the alternative is
deflation leading to unemployment, and that is no longer
socially, morally, or politically acceptable.

This position, if taken in an extreme form—as it often has
been since the war—implies the almost total rejection of
that "external discipline" which, as already stated, requires
internal adjustment to an existing or developing international situation.[7] It calls for the adoption of measures of
economic "self-defense" not only in meeting the special
difficulties of the "dollar shortage,"[8] but whenever the country is in balance-of-payments difficulties from any cause. This
view has been so firmly held by governments since the war
that it is incorporated in many postwar international economic agreements. The Articles of Agreement of the International Monetary Fund and the Charter of the abortive
International Trade Organization, for example, contain provisions that accord certain special privileges to countries in
balance-of-payment difficulties, even if these difficulties are
due to the countries' own domestic policies.

Measures of economic self-defense, even when they are

[6] There is also a school of thought that holds that American productive
efficiency is such that American productivity will always remain greater than
that of other countries, so that these countries will suffer from a "chronic"
shortage of dollars. If that view is accepted, then by virtue of its own efficiency
the American economy must be held responsible for a perpetual set of balance-
of-payments difficulties. Those who hold this gloomy position, however, do
not seem to have made out their case.

[7] See Chapter 6, p. 100.

[8] This much misused term is merely a convenient designation of the sum
total of all the forces contributing to make the dollar a scarce currency after
the war.

imposed for the sake of safeguarding full employment and social welfare programs, and avoiding changes in income distribution that are regarded as ethically undesirable, injure other countries. These countries may be led to take "counter-defensive" action. The harsh consequences of allowing such a chain of defensive action to deteriorate into a state bordering on economic warfare were demonstrated in the interwar period. Consequently, after the war great efforts were put forth to find some more constructive solution to this dilemma.

During the whole recovery effort, to which American assistance programs contributed, great care was taken to avoid too early or too rapid exposure of the economies of the various countries that had suffered from the war to the rigors of full international competition. As conditions improved, advantage was taken of the situation to make a slow but cautious attack on trade restrictions and discriminations. Regional arrangements were introduced in which trade barriers were lessened within the region but maintained against the United States. Shifts of production into channels that would be dollar-earning or dollar-saving were encouraged, largely through the selection of new investment projects. Full employment and the investment of large resources for social welfare programs were characteristic of the period. In general, an inflationary situation was allowed to prevail, in which home demands for resources that were potentially exportable were so strong that a restoration of the external position was made more difficult. It is only very recently that European countries have come to accept the formerly orthodox view that if the external accounts were to be put in balance, monetary and fiscal policies must be followed that would put an end to inflation in all its forms.

INTERNAL STABILITY—RESPONSIBILITIES OF THE UNITED STATES AND OF OTHER COUNTRIES

The question was raised during the recovery period whether the wisest course for the United States would not have been to allow a certain amount of moderate but persistent inflation in its own economy, thereby easing the problems of other countries. The inequities brought about by even moderate inflation, and the serious social and ethical problems certain to arise when inflation is persistent, strongly argued against such a course. The statement on inflation circulated for study by the National Council of Churches, after analyzing the burdens of an inflationary situation, dealt with these problems. It stressed the tendency of major economic groups to accept sacrifices imposed by anti-inflationary measures only on condition that equal or greater sacrifices were made by other groups, and drew two conclusions that underline the kind of problem a country has to face once it allows inflation to become persistent:

1. That if every major economic group—whether workers, farmers, or employers—makes its contribution [to the fight against inflation] contingent on prior action by other groups, and each is continually looking over its shoulder to see what the other is doing, the moral as well as the practical basis for a successful stabilization effort is seriously undermined.

2. That in an inflationary situation every major economic group strives at least to maintain its real income, and that if all such major groups are wholly successful in maintaining their command over goods and services while the basic causes of inflation continue to operate, the real burden of inflation will fall on those parts of the community that are least able to defend themselves.

It is quite clear that American responsibilities for the international repercussions of its own economic behavior do not require it to complicate its own moral and economic

problems by inflation in order to ease the path of other countries. There remains, however, the question whether, after having stabilized its own economy while inflation was continuing in European and other countries—a situation very unfavorable to international balance—the United States had fully discharged its international responsibilities. Did the United States, under such circumstances, have a responsibility for exerting pressure on other countries to carry out domestic anti-inflationary policies which, in its opinion, were necessary for recovery? In particular, should the adoption of such policies have been made a condition of continuing aid to such countries?[9] These questions are substantial and important. They are an essential counterpart to the questions raised about the responsibilities that America should assume in the field of trade and investment in the event of a rapid contraction of American imports relative to exports due to the occurrence of depression in the United States.

There has been in recent years an international debate concerning the nature of these responsibilities. The memory of the 1930s has always been present, and has given to the discussion of this topic an intensity and emotional content that it would never have had if the problems considered had been merely those raised by a mild American recession like that of 1949. During this debate American pressure for nondiscrimination in trade was met by the argument that when economic fluctuations in the United States cause serious international disequilibrium, the United States should not insist that international accounts be put in order by deflationary measures in other countries, leading to unemployment and the abandonment of social welfare measures that rest on enlightened and humanitarian principles. It should rather—as it has done in

[9] See Chapter 10. The limitations of this form of pressure are substantial. For example, inflationary situations in Australia and Brazil could not be influenced by any such conditions, since those countries did not receive aid. In Brazil, however, similar conditions were set in connection with American loans.

large measure since the war—accept with good grace discriminatory measures against its trade, or else provide the necessary credit and investment to make good the current deficiency in the world supply of dollars.

The two underlying principles on which this argument rests have a strong ethical content. They are (1) that when international trading policies and practices come into conflict with domestic full-employment and welfare policies and practices, the trading policies should give way; and (2) that the responsibilities of creditor countries in correcting an unbalanced international trading position in the world are as great as, if not greater than, those of debtors.

The United States has seriously questioned the validity of these two principles as guides to the establishment of a balanced and satisfactorily functioning world economy. Throughout the postwar period it has contended that the morally desirable objectives of full employment and higher standards of living would be better served by a liberal commercial policy than by policies of trade restriction. It has not denied the great responsibilities of creditor countries; but it has resisted the implication that the United States must bear the sole responsibility for remedial action in periods of stress and strain in the world economy.

It is not a correct reading of history to attribute the sole—or, in the view of some authorities, even the primary—responsibility for the outbreak of the Great Depression in the 1930s to the mistaken domestic policies of the United States during the "New Era."[10] The transformations in the American trading position during the last thirty years that have made fluctuations in the American economy so menacing to other countries have been in large measure the result of preparation for wars, the conduct of wars, and the aftermath of wars.

[10] *Course and Phases of the World Economic Depression*, report presented to the Assembly of the League of Nations, Secretariat of the League of Nations, Geneva, 1931, *passim*. This is not, of course, to question the American contribution to the *severity* or the *duration* of the depression.

Many of the difficulties and failures in the postwar period in putting international accounts to rights have been due to the continuation of open or suppressed inflation in other countries. Part of the solution of international difficulties has lain in their domestic credit and financial position. The responsibilities for the disintegration of the world economic system are widely distributed internationally, and the responsibilities of debtors for putting their international accounts in order are not eliminated by a recognition that creditors also have responsibilities.

Yet, when all is said and done, the mere weight of American economic power in the world economy makes the maintenance of a stable and expanding economy in the United States a major international responsibility; and the problem for consideration by Christians is whether this can be discharged in a manner conforming to Christian principles of action.

The high point of admonition to the United States on the scope of its responsibilities as a creditor was contained in a report of United Nations experts in 1949. After recounting the cumulative effects of deflation in a particular country as it is communicated to other countries through declining purchases from them, which result in a fall in the exports of those countries relative to their imports, this report concluded:

The only possible way of preventing this cumulative process of contraction, and of enabling countries to maintain their imports and their real income in the face of fluctuations of foreign demand, is for each country to stabilize its own external currency disbursements on current account in the event of a decline in its own demand for foreign goods and services.[11]

[11] *National and International Measures for Full Employment*, report of a group of experts appointed by the Secretary General, United Nations, December 1949, U.N. Sales No. 1949/II/A/3, p. 95.

Among its specific recommendations was the following:

If, in any given year, the value of the imports of goods and services by a particular country falls as the result of a fall in effective demand within the country, and this fall is not fully offset by a decline in the value of its current exports of goods and services, that country should make a deposit of its own currency with the International Monetary Fund for an amount equal to the fall of its imports less the fall of its exports in the given year as compared with [a] reference year.[12]

This technical language is clear in its import; namely that the United States should always provide the rest of the world with a sufficient supply of dollars to pay for the imports the rest of the world wishes currently to purchase from the United States. The many objections to this extreme proposal have retired it from the forefront of international discussion; but the question of what precisely are the responsibilities of a country like the United States when its imports decline still remains open.

Aside from the extreme suggestion already referred to, many others have been made for international action to remedy the sort of situation arising from the international effects of economic readjustment in the United States.[13] To cite only a few:

(1) Concerted action to ease the terms of borrowing over a wide area in times of deflationary pressure; (2) international arrangements to promote stability of the incomes of the producers of primary commodities; (3) the timing of expenditures on long-term international investment projects to achieve anticyclical results; (4) encouragement of the flow of capital in periods of

[12] *Ibid.*, p. 97.
[13] See, for example, the full recommendations of the United Nations report referred to above, and the conclusions of a later United Nations experts' report—*Measures for International Economic Stability*, United Nations, Department of Economic Affairs, New York, 1951.

wide deflationary pressure to countries whose balance of payments need temporary support; (5) the accumulation of stocks of commodities when international demand is low and the producing countries are depressed, with a view to their resale in better times—the buffer stock technique; (6) the accumulation of stockpiles of strategic materials for defense purposes, and their timing in accordance with changing international situations; (7) undertakings by the United States to purchase certain primary commodities in bulk over a period of years for the purpose of stabilizing their prices; and (8) the creation of new international organizations to engage in antidepression financing of all sorts.

CONFLICTS BETWEEN INTERNATIONAL AND DOMESTIC RESPONSIBILITIES—THE CASE OF AGRICULTURE

Each of the above proposals raises its own problems, on which wide differences of opinion have been inevitable. They have one thing in common, however, which raises a fundamental question for Americans: they are intended to prevent the international spread of unemployment. The question is: *Is the maintenance of high levels of domestic employment and economic activity in this country—or for that matter in any other country—to be treated as a matter exclusively of domestic concern; or is it, in some of its aspects, a matter on which international consultation, cooperation, and joint action is admissable, proper, and necessary?*

If America is to discharge the international responsibilities that are associated with the functioning of the United States economy, the answer to this question must be the acceptance of the latter alternative. If that is the answer, however, further questions are raised concerning the degree of freedom that should be enjoyed by the United States in its selection of the methods of stabilizing its own economy. This is because some of these methods have unfavorable international repercussions. Chief among them are the methods chosen to stabilize the agricultural sector of the American economy.

During the early 1920s and 1930s the inability of farmers to adjust their production to the drastic curtailment of demand placed them at a serious disadvantage. There was general agreement that some sort of public action was necessary to assure them some degree of "economic equality" in relation to other segments of the economy. But there was, and continues to be, a disagreement on the concept of equality to be adopted,[14] and the methods for bringing it about—chiefly rigid and high-price supports based on a parity formula.

Since agricultural policy directly affects the welfare of the entire farm population, it raises such fundamental questions as the preservation of the values of rural life—and particularly of the family farm—the condition of a large group of sub-marginal farmers, the interrelationships between the welfare, prosperity, and stability of American agriculture and that of the economy as a whole, and the effects of American agricultural policy on other countries. Thus the ethical problems raised by American agricultural policy are of great importance to all Christians. This was recognized by the National Council of Churches when it called a conference on agricultural problems at Haverford in June 1951, and circulated for discussion in the churches "A Preliminary Study of the Churches and Agricultural Policy." In this document three important conclusions were reached that directly concern the international responsibilities implicit in the functioning of the American economy. Each of these conclusions is based on ethical rather than on purely economic considerations:

[14] The economists' concept of equality for agriculture (and all other industries) is a condition in which the real return to labor, management, and capital employed in agriculture (and in each of its parts) is equivalent to what the persons or the units of capital could get in any other vocation or use. The approach to such equality requires the highest possible degree of business flexibility and personal freedom; and the concept itself is very different from that embodied in the parity conception that has actually been employed. *Turning the Searchlight on Farm Policy*, The Farm Foundation, 1952, p. 32. This pamphlet represents the conclusions of a conference of eminent agricultural economists.

1. Any system, whether it be of free markets, of government regulated markets, or of a combination of the two, which is to win support, should avoid freezing production in uneconomic patterns, artificially inflating land prices, or producing unmanageable surpluses. Waste is abhorrent to the Christian conscience. Any system that results in loss through spoilage or destruction of commodities is morally indefensible. The carry-over of staples sufficient to protect the nation against drought or other agricultural calamity is legitimate. Anything more than this in a world as hungry as ours is contrary to the Christian conscience.

2. Justice demands that the farmer who produces efficiently should receive economic rewards comparable to those received by persons of similar competence in other vocations.

3. Every aspect of agricultural policy should be examined for its impact upon the general economy both national and worldwide. Programs that seek to advance the interests of agriculture at the expense of other groups or other nations should be shunned.[15]

On several counts the present agricultural policy of the United States falls short of these standards. Whether it is actually a stabilizing or an unstabilizing influence in the economy is open to very serious question. On this point a distinguished group of agricultural economists has recently taken the following firm position:

Since agriculture must continuously adjust to changing situations, a program that is rigid and mechanistic is not stabilizing but rather has the opposite effect. Use of the parity formula may produce practically the same dollar—and—cents price per unit in years of big crops as in years of small crops. From the farm income standpoint, this is definitely unstabilizing and, moreover, tends to impede the adjustments needed to correct over and underproduction. Furthermore, it creates situations in which large accumulations or oversupplies of given farm products may bring on

[15] A *Preliminary Study of the Churches and Agricultural Policy*, Department of the Church and Economic Life, National Council of Churches, 297 Fourth Avenue, New York.

eventually a disastrous break in the agricultural price structure as a whole.[16]

The problem of disposing of these surpluses has led to various suggestions for making them available to meet the needs of countries where famine or distress prevails; but these raise many serious problems, the discussion of which is deferred until the fifth area of American responsibility is taken up (Chapter 11, pp. 176-77).

The present policy frequently results in maintaining American prices above the free-market level, so that products are attracted from other countries. This gives rise to pressure for curbs on imports in order to maintain the high American prices required by the price support program. To prevent the cost of the price support program from being increased and the success of the program endangered, various measures of import restriction have been resorted to.[17] The high-price support system also increases the difficulty of export—particularly of those staples on which large parts of the American agricultural economy are dependent—and leads to the imposition of various measures of export subsidy.

Neither of these results of the agricultural policy can be regarded as in the national interest, or as compatible with the full discharge of America's international responsibilities. Yet the values that the agricultural policy is intended to preserve cannot be disregarded. It is a responsibility of Christians, in their attitude on agricultural policy, to distinguish between those aspects of that policy that reflect merely a desire for ever-increasing high levels of agricultural prices and incomes, and those elements that genuinely contribute to a just relation between the economic positions of the farming population and of other segments of the economy. This is essential if

[16] *Turning the Searchlight on Farm Policy*, p. 40.

[17] A full description of these restrictions is given on pp. 23-29 of the *Report to the President by the Public Advisory Board for Mutual Security* submitted in February 1953, generally known as the Bell Report.

agricultural policy is to contribute definitely to the stability of the whole economy. In addition, search must be continued for methods of achieving these domestic objectives that will not increase the economic difficulties of other countries and make the solution of international economic problems more difficult.

It has been impossible to deal with the first area of American international responsibility—the American economy—without encroaching on the domain of the other four, particularly the second: world trade and investment. This has been due mainly to the important repercussions of the fluctuations in the American national income on the course of international trade, and the problems created thereby. Important as these are, it would be a mistake to exaggerate their influence as compared to the influence of tariffs and other protective measures, and of changes in price relationships. Whether the variations in the American national income have had so preponderant an influence on the volume of imports that other influences must be considered negligible is a question that has been much debated by economists and statisticians. The pendulum of opinion has swung from one side to the other; but the most recent investigations have disclosed that imports—especially imports of finished manufactures—continue to be influenced to a considerable degree by tariffs, and by changes in the prices of American imports relative to other prices.[18] There is therefore no reason for the complacent conclusion that the responsibility of the United States for helping to maintain a stable and expanding world economy will be discharged, once the instability exhibited by the American economy in the past has been eliminated.

[18] The Pattern of United States Import Trade Since 1923, John H. Adler, Eugene R. Schlesinger, and Evelyn Van Westerborg, Federal Reserve Bank of New York, May 1952, pp. 42–43, 45–49.

9

World Trade and Investment

In an accounting sense the international transactions of any country, with all other countries taken together, are always in balance.[1] That is to say, the difference between exports and imports of goods and services (the current account balance) is always offset by some combination of other items —movements of gold and silver, changes in bank deposits and short-term indebtedness, capital movements, and the so-called "unilateral transfers"—mainly foreign assistance. It is customary to speak of these multifarious transactions as the means of financing current-account deficits or surpluses. But this is really an oversimplification, since there is a close interaction between the behavior of many current-account items and many balancing items. No group of items in the international accounts of any country varies independently of changes in other groups of items. Therefore if the international responsibility of the United States in the field of world trade and investment is to be defined as making a maximum contribution to mutually advantageous, expanding, and balanced international trade, the way in which the international accounts of this country are brought into balance becomes all-important. If this is done in such a way as to contribute to higher standards of living throughout the world, as a result of increased production nourished by mutually advantageous trade, then the requirements of a fully responsible foreign economic policy are met. Ever since the outbreak

[1] The transactions need not balance for each of a country's trading partners, since deficits with one country are set off against surpluses with others.

of World War I the United States has been faced with the problem of meeting this responsibility while experiencing large and persistent export surpluses on current account.[2]

It is a truism that exports pay for imports, and that the two must move together. In an international trading system in which only goods and services were exchanged, the strain of making adjustments needed to bring exports and imports into balance would fall exclusively on transactions that heavily affect the welfare and prosperity of the people. If, in addition to trade in goods and services, there is an international flow of capital, of reserves, and of other balancing items, the adjustments can be made in ways that do not have the same serious impact on employment and living standards. But if these balancing items move erratically or perversely, the strains of adjustment may be multiplied.

This principle is well illustrated by the behavior of the current account of the United States from 1921 to 1940. During the first ten of these years, which included a period of large-scale outflow of American capital, exports on current account exceeded imports by an annual average of one and a half billion dollars; but during the second ten years, when the capital flow was reversed, this surplus was reduced to an

[2] From July 1914 through 1952 the United States exported goods and services to the value of $342 billion, and imported goods and services to the value of $222 billion. It thus exported $120 billion more on current account than it imported, or nearly $3 billion a year over a period of 38½ years. If we exclude the war years July 1914 through 1918, when the surplus was financed in large part by war loans, and also 1941 to 1945, when the surplus was largely covered by lend-lease, the United States exported $241 billion and imported $171 billion, leaving an export surplus on current account of $70 billion. If not only the war years but the first two years immediately after each of the two wars are excluded, the current-account exports were $185 billion and the imports $143 billion. Thus in the twenty-five years not dominated by war or its immediate aftermath the current-account surplus of exports over imports was $42 billion. It is striking that of this surplus only $17 billion was built up during the 20 years 1921 to 1940, and $25 billion was accumulated during the five years 1948 to 1952, when the American government was extending large-scale foreign assistance.

annual average of only half a billion. As the total value of both current-account exports and imports fell during the depression, the margin between them also fell. The downward adjustments in our foreign trade were worked out mainly within the current-account transactions, rather than through the balancing items. This was a major consequence of the breakdown in the system of international multilateral trade and investment that occurred during the depression.

The Postwar Attempt to Learn from Experience

In the closing years of the interwar period there was an alarming drift toward anarchy in international economic as well as political relations. The major manifestation of this drift in the economic sphere was the absence of any general system of conducting world trade, and of any general willingness to devise one. This was due in part to a wide variety of measures taken by many countries to ensure internal security, or to promote special national objectives by means incompatible with the effective functioning of such a system. Among these were the special treatment of international trade in agricultural products as a safeguard to various national schemes for stabilizing farm incomes, the private regulation of international trade through cartel arrangements, and the intensification of regional trading arrangements. Foreign-trade policies were being gradually subordinated to domestic employment and development policies.

Such measures and policies made cooperative international economic relations more difficult, but not impossible, given good will and the spirit of accommodation in international negotiations. Far more destructive to such relations was the growth of new philosophies of trade, which led to the acceptance of autarchy[3] as the goal of trade policy, and to efforts

[3] The new name for economic nationalism and doctrines of self-sufficiency.

by many countries to balance their international accounts bilaterally with their trading partners. At the close of the interwar period much of the trade of central Europe, and to some extent the trade of all Europe with Latin America, was on a bilateral basis. Only through increasing government-controlled trade could such policies be carried out. As a consequence, many new administrative techniques of trade, for both offense and defense, were perfected. Among these were various forms of exchange control, whose use constituted in effect a partial breakdown of the world system of payments. The use of these techniques by Germany as instruments of economic warfare was one facet of a developing political crisis that threatened the peace of Europe. Autarchy, bilateralism, and instability became the characteristics of international economic relations.

In the postwar years there was a general consensus that international accounts must never again be balanced by such drastic measures of economic attack and counterattack, destructive both of the welfare of the contestants and of good political international relations. This feeling was eloquently expressed at the opening of the negotiations for the Havana Charter at Geneva on April 11, 1947, by the late Sir Stafford Cripps, then the British Chancellor of the Exchequer:

Many of us have had a vivid experience of the tragedies which beset the world during the years between the two wars, and the slow inexorable drift which led us into the ghastly experience of the Second World War. It was these experiences of the mishandling of the world's economic problems in the interwar period and their influence on the coming of the Second World War that strengthened our convictions that some wiser and better organization of international economic relations was imperatively necessary.

Though the approach to this objective by the creation of an International Trade Organization proved to be unsuccess-

ful, much has been accomplished. There has been a great deal of cooperation in the rebuilding of the world trading system. An organization, The General Agreement on Tariffs and Trade (GATT)—which is too little known by the American people—has come into being, not only to carry out successful negotiations for mutual tariff reductions, but also to provide a forum for the discussion and settlement of differences in the commercial field. It is the only such forum in existence; and has to its credit many unobtrusive but important accomplishments. There has been no relapse into economic warfare, with the exception of the regulation of East-West trade, to which reference will be made later; but there have been occasional glimpses of what might occur if the United States should fail to stabilize its economy. Though there have been numerous efforts by countries in balance-of-payment difficulties to protect themselves by increasing restrictions—including the cancellation of previous measures of trade liberalization —these restrictions have not generally led to a series of baleful retaliations. This is due partly to the fact that many of them have been directed against the United States, which has in this respect displayed a creditable attitude of cooperation and patience, and partly to the fact that many of them have been carried out under international auspices through the European Payments Union. The current deficit of the rest of the world with the United States was reduced from $11.5 billion in 1947 to $5 billion in 1952. If $2.5 billion in exports specially financed in 1952 by military aid[4] are excluded, the deficit was reduced to $2.5 billion. In 1953 it had almost disappeared.

On their face these figures would seem to indicate that the back of the problem has been broken; and that the current deficits—apart from those occasioned by the shipment of

[4] It is still customary for official statisticians to treat such shipments as something apart from normal trade.

military items—could be handled by ordinary balancing trans-actions, particularly United States capital exports. But the situation is still far from satisfactory. American foreign assist-ance has provided the time, and part of the resources, for re-building the productive capacity of other countries, without which a high level of balanced foreign trade would not be possible. These are its two main contributions to the dis-charge of the American international responsibilities in the economic sphere, and they have helped to make possible the great reduction in the world's dollar deficit.

The closing of the "dollar gap" has not, however, been brought about in the most satisfactory way. Though American imports have increased steadily, the rate of increase has been moderate, and American foreign investment until very recently has shown no tendency to rise above a relatively low level. The total of American imports has been increased by the in-clusion of large payments by the American government for off-shore purchases, stock-piling, and the maintenance of Amer-ican troops abroad. These are currently running at a rate of about $3 billion per annum. They must in time be replaced by commercial imports if the situation is not to deteriorate. The major means of closing "the dollar gap" has been through such temporary payments and a decline in that portion of American exports not financed by military aid. Three influ-ences have contributed to this decline: the economic recovery of the countries receiving aid, the improvement in non-dollar sources of supply, and the continued restrictions and discrim-ination against dollar imports.

THE GOOD-CREDITOR POLICY

If major reliance is in practice placed on the contraction of American exports—partly forced by exchange and trade re-strictions by other countries—in order to bring about a man-

ageable relationship between exports and imports on current account, the economic cost will be high. It will take the form of a check on the rate of improvement in the standards of living in the importing countries, and of economic difficulties for the large segments of the American people who are dependent on the production of goods for export. The cost will be heavy also in international economic friction. Such costs will become more serious, unless there is a substantial rise in the rates of the increase of imports into the United States and of the annual outflow of capital from America. To stave off a contraction of American exports by the continuation of large-scale foreign assistance for a long period would—even if it were politically feasible—provide no solution.[5] Indeed, given the recovery of productive capacity already achieved since the war, such a course might serve to postpone a real solution. For these reasons, the United States is being called upon by other countries to follow a "good-creditor" policy; and in the United States itself major attention is being directed to the problem of increasing imports.

On this there is no lack of good advice tendered to the government. Most professional economists in and out of government have pressed for a policy of encouraging imports by such measures as the following: tariff reduction, a simplification of customs procedures far more sweeping than that recently placed on the statute books, the repeal of "Buy American" acts, the elimination of the conflict between American agricultural and commercial policy, the repeal of various forms of special-interest legislation affecting foreign trade, and the elimination of administrative abuses that unnecessarily obstruct imports.[6] Many of these measures have

[5] From the point of view of the assisted country, American aid is an export, which, like any other export, enables that country to increase its purchases in the United States.

[6] A case in point is the use of sanitary restrictions for the purpose of giving economic protection.

been recommended by individual businessmen and by some business groups; and even the general public—if a recent Gallup poll is to be trusted—has come to favor a further reduction in American tariffs. Perhaps even more significant is the growing consensus expressed in official reports to the Government itself. No less than six of these reports, though with somewhat different emphases, have advocated the type of measures just enumerated.[7]

In spite of all these manifestations of a growing general consensus on what should be done, there does not appear to have been a time in recent years when pressure for protectionist legislation from numerous important American interests has been stronger and Congressional response to these pressures more favorable. The explanation of this situation lies in the traditional conflict between the general interest and the interests of special groups that has permeated all American tariff history. It is in recognition of this long-standing conflict of interests that the Bell Report made its first recommendation as follows:

That decisions on trade policy be based on national interest, rather than the interest of particular industries or groups; that in cases where choice must be made between injury to the national interest and hardship to an industry, the industry be helped to make adjustments by means other than excluding imports—such

[7] These six reports are: (1) *Report of the ECA Commerce Mission*, October 1949, published by the Economic Cooperation Administration; (2) *Report to the President on Foreign Economic Policies*, November 10, 1950 (Gray Report); (3) the *First Report to Congress of the Mutual Defense Assistance Control Act of 1951* (the Battle Act), Mutual Security Agency, 1952; (4) *Report to the President* by Ambassador William H. Draper, U. S. Special Representative in Europe, April 22, 1952; (5) *A Trade and Tariff Policy in the National Interest* (the Bell Report), February 1953; and (6) *Report of the Lewis W. Douglas Mission to the President*, August 24, 1953. The *Report of the Commission on Foreign Economic Policy* (the Randall Commission), made public in January 1954, contains a number of recommendations along the same lines, but in many ways this report represents an attempt to reconcile widely divergent views.

as through extension of unemployment insurance, assistance in retaining workers, diversification of production, and conversion to other lines.[8]

It has not been long since the American tariff was proclaimed to be a purely domestic matter, though such statements are not heard today. It is still possible, even under an enlightened trade and tariff policy *in the national interest*, to interpret "the national interest" merely as a reconciliation of competing interests within the country, without taking into account the effect of tariff action on other countries. In this respect, as in so many others, the international responsibilities of the United States will not be fully discharged unless the American national interest is conceived in the broadest terms.[9] The issues at stake are therefore ethical and moral as well as economic. This was recognized by the National Study Conference of the Church and Economic Life held in Detroit, Michigan, in February 1950, when it approved a report that dealt with the first two areas of American responsibility in the following terms:

In assessing the responsibility of our nation for international economic welfare, in the light of the Christian ethic, we set forth the following guiding principles:

1. The United States has a moral obligation to appraise the consequences in other countries of our economic policies, including many policies affecting our internal stability and employment that have hitherto been considered of solely domestic concern. Whenever feasible, the United States should undertake consultations prior to putting into effect policies having major repercussions on other countries.

2. The United States has a corresponding obligation to consider any soundly conceived plans for international action to mitigate severe economic fluctuations. The spread of economic depressions from one country to another has been met in the past by measures

[8] *A Trade and Tariff Policy in the National Interest,* p. 1.
[9] See Chapter 7, pp. 110ff.

of retaliation and counterretaliation. The Christian ethic requires that this practice should not be repeated.

3. The United States, as the greatest creditor and exporting nation, has a responsibility to adopt positive measures to facilitate imports. Such action is required to bring our international accounts into balance at a high level of transactions, to provide our people with the maximum opportunity to enjoy the fruits of mutually advantageous international trade, and to ensure that the economic progress of other countries is not stifled because of inability to pay for the American products necessary for their economic progress.

4. In addition, in order to bring our international accounts into balance at a high level of transactions, it is necessary that our capital should flow abroad in steady and substantial amounts.[10]

The increase of foreign investment referred to in this statement raises a series of very difficult problems of international responsibility.

Unsettled Problems of Foreign Investment

The reconstruction of an international investment network, which is essential for a stable and expanding world economy, has remained an unrealized objective. Intergovernmental lending and the lending of international agencies, though substantial, have not provided a substitute for the flow of private capital, which, both in its volume and in the large amount of technical knowledge that goes with it, remains the chief source from which large-scale and continuous international investment can be derived. The inadequacy of the flow of private capital is due partly to the fact that private capital will not move freely as long as currencies remain inconvertible,

[10] *The Responsibilities of Christians in an Interdependent World*, Detroit Conference, Statement and Reports, Department of the Church and Economic Life, Federal Council of Churches of Christ in America, New York, 1950, pp. 22–23.

and partly to the existence of certain specific obstacles to the revival of foreign investment.

In the course of prolonged national and international discussions on the revival of private foreign investment, the list of these obstacles has become somewhat stereotyped. Private capital hesitates to enter countries that are politically unstable, in which nationalization or confiscation is ever to be feared, and from which adequate, prompt, and effective compensation cannot be confidently relied on. It hesitates also to move to countries in which foreign enterprise encounters various discriminations, is not allowed fully to control operations over an indefinite period, and is subject to discriminatory and even double taxation; nor will it move freely to countries from which it cannot be withdrawn with a fair proportion of profit.

On the other hand, countries in need of foreign capital hesitate to grant it free rights of entry, for fear that scarce labor and resources may be withheld from employment in those types of production called for by economic development plans, and may be applied to less essential uses. They fear that foreign—and particularly American—capital and management will be so efficient that Americans will come to control one industry after another, and that their countries will thus become American economic colonies. This fear is often reinforced by strong protectionist sentiment on the part of local enterprises with which foreign capital would become competitive. It is the ambition of most capital-deficient countries to see their own nationals in control of all their major industrial and other productive enterprises; and they do not feel that in times of currency difficulties they can give to foreign investors an absolute priority on scarce foreign exchange.

A great deal of progress has been made, in particular countries and enterprises, in overcoming some of these obstacles.

Among many examples that could be cited is the experience of such a company as Sears-Roebuck in South America and the arrangements made by American oil companies for building petroleum refineries in India. It is moreover the policy of the United States, as stated in President Truman's inaugural address of January 1949, that in the future our foreign investment shall serve the interests of the countries in which it is made, as well as the interests of the investors. There is really no disagreement on this policy; moreover it is less of a departure from past practice than those who continually emphasize the exploitative nature of past foreign investments would have us believe. Nevertheless, the examples of progress do not add up to a victory over the general problem. Several extremely difficult questions, with serious moral and ethical connotations, have still to be faced.

Since there are now unusual and serious risks peculiar to foreign investment, who should carry them? Attempts have been made to transfer, by a system of guaranties, some of these risks from the shoulders of new private investors to our Government. These attempts have not been of great practical importance, and have been opposed in principle on various grounds—among them the view that if guaranties must be given to induce American foreign capital to go abroad, they should be given not by the United States but by the receiving countries. These countries, it is argued, cannot expect to enjoy the benefits of foreign capital in their territories unless they are willing to create a climate favorable to such investment. To encourage them to do so, rather than to rely on the possibility of intergovernmental loans, it is frequently contended that a sharp line of division should be made between the areas in which government lending to other countries is suitable—power, transportation, communications, irrigation—and the areas in which private investment is suitable. The Government is asked to make it clear that it will not

trespass on the field reserved for private investment. The basic issue here may be formulated as follows: Can the responsibilities of the United States for getting the world economy going again on an expanding and stable basis be reconciled with insistence on the creation of a climate in other countries favorable to private United States investment?

This question should be approached in the light of two important facts: first, there can be no assurance that, even if great efforts are made to improve the climate for private foreign investment, such investment will be forthcoming in the amounts necessary to solve the American balance-of-payments problem and to meet the minimum legitimate needs of the receiving countries; and, second, if total foreign investment, public and private, from the United States does not solve the American balance-of-payments problem, the burden of adjusting America's international accounts will continue to fall on American exports.

In recent years several suggestions have been made for additional financial institutions of a public character to finance economic development, by supplementing rather than supplanting private investment. To these institutions the United States would of course be the greatest contributor. There have also been proposals that in the event of a downward movement in the business cycle, accompanied by a sharp decline in American imports, the United States should maintain the supply of dollars available to the rest of the world by expanding its foreign lending. Such proposals imply the continuation of a considerable amount of public lending, since private foreign investment cannot easily be timed so as to counteract cyclical forces.

The question therefore narrows down to whether, if private investment is not forthcoming, the United States Government has a responsibility for making up the deficiency through some form of public lending. Though there is good reason not

to allow private American interests to adopt a "dog in the manger" attitude with respect to the outflow of foreign investment, there is also some danger in accepting too readily the principle that whenever private investment is not forthcoming public investment should be made available. There is a danger that such an attitude may lend support to the view that countries in need of foreign capital have some sort of *moral right* to demand it of the United States in forms and on conditions acceptable to them.[11] The international responsibilities of the United States do not require it to make its capital available to other countries on terms laid down by them, simply because these countries are capital-deficient; but a strong case can be made for an investment policy, as well as a trade policy, in the national interest.

Such a policy, while making every legitimate and proper effort to encourage the creation of a climate favorable to foreign private investment—the form of investment best suited to the organization and economic philosophy of the United States—will endeavor to make a maximum contribution, through public as well as private investment, to the solution of the problems that still obstruct the full reconstruction of the world's economy. Whether a successful investment policy can be devised depends, it must be remembered, to a considerable extent on action by other countries; in this respect investment does not differ from other major aspects of American foreign policy. The responsibilities of capital-receiving countries with regard to the admission and treatment of foreign capital are not in any way reduced by steps taken by the United States Government to make such capital more readily available. In the field of investment, as in other fields, mutuality of interest provides the firmest basis for good international relations.

[11] See Chapter 11, pp. 168–170.

10

Strengthening the Free World

To the extent that the international economic responsibilities already described are successfully discharged, the United States will make a contribution to strengthening the free world. Even if the world were not divided by an iron curtain these responsibilities would not disappear, for they are responsibilities toward the whole community of nations. But since the world is half totalitarian and half free they have been in some ways increased, and an extremely complex set of problems has been raised. For this reason strengthening the free world may be treated as a separate area of responsibility. It was accepted by the United States only after free institutions and free countries, for the second time in a generation, were menaced or overrun by totalitarian powers.

Though the analogies cannot be pressed too far, there are striking resemblances between the situation that has developed during the past seven or eight years and the situation prevailing at the close of the interwar period. The United States was then confronted by a developing threat to all its major foreign policy objectives. One by one small countries were being absorbed by an expanding totalitarian imperialism. Claims were being advanced by totalitarian powers that they alone could solve the alleged evils of a capitalist organization of society, by introducing an economic order completely antithetical to that practiced and believed in by the United States and other democratic countries. The infiltration of totalitarian ideas and influences in areas not under totalitarian rule was being promoted by all available means. In countries

directly menaced, normal peacetime economic objectives had to be subordinated to the urgent requirements of defense. The techniques of economic warfare were being developed. Civil war, aggression, and appeasement were the characteristics of political relations. The system of peace treaties concluded after World War I was in process of being destroyed; and all efforts to achieve collective security through the League of Nations were ending in failure.

Both the similarities and the differences between this situation and the contemporary one are significant for the present discussion. In 1938 Secretary of State Hull called the attention of the American people to the gravity of the threat to American objectives. He enumerated these objectives as follows: (1) the maintenance of basic principles of international law; (2) respect for treaties and observance of them; (3) cooperation to abstain from force as an arm of policy, and to limit and progressively to reduce armaments; (4) cooperation to reconstruct world economic activity; (5) the attainment of as free as possible intellectual intercourse between peoples. These continue to be basic objectives of American foreign policy. Every one of them is jeopardized today by the advance of communism, just as they were jeopardized by the disintegration of international economic and political relations before the outbreak of World War II in Europe in 1939. At that time the United States was not so well prepared to meet a challenge of this sort as it is now. It was not prepared to mobilize its strength in defense of the kind of world that its own national interest should have prompted it to protect and preserve. That the United States has since become increasingly willing to do so is evidence of an enlargement and deepening of the conception of the American national interest.

During World War II strong currents of economic nationalism were set in motion. In many countries economic security and full employment became primary objectives of postwar policy. In nonindustrialized countries there was a

drive for economic development that had no previous parallel. Peaceful and cooperative international relations were unobtainable in the postwar world without the recognition—and to some extent the satisfaction—of these national aspirations. They were also unobtainable unless another and more fundamental condition was fulfilled—the preservation of human freedom in the face of a threat of communist aggression. Under these circumstances the American people came to recognize—and even to take for granted—that the influence and strength of the United States must be used, in its own national interest, to bring about as far as possible world-wide conditions favorable to peaceful and mutually beneficial political and economic relations. Had this not been the attitude of the American people, the public support needed to carry out large programs of foreign assistance would not have been forthcoming.

ECONOMIC AND MILITARY AID—THE PROBLEM OF PRIORITY

If the wartime hope for good political relations with the Soviet Union had been realized, it would have been possible, in planning and carrying out programs of assistance, to give single-minded attention to the solution of the basic economic problems of a world in transition from war to peace. The mounting evidence not only of the unwillingness of the Soviet Union to collaborate, but of its program of communist expansion, made impossible a concentration on world-wide economic problems, and introduced a dualism into all aspects of American foreign-assistance operations. American assistance was directed increasingly toward checking the advance of communism by economic means. Economic recovery as an end in itself was pushed gradually into the background, and came to be regarded chiefly as a means of advancing political and security objectives.

Until June 1950, when the communist invasion of South Korea took place, it had been American policy in extending assistance to Europe to give absolute priority to economic recovery as compared to military strength. The United States wished to use none of its resources to finance a world armament race, and conceived that the major danger from communism was its infiltration of the political and economic life of noncommunist countries. After June 1950 this priority was dropped, and the pendulum swung to the other extreme. A year later, on June 29, 1951, the proper relation between defense and recovery as elements in an American assistance program was stated by Secretary of State Acheson as follows:

We must be aware of both the fallacy of recovery without defensive strength, and the fallacy of military strength upon a shaky economic foundation. These two things are of vital importance. They go together and they are at the heart of our efforts at the present time in the North Atlantic Treaty countries. . . . Economic well-being is not enough by itself. The countries which we have aided along the upward road now see that the situation demands a tremendous effort to build up along with us military strength as well as economic strength. Defensive strength is as integral to recovery as a fence is to a corn field. Yet in seeking to replenish military strength it is necessary to avoid putting too great a load on our allies or on ourselves for that matter. There must be a very carefully worked out balance between the firm economic foundation and the strong military defense so that the military defense does not bring down the economic structure in ruins and so that the economic structure is built up for the purpose of defending itself with its military components.[1]

This view does not run counter to Christian ethics, unless Christian ethics is identified with the pacifist position.

Indeed, there has never been a time during the past decade

[1] "Summary of Remarks of Secretary Acheson to Magazine and Book Publishers," *Department of State Bulletin*, Volume XXV, No. 630, July 23, 1951, p. 126.

when defensive strength was not as integral, not only to recovery but to the existence of the kind of world in which values cherished by the American people can flourish, "as a fence is to a corn field." But war is by no means inevitable; and programs of military defense must not be allowed to distract attention from programs that contribute to the welfare and moral quality of the society to be defended. This was recognized by the Detroit Conference in the report already mentioned:

We believe that the economic measures required for the stability and health of both our own nation and the nations jointly committed with us to the principles of a free society should be part of a general political program. The total purpose of this program should be to create a more genuine sense of community among all peoples. We repeat that war is not inevitable. While we recognize the existing necessity for military defense against the menace of totalitarianism, we hold [that the] moral, political, and economic programs [elaborated in the report] are the primary essential for the positive achievement of an enduring peace. The best way of avoiding a military encounter with totalitarianism lies in proving that only a free world can achieve standards of unity, justice, and progress which increasingly satisfy the needs and conscience of all people.[2]

It cannot be said that the viewpoints reflected in the last two quotations have dominated recent American assistance policy. All American assistance programs have been made subordinate to security considerations. Economic assistance has been rechristened "defense support," and there is danger of losing sight of the economic objectives for which great amounts of American assistance have been expended. The United States will not fully discharge its international re-

[2] *The Responsibility of Christians in an Interdependent Economic World*, Department of the Church and Economic Life, Federal Council of Churches of Christ in America, New York, 1950, pp. 25–26.

sponsibilities if such vacillations as these continue to characterize its use of economic power.

CONDITIONS ATTACHED TO THE GRANT OF AID

As the emphasis in American assistance operations has shifted more and more to military aid, there has been a tendency for the United States to attach increasingly severe conditions to this aid. It is clear that assistance cannot be given by one country to another without any conditions. It should be clear also that the country giving aid cannot obtain from the country receiving it—unless that country is very weak— the adoption of policies affecting its vital interests, its basic economic, social, and political institutions, and its long-range welfare, in return for temporary assistance, however large. The giving country can obtain such agreement if the receiving country finds that the action or policies in question are in its own interest. Then the real basis of the cooperation becomes mutuality of interest, and not pressure by threat of the withdrawal of aid.

The American attitude toward European integration and its relation to American assistance well illustrates these points. It is doubtful whether French fears of German domination of Europe, or German fears that membership in the European Defense Community (EDC) may postpone German unification, will be much relieved by the action of Congress in 1953 in requiring the President to make part of American assistance available only to EDC or to countries that became members of EDC. It is doubtful whether American legislative declarations that it is the policy of the people of the United States to encourage European unification, and indications by the dispenser of American assistance that the attitude of the United States toward further assistance would be influenced by progress made toward unification, have been really major

factors in such progress toward this end as was actually achieved.

At a time when many demands were being made in Congress for major policy commitments by Great Britain as a condition for the grant of the British loan of 1946, the executive branch replied that among self-respecting peoples such concessions could not be bought with money. This was the voice of responsible and practical statesmanship. The principle involved applied as well to American pressure for European economic integration, at a time when large-scale assistance was being rendered, as to any other similar demand. European unification is a perfect example of something the United States cannot buy with money, even though the United States may feel that it is essential for the defense of the free world. It is not implied, however, that the United States should not be perfectly free to press toward this objective, using other available means of consultation and cooperation with the powers affected, and avoiding disrespect for national traditions and national consciousness.

THE TEMPTATION TO DICTATE

The fact that the United States is the strongest single partner in the mutual enterprise of strengthening the free world offers a strong temptation to the American people to press on other countries courses of action they are not prepared to follow themselves. It inclines them to ignore the full implications of membership in international organizations; and it often leads them to assume that other free countries should almost as a matter of course accept unilateral policy decisions by the United States that affect matters of common concern.

The long-continued American pressure for European unification well illustrates the first of these tendencies. The United

States Government, in both its administrative and legislative branches, and with a great deal of enthusiastic support from American public opinion, has persistently pointed out the dangers of excessive nationalism in Europe. As has been noted above, it has told European recipients of American aid that the American people insist on the breakdown of European trade barriers, and the creation of a single market in which there shall be free movement of men, goods, and capital. European countries have continually been urged to merge their sovereignty, and to move toward a United States of Europe.

These are radical demands to come from a country that shows few signs of willingness to move in the same direction, and that is seriously considering amending its constitution to meet any possible infringement of its sovereignty through freely negotiated international treaties. There are many more Americans who favor the merger of European sovereignties in a European Union than favor the merger of American sovereignty in an Atlantic Union; more who believe in the free movement of workers across European boundaries than favor a substantial relaxation of American immigration laws; and more who favor a complete abolition of all intra-European trade barriers than favor a complete abolition of the American tariff. Those Americans are mistaken who think it is easier for Europeans to do these things than it would be for themselves. They are arrogant if they think that because the United States is strong and is giving European countries various forms of assistance it can impose on them a unity they themselves do not feel.

There is in Europe a loyalty to European culture and civilization that binds all Europeans together. But there is not yet, and there will not be for a long time, a political loyalty to the idea of the United States of Europe superior to the loyalty felt by Belgians for Belgium, Frenchmen for France,

and Dutchmen for the Netherlands, any more than there is in America a loyalty to the United Nations superior to the loyalty to the United States. Love of country is among the deepest of human emotions. Americans share it and cherish it; and if they hope to see it supplanted in Europe by a larger loyalty, they must base that hope on something more solid than American pressure or advice. Fortunately there is something more solid to rest these hopes on; it is the gradual strengthening of Europe's own will and desire to emerge from the evils of excessive nationalism.

These considerations suggest that Americans, as they approach the enormous problems that affect the vital interests of friendly countries, should display a more patient, a more understanding, and a more analytical approach. Such an approach would call for a careful weighing of the effects of European integration on Europe's relations with the rest of the world. It would require a consideration of the contribution that America might make to the solution of some of Europe's economic problems—by refraining from such acts as the exclusion of Danish cheese from the American market, by checking inflation at home, by investing more abroad, by following in general a more liberal policy in our foreign economic relations than we have been following, and by receiving more displaced persons in this country. Above all, it would require a full realization of the fact that Europe's problems are not merely—not even mainly—regional problems, but are world problems in which the United States itself is inextricably involved. The United States will not fully discharge its responsibilities for strengthening the free world if it continues to urge on others courses of action it will not take itself. Exhortation and pressure will continue to be weak weapons unless they are reinforced by example. The strength of America in the free world is such that much more can be accomplished in achieving American objectives by the force of

example than most Americans realize. For America to urge one policy on others and to follow a different one itself weakens every aspect of American policy in this area.

A striking example of the unwillingness of the American people to accept the full implications of membership in international organizations and enterprises was the tendency of the American Congress to treat UNRRA as if it were an agency of the United States Government, simply because America made the largest contribution. A similar attitude has permeated many aspects of the American participation in joint efforts to strengthen the free world.

For example, in negotiating bilateral agreements under the Mutual Defense Assistance Program—the first military aid program after the war—the United States proposed conditions that might have given it the power to determine whether the currencies of the countries receiving aid should or should not be devalued, and to interfere with long-established trade patterns by a rigid prohibition on the export of commodities similar to those furnished as aid.

Under the Mutual Security Act of 1951 no country was to receive assistance unless it agreed, *inter alia*, to join in promoting international understanding and good will and in maintaining world peace, and to take such action as might be mutually agreed on to eliminate causes of international tension. The action to be taken was not to be mutually agreed on by any regional organization like the North Atlantic Treaty Organization, but bilaterally by the recipient country and the United States. If the recipient country did not agree to action desired by the United States, it risked the loss of aid. Assistance could be terminated by a joint resolution of Congress a: any time without giving any reason, even though the recipient country might have embarked on long-range programs on the understanding that American assistance would be continued. Other examples could be cited, particularly the

de facto limitation placed on the authority of the North Atlantic Treaty Organization to distribute the burdens of rearmament by collective decision, as long as the actual allocations of United States aid are made bilaterally.

It is dangerous to assume that if, in a mutual enterprise, the contribution of one partner takes the form of a unilateral transfer of goods or services to the others, that partner acquires the right to dictate to them. A decent respect for the opinions of friends and allies is necessary for the moral strength and unity on which the success of the enterprise largely depends, though it need not rob the stronger partner of great and even major influence.

In dealing with the peculiarly difficult problems growing out of trade between the free world and the Soviet orbit, the American government has put forth great efforts to achieve a mutually agreed-on program of action; and it has largely succeeded. But it has done so only by overcoming very strong Congressional pressure for making conformity with unilaterally determined American views a condition for the continuation of aid to other countries. Some features of the most recent legislation on this subject, the Mutual Security Control Act of 1951 mentioned above, still require, as a condition of receiving aid, conformity with American decisions; but flexibility of administration has been preserved.

The Influence of Public Opinion

The special significance of these particular problems in a discussion of America's responsibilities in strengthening the free world is that situations may arise in which the Government cannot act responsibly because public opinion will not allow it to do so. No question seems simpler on the surface than whether or not the United States and other free countries should send goods to China or the USSR, to be used in shoot-

ing down our soldiers in Korea, or in general adding to communist war potential. There is no disagreement on the fundamental issue of supplying arms and ammunition to potential enemies of free countries; but on the question of general trade there is ample room for disagreement. This problem cannot be worked out on a satisfactory basis if an aroused public opinion, not fully informed on the intricacies of the issues, interposes a veto. On such issues as this a very large measure of responsibility rests on individual citizens, and particularly on Christians, to secure a calm, objective appraisal of all the issues by the American people.

One of these issues is whether the United States must assume responsibility for providing markets and supplies to countries formerly dependent on "Iron Curtain" markets. The main case in point is that of Japan. It is a hard case, because of the fear in the United States and Australia and most European countries of being flooded with low-cost Japanese goods. It is clear, however, that American responsibility for the strengthening of the free world must include the acceptance of the consequences of any action taken for that purpose. When these appear to involve possible readjustments in the American economy, as in the case of Japanese trade, responsible action must be supported by a responsible public opinion.

It is often said that the major responsibility of the United States in strengthening the free world is in keeping its own economy strong. No one can deny the truth of this statement, but nothing is easier than to use it as an excuse for evading the full burdens imposed by other international responsibilities. A minor example is the strong opposition of special American interests, and their representatives in Congress, to the operation of the International Materials Conference, an international body set up in 1951 with American participation to expand the production, increase the availability, and assure

the most effective distribution and utilization of the supplies of scarce raw materials. The American economy, it was argued, should not be deprived of the raw materials necessary to keep American industry fully employed, which America was in the position to purchase if no international restraints were interposed. This episode was not actually too important, but it occurred at a time when the United States was being charged by other countries with responsibility for the scarcity of many raw materials because it would not restrict domestic consumption in order to free resources for the needs of re-armament. This was regarded as an irresponsible and even unfriendly policy by many countries, who felt that they were being called on to bear an undue portion of the burdens imposed by the defense build-up that was in progress.

Nothing is more difficult than to apply in any meaningful way the principle of the equality of sacrifice to the problem of strengthening the free world. But it is not seemly or responsible for a country situated as is the United States to urge belt-tightening on other countries in a common cause, unless it is prepared to do the same. In all such matters the moral and intellectual support given by the public to responsible and cooperative action by the United States Government may be decisive.

Leadership in strengthening the free world imposes on the United States a series of hard choices. It is incumbent on those who are in a position to influence public opinion not to shirk these hard choices, but to arrive at a settled judgment concerning them. If the problems are to be solved, some things that are desirable must be subordinated to others that are more desirable; and the solution may require a good deal of soul-searching on the part of people who are enthusiastically devoted to one or another constructive aspect of American foreign policy. This applies with particular force, under present circumstances, to the whole area of activity generally

known as Point IV. The need for strengthening the free world imposes serious problems of priority in the relations of the United States and underdeveloped countries; for example:

1. How far should the requirements of these countries for manufactured goods and materials be satisfied, when these same goods and materials are sorely needed for the defense efforts of this country and of Western Europe?

2. How far should the United States go in asking or forcing these countries to concentrate, in their plans for economic development, on the production of strategic materials needed by the United States, even if this may later get them into economic difficulties?

Difficult as these questions are, they are by no means the most fundamental confronted by the United States in its relations with less developed countries.

11

Economic Development and Response to Human Need

For many years the latent economic resources of the United States were developed with the aid of foreign capital and foreign technical knowledge; but the United States was not an underdeveloped country, in the sense in which that term is used today. Such a country is generally understood to be one in which capital investment is small, per capita productivity is low, and the standard of living of the large part of the people is at or near the subsistence level. The depths of poverty that prevail in many such countries, particularly in Asia, is apparent to all who travel through them. A good indication of its extent can be obtained by a comparison of the difference in the per capita national income of various countries given in the attached table.

PROPOSALS FOR SHARING WEALTH AND EQUALIZING INCOMES INTERNATIONALLY

The enormous differences in wealth and standards of living between developed and underdeveloped countries have long troubled the conscience of men of good will. The spectacle of the American people living at the highest per capita income in the history of the world in the midst of so much poverty presents for Christians a serious moral problem. To many the solution that seems most obvious is that of sharing our wealth with other countries. From this it is but a step—one not

Table I. Levels and Sources of Income in Various Countries
(Per Capita Income in 1949 of Countries in Continental Divisions)

Income per capita in US dollars	Total Population Number (millions)	Per cent	Africa	North America	South America	Asia	Europe and USSR	Oceania
Under 100	509	34	Kenya N. Rhodesia	Dominican Republic	Ecuador Paraguay	Burma Ceylon India Iran Pakistan Philippines Thailand		
100–200	284	19	Egypt S. Rhodesia	Mexico	Brazil Chile Colombia Peru Surinam	Japan Syria Turkey	Bulgaria Greece Spain Yugoslavia	
200–300	82	6	Union of S. Africa	Cuba Puerto Rico			Austria Hungary Italy	
300–450	305	20			Argentina Uruguay	Israel	Czechoslovakia Finland Germany (Western) Ireland Poland USSR	

450–600	69	5		Venezuela	Belgium France Iceland Luxembourg Netherlands Norway
					Australia New Zealand
600–900	89	6	Canada		Denmark Sweden Switzerland United Kingdom
900 and over	149	10	USA		
	1,487	100			

GENERAL NOTE: The countries are listed alphabetically in each group. The concept of income used to calculate the per capita data is national income produced within the territorial boundaries of the country, or net geographical product at factor cost.

SOURCE: *National Income and Its Distribution in Under-Developed Countries*, United Nations, New York, 1951, Statistical Papers, Series E, No. 3, Sales No. 1951, XVII.3, p. 3.

often taken even by those who feel morally disturbed by this problem—to the acceptance of an egalitarian concept of social justice in international relations. The argument is made that the redistribution of incomes within nations by taxation and other social measures is now accepted not only as morally defensible but as a moral imperative; and that the time has come to apply the same principles to the international scene. This concept of the international equalization of incomes has found support not only in communist propaganda,[1] but in responsible quarters in underdeveloped countries. It underlies a current assumption on the part of many in these countries that they have a right to demand assistance from the United States, and that the United States has an obligation to grant it. This assumption requires careful examination.

The concept that the United States is morally obligated to share its wealth with other nations in order to diminish the inequality in national incomes cannot be the foundation underlying American relations with underdeveloped countries. It suffers from all the defects of other share-the-wealth schemes. It cannot apply to previously accumulated wealth, since it has often been demonstrated statistically that the lot of the many cannot be appreciably improved by taking from the few, because the many are too many and the amount of wealth in the possession of the few is too small. All such proposals therefore resolve themselves into schemes for distributing current income.

If the principle of the international equalization of income were applied, it would not be the United States only that would be expected to share in a world-wide leveling process. Many countries—including those European countries that have received most assistance from the United States—would on this principle have to tighten their belts to help others. The

[1] It has been a major theme of the World Federation of Trade Unions, the communist-dominated international federation put together after the war.

confusion in the conduct of ordinary economic relations between nations that would be occasioned by attempting to act on this principle can hardly be imagined.

A program for sharing the wealth of America with other nations could be carried out only in one of the two following forms: First, the regular transfer by grant from the United States to other countries of goods and services that enter into current consumption. By the mere weight of numbers no such program could be effective in raising living standards significantly without wrecking the United States economy. Or, second, the provision from United States resources of enough capital every year to produce the desired result. That such a transfer of capital is in the realm of fantasy is shown by an estimate made by United Nations experts, to the effect that an annual investment of $19 billion in industry and agriculture would be needed to increase the per capita national income in the underdeveloped countries by 2 per cent annually; and that the total capital requirement, including social overheads, would greatly exceed that amount. Net savings in these countries were only about $5 billion per annum. That is to say, an annual capital export from developed countries of $14 billion would be needed for this very modest achievement in raising national incomes.[2] It is necessary, moreover, to recognize that this estimate is one of the industrial and agricultural needs of underdeveloped countries, and does not give any indication of their capacity to absorb foreign capital or technical knowledge. There are not enough feasible projects to make it possible for such amounts of foreign capital to be fruitfully invested in these countries each year.

Transfers of capital resources on a scale sufficient to equalize incomes internationally would mean on the part of the

[2] *Measures for the Economic Development of Under-Developed Countries*, report by a group of experts, United Nations, May 1951, Sales No. 1951 II.B.2, pp. 75-77.

United States Government a massive intervention in the affairs of its citizens. Through the use of taxation for this purpose many Americans would be deprived of the product of their industry, and the Government would in fact be giving to other countries more than was its own.[3] Moreover, a perpetual relation of giver and receiver among nations would be established; for unfortunately it would be a long time before the great disparities could be substantially reduced. Such a relation between states is degrading if it is too long continued; and it could not be maintained without the raising of serious problems of interference by the giver in the internal affairs of the receiver.

THE PROBLEM OF PROVIDING CAPITAL
FOR ECONOMIC DEVELOPMENT

To criticize the concept of the international equalization of incomes is, however, not to minimize the importance of providing a very considerable international transfer of capital from highly industrialized countries to underdeveloped countries. Economic development in its early stages always results in an increased demand for the import of capital goods without a corresponding increase in exports. But no country can compel other countries to provide it with capital. If this demand is to be satisfied, capital must be attracted to the underdeveloped countries, and its outward flow encouraged by the industrialized countries. Economic development also tends to produce inflation in countries where there is no substantial amount of domestic savings; and, if this is not resisted, the slender resources of potential savers may be dissipated in rising prices, instead of being used to contribute to development.

The major responsibility for solving these problems rests on the underdeveloped countries. It is their responsibility to work

[3] See Chapter 7, pp. 109–110.

out well-conceived, long-range development plans; to create the financial institutions needed to direct their own savings into channels consistent with these plans; to resist inflationary forces; and to adopt a fair and reasonable attitude toward the foreign capital essential to meet their development needs. But countries in a position to provide capital also have important responsibilities: to recognize the right of underdeveloped countries to manage their internal affairs without foreign interference; to conduct their operations in ways that will confer real benefits on the peoples of these countries; and to cooperate with them in removing the many obstacles that impede the flow of capital for development.

There has been some progress in recent years in reducing these obstacles; but the flow of foreign capital to underdeveloped countries continues to be wholly inadequate to meet their immediate and long-range needs as measured by any reasonable criterion.

Some of these needs can best be met by public lending—through such national agencies as the Export-Import Bank of the United States, or through the International Bank for Reconstruction and Development. Public lending is essential for financing the creation of such basic utilities as power, transportation, communications, and flood control. But if the underdeveloped countries are to build on this foundation, much greater efforts must be made to solve the stubborn problems that impede the international flow of private investment.

An important objective of American foreign policy is to help the people of the underdeveloped countries to realize the economic progress and political freedom that are the common aspirations of the common man wherever he may be. It is therefore incumbent on the Government of the United States, not only to continue some forms of public lending, but to take such steps as lie in its power to encourage the flow of develop-

ment capital from this country in the form that the United States is best suited to provide—private investment.

Some of the most constructive steps that can be taken lie in the field of taxation and the negotiation of investment treaties. If sound development plans cannot be postponed or abandoned without the intensification of grave social and political tensions, moderate grants-in-aid are in the common interest of both the United States and the underdeveloped countries. Such grants may also play a strategic role in the early stages of those development programs that could not otherwise be started effectively without resort to totalitarian methods.

The case is much less clear, from both an economic and an ethical point of view, when very ambitious schemes are put forward for new international institutions to provide development capital by large-scale grants, or by loans that do not measure up to any criterion of sound international lending. Pressures have been very strong within the United Nations to provide capital on these terms through a Special United Nations Fund for Economic Development, to which the United States would be the major contributor, but in which it would not have the major voice. But such a fund would not rest on good moral foundations if it served only to perpetuate a world system in which some countries relied for their own development on the bounty of others.

INDIVIDUAL AND NATIONAL MOTIVATIONS IN PROVIDING TECHNICAL ASSISTANCE

A situation in which underdeveloped countries assert a *right* to American aid, and the United States denies it has an *obligation* to meet their demands, is not conducive to friendly international relations. What is needed is an effort to find a point of concurrence between the interests of the underdeveloped countries and those of the United States, and to

devise ways and means of promoting what is recognized as a mutual interest. This does not by any means rule out the humanitarian impulse to go to the aid of people less fortunate than ourselves, as a force guiding American action. The Point IV program of technical aid has from the beginning made a strong appeal to Christians and to all men of good will in the United States, because it strikes a warm, humanitarian, and recognizably Christian note in a statement of national objectives and a program of national action. In no area of international relations in which the Government participates has a greater opportunity been provided for the development of mutual understanding through cooperative action. It is a field in which the individual can contribute much to the human understanding and friendship that is in the mutual interest of all the countries concerned.

As formulated by President Truman, the program of technical assistance is based on a deep concern for the peoples of the world who were living in a condition approaching misery, and on a recognition that improvement in their lives would benefit all other countries:

> Only by helping the least fortunate of its members to help themselves can the human family achieve the decent, satisfying life that is the right of all people. Democracy alone can supply the vitalizing force to stir the peoples of this world into triumphant action not only against their human oppressors but also against their ancient enemies—hunger, misery, and despair.[4]

The President, however, made it clear in his message to Congress on June 29, 1949, on Point IV legislation, that as a part of the foreign policy of the United States the program was designed to serve four primary American interests: (1) to have new and stronger nations associated with us in the cause

---

[4] President Truman's inaugural address of January 1949, "A Decade of American Foreign Policy," *Basic Documents 1941–9*, Government Printing Office, Washington, 1950, p. 1367.

of human freedom; (2) to strengthen the United Nations and the fabric of world peace; (3) to contribute to restoring the economies of free European countries; and (4) to increase our trade and economic stability by increasing the output and national income of underdeveloped countries.[5] The first of these objectives raises a serious moral dilemma in cases where Point IV assistance is furnished to governments with despotic, reactionary, and, in some cases, even feudal ruling powers.

In many fields during its short life the Point IV program, as well as the related United Nations technical assistance programs, and the provision of what may be called Point-IV-type aid in many other American programs, have demonstrated how much can be accomplished by this method. At the same time many of the countries in which such programs are in effect have been acutely aware that the United States interest in their welfare seems to have begun when the problem of resisting communism became important to the United States, and they fear that this interest might evaporate were the communist menace to diminish. Therefore the two questions concerning the priorities mentioned above have become part of a greater question concerning American responsibility in this area.

This greater question is whether the mutual, long-range interests that were the foundation of the Point IV program as originally conceived are to be lost sight of, and the program is to become merely one of the weapons employed in the fight against communism. If this should be the fate of the Point IV program, it would no longer represent a point of concurrence between the interests of the United States and those of many countries in which the program is being carried forward. The problem of economic development is essentially long-range; and if international programs for its solution are to be carried out successfully they cannot be made an adjunct

[5] op. cit., pp. 1367–1372.

of other policies, no matter how pressing. This is not to say that in emergency situations the extent and character of the cooperation may not have to be modified. The great danger is that the nature of the program and its true objectives may become permanently distorted. It is one of the great advantages of increased American participation in United Nations technical assistance programs, including those of the specialized agencies, that this danger is avoided.

GOVERNMENT ACTION IN RESPONSE TO HUMAN NEED

The American people have to their credit a long record of generous response to the call of human need from other countries. In times of flood, famine, or other disaster, help from individuals and private organizations has been readily forthcoming. The hardships inflicted on civilian populations by war and its aftermath have called forth generous American aid in many ways. The humanitarian impulses of the American people have long been an important factor in American foreign relations, and in many circumstances it has been necessary to give them expression through government action. If the American Government is to discharge its responsibility for giving practical expression to the wishes of the American people to bring help and comfort to others in times of distress or disaster, it must do so, whenever the occasion arises, in a steady and effective manner. This is not easily accomplished. Sometimes actions by the United States Government that appear to be humanitarian have been motivated by their contribution to the solution of domestic problems rather than by the need of other countries.

Government action in helping other countries is almost always inspired by mixed motives. This is well illustrated by the motives underlying the Point IV program that have already been mentioned. It is also illustrated by the tendency

of the Congress to see in almost every proposal for a relief or assistance operation abroad an opportunity for disposing of surplus agricultural products. Though it may be convenient to arrange a marriage between the satisfaction of the humane and generous feelings of American citizens toward others in distress and the satisfaction of special interests in the disposal of their products, such a marriage cannot for long be a happy one.

There is, for example, a strong humanitarian and Christian appeal in two basic ideas that are of growing influence in agricultural policy in the world today. One is that since there is no absolute overproduction of any major agricultural product as far as human need is concerned, the basic world agricultural policy should be the expansion of production. The second is that when, under a policy of expansion, "surpluses" develop, they should be distributed through noncommercial channels to those who need them most. The application of these ideas, however, raises many problems. Agricultural "surpluses" may be created by such high supports to farmers that the whole output cannot be sold in the market at or near support prices, even over a long period of time. The Government then continues to hold a portion of the supply off the market; and the adjustments in production that are required from an economic point of view do not take place.

Quite apart from the foreign trade problems to which this may lead, other questions must be answered—questions that arise from a strong desire not to allow these "surpluses" to go to waste. These raise profound issues of equity. Is it, for example, just that agricultural "surpluses" of the United States should be distributed at special prices to needy areas in the rest of the world at the expense of the general body of consumers (many of them needy) in the United States itself, and of consumers in countries not judged to be especially needy? Should those producers whose interest is directly involved have the predominant voice in determining what

should be considered "surplus"? Should the needy areas receive aid of this kind only when a "surplus" appears, and at other times be left to shift for themselves? By what criteria should the needy areas be selected?

In the great complex of international commerce, in which producers of the same commodities in other countries and consumers in countries that are not in desperate need are vitally affected, the disposal of surplus agricultural products cannot be conducted on the simple principles that govern the conduct of an individual in relieving his fellow man. Account must be taken also of the long-range economic problems of the receiving countries. It is quite possible that what is needed most in such countries is an increase in their own production, for which a large-scale program of surplus disposal, carried on intermittently at special prices destructive of market relations, is certainly no substitute. American responsibility for responding to the call of human need is not discharged if the response to that call must be dovetailed with a domestic agricultural support program. The United States should at least be ready, even in time of shortage, to play its role in alleviating suffering.

It is therefore incumbent on those who from purely humanitarian motives insist strongly on measures of agricultural surplus disposal to familiarize themselves with the issues, difficulties, and pitfalls that surround such a program. Brains as well as hearts are required in urging the United States to discharge its responsibilities in meeting human needs. It is, moreover, incumbent on Christians to be sensitive to attempts to cloak other activities and policies of the Government under the guise of humanitarian action. The provision of food primarily to obtain a political objective is not humanitarian; and in general the use of food as a political weapon is not in accord with the highest sense of international responsibility and obligation. All aspects of American policies should be imbued with some element of humanitarian concern

for the welfare of others; and those parts of American policy that are proclaimed as purely humanitarian should be confined to clear cases in which there can be no question of ulterior motives.

However great the contribution of technical aid to the solution of economic, social, and administrative problems in underdeveloped areas, and however devoted the service and broad the vision of the persons taking part in these programs, the hope for big increases in living standards cannot be realized without large-scale investment. The responsibilities of the United States in the field of economic development cannot be separated, therefore, from its responsibilities in the field of investment; and, as has been shown, these in turn cannot be separated from its responsibilities in the field of trade. All these fields are intimately related to the functioning of the United States economy; and all are deeply affected by the necessity of American leadership in strengthening the free world. Even when serving as a channel for the response of the American people to the call of human need, the Government must take into account the economic consequences of its action at home and abroad. A supreme responsibility of the United States in conducting its international affairs is, therefore, to make its action in all these fields mutually supporting and harmonious. Pressure brought to bear on the Government by individuals and groups concerned with one or another aspect of policy increases the inherent difficulties of achieving a well-balanced and responsible foreign policy in the economic sphere. And this is as true of pressure from uncritical enthusiasts for programs that have not been carefully thought out, as of pressure from special interests. Therefore the individual citizen and private groups must bear an ultimate responsibility for the quality of the policy that is actually followed.

SUMMARY OF THE ARGUMENT

The implications of Christian economic ethics for the conduct of international relations, drawn out in this Part, have been discussed exclusively in terms of American international responsibilities. The treatment, therefore, has been partial and incomplete. No attempt has been made to give a fully rounded, ethical interpretation of the great issues involved. Instead, this discussion has been directed to the development of the following sequence of ideas:

1. The degree and kind of economic interdependence existing within our own country (or any country with significant international economic relations) is determined not only by its domestic economic structure but by its economic relations with other countries.

2. The community of interest that binds and the conflicts of interest that separate individuals or groups within the country cannot be understood or analyzed satisfactorily without reference to these international economic relations.

3. Consequently no sharp line of distinction can be drawn between the ethical issues that arise from attempts to apply Christian principles to the conduct of our domestic economic affairs, and those that arise in the conduct of our international economic relations.

4. A distinction has nevertheless to be drawn between the responsibilities of individuals or groups in reconciling their economic conduct with Christian principles, and the responsibilities of government in influencing or conducting international economic relations.

5. The question how far the general conclusions reached in Parts I and II can be applied to relations between sovereign states has to be faced squarely.

6. Though the actions of the government of a sovereign state are limited to what is regarded as national self-interest, the conceptions of the national interest may easily become too narrow

and short-range. It is therefore important to emphasize the concern of individual citizens of a nation for values that serve to broaden the concept of national interest.

7. The promotion and safeguarding of America's national interest calls for the creation, maintenance, development, and defense of the kind of world order in which a set of values accepted by the American people can be advanced and defended.

8. The quality of American leadership in contributing to a better world political and economic order depends fundamentally on what these values are.

9. What these values are or may become depends on how the ethical issues raised in this series are approached and dealt with in practice.

10. Whether these values are reflected in the conduct of our international economic relations depends on the degree to which the American people understand the intricate problems involved, and accept the consequences of national action that is in consonance with these values.

11. In every area in which the United States, by virtue of its great economic and military strength and political influence, has great responsibilities, there are extremely hard choices to be made, often among objectives that are defensible on ethical and moral grounds but that cannot all be equally served in a given set of circumstances.

It is one of the duties of the Church to face these moral and intellectual dilemmas squarely—a duty additional to its duty of reaffirming and restating the basic Christian approach to all social and personal problems. If it does not continue to perform the latter, there is the risk—to which Protestantism is peculiarly subject—of identifying Christianity with enlightened self-interest. If it does not perform the former, there is the risk of failure to relate the message of the Church to the realities of the world we live in.

PART IV

The Main Issue

Howard R. Bowen and John C. Bennett

12

Ethics and Economics

by Howard R. Bowen

The connection between ethics and economics is by no means obvious, and is often overlooked or imperfectly understood. Economic life takes place in a mundane atmosphere of money, machines, profits, and prices. It often appears as a unique and separable part of human existence in which calculating self-interest is the appropriate motive and the dollar is the adequate criterion of value. Thus, in the economic part of life, ethics often seems unnecessary—except, of course, for certain "self-evident" rules pertaining to respect for property, observance of contract, and abstinence from fraud and coercion.

Actually, it is a dangerous delusion to suppose that ethics touches economics only with respect to these elementary rules of "common honesty." Economic life is, by its very nature, suffused throughout with ethical problems and implications.

Economic activity is an important part of human experience. It fills most of our waking hours, and to it we devote much energy and talent. It supplies the goods (and bads) which make up our scale of living. It involves us in many of our most rewarding (and most difficult) human relationships. It requires us to meet competition. It places heavy responsibilities on us. It influences our family life, our religious observances, and our cultural attainments. It partly determines our sense of personal tranquillity (or fear and uncertainty).

It provides us with opportunities for creative satisfactions (or monotonous drudgery). Altogether, economic activity places an indelible stamp on human personality and on the quality of human life. As Alfred Marshall, the great Cambridge economist, said:[1]

> For man's character has been moulded by his every-day work, and the material resources which he thereby procures, more than by any other influence unless it be that of his religious ideals; and the two great forming agencies of the world's history have been the religious and the economic. . . . Religious motives are more intense than economic, but their direct action seldom extends over so large a part of life. For the business by which a person earns his livelihood generally fills his thoughts during by far the greater part of those hours in which his mind is at its best; during them his character is being formed by the way in which he uses his faculties in his work, by the thoughts and the feelings which it suggests, and by his relation to his associates in work, his employers or his employees. . . . And very often the influence exerted on a person's character by the amount of his income is hardly less, if it is less, than that exerted by the way in which it is earned.

Any activity which occupies so large and so significant a part of our existence and which touches our lives at so many points has profound ethical significance far beyond the conventionalized rules of "common honesty"—important though these be. Economic activity must be considered in terms of the ultimate meaning of life itself. The basic ethical questions to be considered are: What are the ultimate values of human existence? And how may economic activities and institutions contribute to the achievement of these ultimate values?

In everyday life, the ethical principles underlying our economic behavior tend to become imbedded in rules-of-thumb that we accept uncritically and for the most part unconsciously. We commonly assume, for example, that more income is better than less, that thrift and hard work are virtues,

[1] *Principles of Economics*, 8th ed., Macmillan, London, 1920, pp. 1–2.

that productive progress is good, that things are worth what they cost, that those things should be produced that promise the greatest profit, that each person is the best judge of his own interests, that lower cost of production is preferable to higher cost, that each family head is responsible for the support of his own, that people deserve the incomes they earn, that monopoly and "profiteering" are evil, etc.

Each of these axioms is, of course, at least partly defensible, but not one of them is completely valid without qualification. But this is not the place to debate the merits of these principles. The point is that by means of axioms such as these, axioms which we regard as so self-evident that they need scarcely be thought about, we fall into the illusion that economic life lies largely outside the sphere of ethics.

The neglect of the ethical side of economic behavior in our daily conduct is perhaps understandable. Axiomatic principles are essential, because the onrush of events does not permit us to examine all the ethical implications of our actions all the time. Yet it is hazardous to relegate ethics to the habitual and the subconscious, and to accept our moral codes without frequent reappraisal. To do so tempts us to forget the moral aspects of economic decisions by assuming that they do not exist. To an alarming degree, this is precisely what has happened in the modern world.

Because of the all-too-easy tendency to slight the ethical side of economic life, it may be worth while to examine precisely the role of ethics in economic life. This will require a consideration of the nature of economic *means*, and the nature of the *values* sought with these means.

ECONOMIC MEANS

Economic life is concerned mainly with decisions about the use of means (primarily labor and wealth) that are scarce. In this context scarcity implies that the supply of

these means is less than the amount people would like to have. Whenever economic means are used to provide goods for any one person or group, this use tends to reduce the amount of goods that can be enjoyed by others. Scarcity, therefore, usually leads to rivalry for the use of these means or their products; and this rivalry is a potential source of conflict, or a potential source of economic oppression of the weak by the powerful.

It has sometimes been hoped, optimistically, that the great increase in productivity, which in a few countries has relieved the pressure for survival, would reduce the intensity of this rivalry and eliminate a major source of conflict. This hope has proved to be vain. Instead, it has been found that economic means are used not only for the necessities and amenities of life but also to provide status and power. As a result, no foreseeable increase in the quantity of economic means appears to be sufficient to overcome the harshness of the struggle for wealth. Even in fabulously rich America we are daily witnesses to conflict that is fully as intense as in earlier times or in poorer countries. This involves rivalry not only among individuals and firms, but also among great organized power blocs which divide us into opposing camps.

It is true that in modern America and a few other Western countries many of the conditions of economic oppression—so evident in early nineteenth-century capitalism—have been corrected. Much of the improvement in this respect has been achieved under the leadership of social reformers who have been actuated by Christian ideals. Yet the relatively favorable conditions in a few Western countries should not blind us to the essential and inescapable fact of scarcity and its potential consequences. We cannot complacently assume that further progress will be achieved or that we shall be permanently immune to new forms of economic oppression arising from new concentrations of power.

One of the major problems of any society is to achieve rules of conduct under which this rivalry may be carried on peaceably and justly. In our society, these rules are in the form of an elaborate system of laws, customs, and usages governing the acquisition and use of labor and wealth. A large part of what we call government pertains to the formulation and enforcement of these rules. And a large part of what we conventionally call morality pertains to obligations, rights, immunities, and freedoms in the acquisition and use of economic means.

Despite the multiplicity of rules and our elaborate machinery for indoctrinating and enforcing them, the underlying rivalry that grows out of scarcity is always a potential source of conflict. Individuals and groups are always liable to break away from the established rules, or, more importantly, the established rules are liable to become outmoded by new developments in technology and social organization. Ethical considerations are involved, both in the development of our institutions to deal with the explosive problem of economic rivalry, and also in the conduct of individuals and groups within the given institutional framework.

Moreover, if these scarce economic means are to be used efficiently, they must be so organized as to reap the gains from specialization. Hence each individual must surrender his ability to provide directly for his own needs; he must rely on the market to accept his particular productive services in exchange for the goods produced by others. The result is an intricate network of mutual relationships in which the individual becomes utterly dependent on others for his very life, and at the same time the welfare of all is dependent on the productiveness and efficiency of each individual.

This extreme interdependence raises a host of ethical issues. These pertain partly to the obligation of those in power to protect the integrity of the virtually helpless individual—to

assure his rights, his security, and his personality. And these ethical issues are partly concerned with the obligation of all persons—from obscure artisans to great industrial leaders—to perform their economic functions effectively and coordinately; i.e., to contribute their share to the common enterprise.

But the close connection between ethics and economics arises not only because of scarcity and interdependence, but also because of the nature of the values that are sought through economic life.

VALUES

We commonly associate economic activity with the businesslike, unsentimental, and materialistic aspects of life. But this is a grossly inadequate view. Economic activity yields not alone material values such as food, clothing, and shelter. It also is involved in the quest of virtually all values, including those we regard as the noblest.

Aesthetic experience, for example, often requires artists, galleries, or musical instruments. Religious worship calls for clergymen, churches, and hymnbooks. Indeed, we recognize the economic base of organized religious life by including the offering as part of the standard ritual. Sport demands fishing tackle, baseballs, and stadia. Education and research require teachers, buildings, and laboratories. Friendship and courtship require telephones and facilities for entertainment. Birth requires obstetricians and hospitals. Social status is sometimes linked with conspicuous consumption. Power and influence can be had with great wealth. Government needs policemen, judges, and battleships.[2]

---

[2] Even in primitive society, the values sought through economic life are not exclusively those concerned with survival and physical comfort. See *Goals*, pp. 85–88, 322–3, 332–3.

To whatever department of life one turns, economic means are involved. This is not to say that they are sufficient for attaining all our values. A magnificent cathedral does not guarantee spirituality or appreciation of beauty. Costly sporting goods do not always give genuine recreation. Expensive courtships do not necessarily end in happy marriages. Rich food may not lead to good nutrition. Conspicuous consumption does not insure high social status. And great wealth does not always confer power. Yet economic means are used for all of these purposes, and in most cases are essential.

Because economic means are used in connection with the full spectrum of human values, the way in which they are used by a society reflects its total pattern of values. Just as the way of life of a family is revealed by the way it spends its money, so the way of life and the values of a whole society are reflected in the array of economic goods it produces ard consumes.

What distinguishes the economic aspect of life is not the nature of the values sought, but rather the nature of the means used to attain these values. Economics is concerned with the use of scarce means for the attainment of any values whatsoever. Decisions regarding the use of economic means are usually in the form of choices among values. They involve the appraisal of alternative ends—ends that range all the way from nutrition to aesthetics. Such a process of valuation is essentially ethical.[3]

But the goods and services derived from economic means are not the only products emanating from the economic system. Another product is the experiences of people as they participate in the system. True welfare is influenced fully as much by what happens to people in the productive process itself as by the quantity of goods that flows from that process.

[3] Cf. A. B. Wolfe, "On the Content of Welfare," *American Economic Review*, June 1931, p. 207.

Much of our lives is spent in work as well as in other pursuits. This working part of our lives (the part spent in production of any kind) surely has much to do with our welfare.

Though this portion of our lives may for certain purposes be thought of as *means* directed toward ulterior ends, yet it must also be regarded as part of the ends themselves. This is an application to economics of Kant's famous dictum: "Act so that you treat humanity . . . always as an end as well as a means, never merely as a means." Work forms so large and important a part of life's experiences, affects human well-being in so many ways, and stamps human personality so indelibly, that it must be regarded as one of the products of the economic system.[4] As such, it has both its negative and its positive effects.

On the negative side, work sometimes involves monotony, fatigue, disagreeable tasks, and the use of time that might preferably be spent in other ways. It may impair physical or mental health.[5] It may be irregular and uncertain, and thus cause fear and insecurity. Work sometimes involves unwholesome or unpleasant human relations. It may cause deterioration of family life, of community life, or of the quality of government. Work may subject people to injustice and contempt. It may lead to the destruction of social unity through the creation of divisive power blocs. It may produce undesirable personalities—make people aggressive or servile or officious or deceitful; and so on.

But work has its positive aspects, which may well outweigh its negative effects. It may minister to the need of individuals for creative activity, self-expression, and interesting experience. It may offer fellowship, enlarged human relationships, and a sense of belonging and participating. It may offer scope for

[4] Cf. J. A. Hobson, *Economics and Ethics*, D. C. Heath, New York, 1929, p. 108.

[5] For a discussion of the relation of economic life to emotional health and illness, see *Am. Ec.*

altruistic and service motives. It may give opportunities for self-development. It may fill time and prevent boredom. It may be an avenue to self-respect and social status.

In short, when we speak of the values flowing from economic life, we must look not only at the quantity of final goods flowing off the assembly lines but also at the satisfactions and the costs involved in producing these goods. And it is not at all clear that true welfare is to be found more largely in the products than in the process. The economic system produces a great deal more than goods and services for "consumption." It also produces the conditions under which people spend a major portion of their lives, and thereby places a marked imprint on character.[6]

To summarize, economic life in all its ramifications is of profound ethical significance. This is so because of scarcity which gives rise to conflict, because of interdependence which creates mutual obligations, because of the wide range of values sought through economic activity, and because of the significance for human life of the economic process itself. When we judge the economic system or its parts, when we consider proposals for changes in economic institutions, or when we face economic decisions as individuals, the final criteria must be those ultimate values that express the meaning of human life itself. One of the urgent needs of the modern world is to recognize that the great moral principles that express our highest aspirations are as germane to economic life as to any other area of human experience. That is why economic life is properly and necessarily of concern to the Christian Church. The first task in bringing ethics to bear on economic life is to discover the basic values or goals that

[6] Indeed, there may be logic in reversing the customary definitions of ends and means in economic life. A case can be made for regarding as means the goods and services we ordinarily think of as ends, and for regarding as ends the process we ordinarily think of as means.

ought to be achieved through economic life. It is in terms of these goals that economic institutions, decisions, and policies are to be judged.

THE SEPARATION OF ETHICS AND ECONOMICS

In view of the intimate connection between ethics and economics, it is not surprising that during most of recorded intellectual history economics has been treated as a branch of ethics. The central problem has been the ordering of the use of labor and wealth for the purpose of promoting the good life. Until fairly recent times, the great figures of economic thought have been religious leaders or philosophers—among them the Hebrew prophets, the Greek philosophers, St. Augustine, St. Thomas Aquinas, Smith, Bentham, and J. S. Mill.[7]

During the past century, however, the connection between ethics and economics as intellectual disciplines has become attenuated. This has been due in part to the process of academic specialization by which communication among scholars in different fields of study—even in closely related fields—has become progressively more difficult. But, to make the separation more complete, many economists have consciously sought to convert their discipline into a "science."

[7] But economics has not always been treated merely as a branch of ethics. At times, curiously, ethics has come close to being a branch of economics. This was true especially when the utilitarians interpreted ethical conduct as that use of means that permits a maximization of human happiness. The ethical problem, as they saw it, was to arrange so that means would not be squandered on lesser quantities of happiness when they might be used to "produce" greater quantities of happiness. Ethical behavior was construed as a process of economizing. The viewpoint and the principles of economics were thus applied to all aspects of human conduct, and ethics became a kind of "super" economics. It was no accident that many of the utilitarian philosophers were also economists, e.g., Bentham, James Mill, J. S. Mill, and Sidgwick. And it was no accident that utilitarian ethics has exerted a powerful influence on economists, extending even to the present time. Cf. F. H. Knight, The Ethics of Competition, Harper & Brothers, New York, 1935, pp. 1–40.

They have tried to banish normative questions from their purview. In so doing, they have not necessarily repudiated ethics, but rather have elected to concentrate on the development of positive knowledge, leaving normative questions to others. Also, in their effort to be scientific, economists have attempted to restrict themselves to those values that are susceptible to measurement. This has meant, in practice, that only those values are considered that can be measured in terms of money.

The separation of ethics and economics can be explained also by the marked fragmentation of life itself, which has become one of the characteristics of modern civilization. In less complex societies, the several facets of human experience which we are inclined to think of as sharply distinctive— the religious, the familial, the aesthetic, the economic, etc.— have been closely integrated into a single pattern and interpreted by a single philosophy. Today, in our society, each part of human experience has its own particular institutions and behavior patterns, its own specialized functionaries, and its own value system. For example, religion has its own behavior patterns and value systems, which in practice do not seem to impinge very directly on other parts of life; these are all too often reserved for Sunday. The state consists of another set of institutions, behavior patterns, and value systems. The family is still another relatively separate social grouping, with its own way of life and thought, etc. Thus a person may be a church member, a citizen, a father, a sportsman, a Rotarian, and a businessman, and in each of these roles follow different behavior patterns, seek different values, and accept different moral codes.

The economic aspect of life is, of course, conspicuous for the degree of its isolation. Though it is directed toward a wide range of values, it takes place within a clear-cut set of distinctively economic institutions; among these, the store,

the factory, the labor union, the government bureau, the trade association, etc. Individuals are accustomed to reserving a definite part of their time for their highly specialized economic tasks. And in these functions they are likely to be moved by a devotion to material advantage that would be despised in most other areas of life.

It is scarcely surprising that the study of economics should, like its subject matter, have become insulated from broader ethical issues.

The final blow, by which economics was all but cut off from ethics, was the ascendancy of the doctrine of natural order or *laissez faire*. Under this theory, which is still influential, private self-interest and the general social interest were considered to be miraculously in harmony. It was thought that there would be no need for ethics (beyond the elementary rules of honesty), because the "invisible hand" would look out for the common weal while each individual was busy looking out for himself. The more thoughtful advocates of *laissez faire*, of course, never intended to throw ethics out of economics.[8] But in its actual effect their doctrine diverted attention away from ethics.

The profound historic movements that have been so briefly sketched have made comparative strangers of economics and ethics. Value theory, once the very heart of economics, has become price theory. Few economists are concerned about ethical questions, or permit themselves the luxury of considering economics in the context of the larger goals of *life* as distinct from the narrower goals of economic efficiency expressed in pecuniary terms. While most economists have been drawing away from ethics, no other vigorous or effective group has come forward to close the gap between the two disciplines. The result is a kind of intellectual vacuum—a vacuum which, one can hope, nature will abhor.

[8] For a discussion of the ethical postulates of laissez faire, see *Soc. Resp.*, pp. 19–20.

ECONÓMICS AND VALUES

From all this, it should not be inferred that practicing economists have withdrawn from the arena of public affairs, or that they have been reluctant to offer recommendations for public policy. As everyone knows, few economists, however devoted to scientific purity, have been able to resist converting their abstraction into proposals.

Many of the greatest contributions to economics have been made by men struggling with important public issues—men whose scientific contributions were largely by-products of their efforts to find solutions to practical problems, or sometimes by-products of their efforts to find propaganda weapons in support of their policies. Yet few modern economists have given explicit and detailed attention to values; that is, to the question of what goods are to be sought through economic life. On the whole, they have been content—at least for purposes of their professional work—with the conventional assumption that the goal of economic life is to maximize national income. This goal implies that available economic means should be so employed that the pecuniary value of all the goods and services produced by the economy will be as great as technology will permit.

Economists have devoted enormous energy to detailed analysis of the conditions under which maximum national income may be realized. This line of investigation has come to be known, somewhat inaccurately, as *welfare economics.* Its purpose is to distill out of economic theory the principles to be followed if the goal of maximum national income is to be realized.[9] This has been commendable effort, and has un-

---

[9] For excellent critical summaries of welfare economics, see Hla Myint, *Theories of Welfare Economics,* Harvard University Press, Cambridge, 1948; I. M. D. Little, *A Critique of Welfare Economics,* Oxford University Press, Oxford, 1950; Kenneth Boulding, "Welfare Economics," in *A Survey of Contemporary Economics* (B. F. Haley, ed.), Richard D. Irwin, Inc., Homewood, Ill., 1952, pp. 1–38.

doubtedly produced useful results—or first approximations to useful results. But the contribution of economists in charting the course toward social welfare has been limited because of their preoccupation with pecuniary values; i.e., their tendency to ignore values that are not measurable in monetary terms.

In effect, economists have been inclined to limit themselves to problems that can be reduced to quantitative terms. They have been willing to leave to others the task of introducing broader value assumptions. This is all very well, except that it is never clear just who the others are to be.

Economists themselves probably ought not try to assume the role of moral philosophers; they should continue to aspire to the role of scientists. They should not attempt—at least in their professional capacity—to become arbiters of values. For this task they have no special competence, and it would be arrogant and out of character for them to assume it.

But economists should not hold values at arm's length. They should become careful observers of values. They should try to inquire into the values that are held by people of various classes, and by such specialists in values as moral philosophers and religious leaders. A place should be found in welfare economics for values like human dignity, aesthetic enjoyment, new experience, security, freedom, and justice.[10] They should face more directly the fact that only a fractional part of human welfare is measurable in money. Though a high national income is a legitimate goal, it does not follow that an economy that maximizes the money value of goods is necessarily the best economy.[11] The ultimate product of the economic system is not a quantity of goods, but a quality of life. As Carlyle said, "What constitutes the well-being of a man? Many things; of which the wages he gets and the bread he

[10] See Chapter 4.
[11] Goals, p. 455.

buys with them, are but one preliminary item." Ruskin referred to the manufacture of "souls of good quality." And in Hobson's words: "To perform with scientific precision the task of translating economic values into ethical or human values is manifestly impossible. For economic values in their first intent are quantities of money, while ethical or human values are qualities of life."[12]

It should be re-emphasized that the economist should not become an arbiter of values. Rather he should help to identify the values of society, define these values operationally and with some precision, point out ambiguities and conflicts among them, appraise the operation of the economic system in terms of these values, and translate them into relevant economic policies.

If economists are to admit broader values, it is obvious that their work will lose much of its quantitative precision and mathematical elegance. In the past, economists have paid a high price for this precision; namely, inability to consider many important problems, and a consistent bias toward pecuniary values.[13] Perhaps they should give up some of this pseudo-precision in order to deal realistically with the great questions. This will require new research techniques. It will not be possible to find all the values quoted daily in the market reports. It will be necessary to appropriate some of the data and the methods of social psychologists who have developed considerable facility in the measurement of attitudes and opinions; doubtless it will be necessary to invent new methods for identifying values, and determining the degree to which they are attained. The job of the welfare economist will be to find new methods of measuring welfare,

[12] See F. A. Fetter, "Price Economics vs. Welfare Economics," *American Economic Review*, September 1920, pp. 476-9.
[13] *Ibid.*, pp. 101, 106f.

rather than to persist in searching for it only in the vicinity of the cash register.

When economists are asked to depart from the world of money values, they often ask: But how can we measure if we do not have a precise unit of measurement? The answer is only that the problems exist and must be solved by someone. When economists reject the problems, these are likely to be taken up by more biased groups with special interests to serve, who on precisely that account will also leave out much that ought to be included. As Barbara Wootton has said, "It is true that all the problems of social organization would be greatly simplified if we had an infallible automatic criterion of economy; but it does not follow from this that, in the absence of such a criterion, the ordinary human faculties of judgment are completely atrophied."[14] After all, we do choose wives (or husbands), we deploy military forces in a battle, we decide on educational curricula, we dispense goods to the various members of a family, and we make a host of other choices without reliance on precise measurements. All these things we might do better if we defined our ends carefully, and used all the data at our command—quantitative or non-quantitative—for reaching our decisions.

This is precisely what is advocated for economic decisions. For example, the thing that makes curricular policy in education so difficult is that we seldom define our ends precisely, and seldom make careful investigations to determine the effects of various curricula on the attainment of our ends. As a result our policy tends to be one of groping, and frequently issues are settled through contests between vested interests. Exactly the same thing happens in economic life. It is the duty of the economist to help clarify our ends, and to help

[14] Barbara Wootton, *Lament for Economics*, George Allen and Unwin, London, 1938, p. 262.

us, by whatever data and techniques he can muster, to use our economic resources wisely in relation to these ends.

But the entire onus of constructing economic policy should not rest on the economist. Moral philosophers, religious leaders, social scientists, and other specialists in values also have obligations. They could help to formulate values in meaningful terms. They could consider the practical implications of the values they advance, and be prepared to reconcile through compromise the inconsistencies among these values. As the then Archbishop of York (William Temple) said at the Malvern Conference of 1941: "We know the ultimate moral principle of all human relationships—'thou shalt love thy neighbor as thyself.' But we do not know at all clearly how this is to find expression in the relations to one another of corporate groups such as Employers' Federations and Trade Unions, or different nations, nor how it bears on the actions of trustees such as the Directors of a Company or the Government of a country. We lack what one school of Greek moralists called the 'middle axioms'—those subordinate maxims which connect the ultimate principles with the complexities of the actual historical situations in which action has to be taken."[15] In other words, good judgment and knowledge of the consequences of acts "is a necessary part of virtue."[16] As Professor Knight has said, "I wish to insist on the moral obligation to understand before acting . . . and not simply to 'monkey' with complex and sensitive machinery, or apply snap judgments drawn from sentimental principles. . . ."[17] Or as Walter Lippmann has said, "The disesteem into which moralists have fallen is due at bottom to their failure to see

[15] Malvern, 1941, p. 10. For a discussion of the problem of the middle axioms, see John C. Bennett, *Christian Ethics and Social Policy*, Scribner's, New York, 1946.

[16] C. E. M. Joad, *Guide to the Philosophy of Morals and Politics*, Random House, New York, 1937, pp. 316, 462.

[17] F. H. Knight, *Economic Freedom and Social Responsibility*, Emory University, 1952, p. 3.

that in an age like this one, the function of the moralist is not to exhort men to be good, but to elucidate what the good is."[18]

What is being advocated, then, is a narrowing of the distance between ethics and economics, so that the contributions of each can be joined for the purpose of achieving more coherent social policy.[19]

The above conclusions have in no sense been intended as an attack on conventional economic theory. This branch of knowledge has made and will continue to make important contributions. It is more relevant and useful in describing what occurs in the market place than as a basis for the principles of welfare; nevertheless, it is useful as a first step even in the welfare problem. Professor Knight summed up the matter acutely when he said: "My own feeling about price and utility mechanics tends to be one of impatience. What such inquiry has to say about real social problems is relatively little, though extremely vital. Also, it is rather preliminary. It should be, and could be, said without gross error in limited compass and the way cleared for discussion of larger issues. Failure to do this leads naturally to the tendency to repudiate it altogether."[20]

[18] *Preface to Morals*, Macmillan, New York, 1929, p. 318.
[19] Cf. Barbara Wootton, *op. cit.*, p. 267; K. E. Boulding, *Org. Rev.*, p. 69.
[20] F. H. Knight, "Economic Science in Recent Discussion," *American Economic Review*, June 1934, p. 238.

13

Christian Ethics in Economic Life

by John C. Bennett

One of the remarkable aspects of this study is the extent
to which those who have specialized in Christian theology
and ethics find themselves in agreement with the economists
who are their colleagues in the study. There are differences
of emphasis among the economists themselves, as there are
between the economists and the theologians; but the emer-
gence of a large area of common convictions is the chief impression that this study as a whole makes upon this reader.
All the authors have denied themselves the privilege of de-
pending on a doctrinaire combination of economics and ethics
that provides easy or absolute answers to the questions raised.
The economists and those who represent the social sciences
generally are aware of the immense complexity of the problems with which they deal; and they cannot find moral security
by appealing to any natural harmony between economic
"laws" and the moral welfare of the community, nor can they
suggest any pattern of economic institutions which will guarantee a way out of our present difficulties. Those of us who
try to understand economic life from the standpoint of
Christian faith and ethics are not able to point to any Christian laws that prescribe economic behavior in all cultures and
under all circumstances, nor to advocate a "Christian socialism" or a "Christian capitalism" as the goal of all our striving.

The Nature of Christian Ethics

Christian ethics is the name given to the attempt to think through the implications of Christian faith for the moral life. In the first instance the reference is to the moral life of *Christians*. This is very clear in the New Testament, where ethical teaching is intended for those who belong to the Christian community. But it was never possible to isolate Christians completely from the larger community, and so the New Testament contains specific references to the behavior of Christians in relation to the state and the market place. When the Church came to include the majority of the population, and when its members came to have positions of influence and power, and when, finally, there developed the conception of a "Christian civilization" or a "Christian nation," Christian ethics came to be ethics for civilizations and nations as well as for Christians and churches. There were many and great confusions in this development. The Christians who longed for a purer form of Christian conduct often sought it in monasteries or in various limited communities such as contemporary Mennonite communities. The ethics of churches and of Christian citizens became so secularized, so much adjusted to the institutions of the prevailing culture, that it has often been difficult to distinguish between Christianity and culture, between Church and world.

This discussion of Christian ethics is based on the conviction that neither the complacent assumption that civilizations and nations are "Christian," or in the process of becoming "Christian," nor the escape from the world into monasteries or into limited communities is acceptable. Instead of either of these approaches I am assuming the possibility of a third approach that has the following characteristics: (1) the setting forth of the Christian ethic in its fullness without dilution or compromise; (2) the recognition that within the

Christian Church all norms for action in society remain under the judgment of this radical ethic; (3) the responsibility of Christians to find the best course of action in the world in the light of this judgment; (4) the possibility of developing structures and institutions in the world that are more in harmony than others with a Christian ethic, and in which Christians can live according to their vocation as Christians.

Most of this chapter will be devoted to the elaboration of that fourth point. We shall be concerned with the kinds of decisions that are most appropriate for Christians as participants in the economic life of the community, and with the kinds of institutions and structures they should favor in their many roles as citizens of the nation and the world. In all this discussion we shall never escape tensions between Christian faith and ethics on the one hand and cultural institutions and the public life of nations on the other. The Christian lives amidst these tensions. He should do so with rigorous honesty concerning the nature of the tensions, and with a sense of responsibility to find in every situation next steps toward a better order of society.

Christian ethics can never be separated from Christian faith. The love for the neighbor which is central in Christian ethics is within the Christian life a response to God's love for us and for all our neighbors. To put it in this way may seem to some readers to inject a religious premise that is divisive into a discussion of ethics on which widespread agreement is sought. I have respect for that objection. People come in different ways to perceive the truth and relevance of the various aspects of Christianity.

In our culture people are often sure of the validity of Christian ethics when they are doubtful about the claims of Christian faith. Bertrand Russell has recently given eloquent expression to the belief that the nature of modern life drives

us to acceptance of Christian love as the norm. In this study as a whole it is evident that aspects of Christian ethics are the unifying factor, rather than Christian faith in God's love. If there were not many pointers to Christian ethics as the ultimate norm in our experience as a whole, it is doubtful that many of us would accept it. If God is the creator of the world, we should expect some marks of His own highest purpose for man to pervade His creation.

Yet at three points the Christian faith in God's love for man is basic to Christian ethical life. (1) We see it as the deepest source of motive. We may know what is right, but the motive for doing it is a gift that Christians understand best in the context of man's relation to God. (2) We see it in the case of love for those who seem to lack all claims upon us. They may be our opponents or enemies. They may be people who are obstacles to all that we regard as good, or they may seem to us to be lost in a mediocre human mass. Yet our responsibility for them is in principle as great as it is for those we respect and most gladly serve. (3) If we are clear about the radical demands of Christian love, and about the real inadequacies of our own response, we find in Christian faith a dimension that enables us to face these realities about ourselves without covering up the facts, and without being crippled by a sense of guilt. Confession and the sense of being forgiven enable us to go on without self-deception and without despair. Morale for action amidst the most difficult situations is best assured in this context of faith. I do not deny that many people, without any conscious reference to God or religion, are able to combine humility with resolute action in the most trying circumstances. Any way of stating the relationship between faith and ethics is false if it leads a Christian who shares the faith to assume that he is superior to others who know only the ethics. And yet it is a Christian conviction, which I share, that in the context of Christian

faith all the dimensions of a life of love and humility can best be understood and most adequately safeguarded in the long run against distortions and corruptions.

THE RADICAL DEMANDS OF CHRISTIAN ETHICS

Much of what has been said will seem irrelevant unless there is a clear understanding of the radical nature of Christian ethics. There is the unlimited range of Christian love. The nature of love is one of the most discussed subjects in contemporary Christian thought; but it is beyond debate that Christian love means caring for the dignity and the welfare of all persons. We should emphasize our responsibility for those persons who are affected by anything that we may do or leave undone, but in our interdependent world there is no one who may not be so affected. None of the barriers the world erects to separate people have any significance from the standpoint of Christian love. The parable of the good Samaritan illustrates this strongly, for the victim was anonymous, and the hero of the parable belonged to a group despised among the Jews who first heard the story. This liability for all people everywhere has great importance for economic behavior, because it brings under judgment all the complacencies that make it so easy to emphasize chiefly the economic interests of a particular class or race or nation.

This unlimited responsibility involved in Christian love means also that we should be willing to undergo costly sacrifice for others. This is a hard saying at any time, but it is perhaps hardest in connection with conventional economic behavior. There are emergencies in which this ethic, this responsibility, is widely accepted in our culture. We see it in the law of the sea in times of emergency, and we recognize its claim in many situations in which life is given for life. The obligation to sacrifice comfort or property, or even life, rather

than become party to some obvious treachery, is generally accepted. In Christian ethics we find at the center this obligation to give, to sacrifice, to suffer for others; and it lends a quality to every other obligation.

The unlimited claims on us that are implicit in Christian love for the neighbor make it difficult to find a place for the claims of the self. Yet it would be a mistake to suppose that Christian ethics knows no concern for the self. Even though our own concern for our welfare usually claims too much of our attention, and we therefore have to be warned against self-love, the welfare of one's own self or one's family is as important to God as the welfare of the neighbor. To neglect the welfare of the self may throw a burden on others and on society. There is much in the way of prudent planning in the interests of our families and ourselves which is our own responsibility. This needs emphasis; it is an essential point of contact between Christian ethics and our economic activities in a competitive economy. Yet it remains true that in an economy that puts major stress on personal acquisitiveness any really substantial limitation of the claims of self-interest is an alien factor. I believe that there is a deep conflict in spirit between Christianity and modern economic life at this point.

Another indication of the unlimited character of the Christian ethical demand is in the sphere of motive and attitude. The first commandment is that we love God with all our hearts and minds; this wholeness of commitment is emphasized throughout the New Testament. We are asked to be single-minded. Two of the sayings of Jesus which have most relevance for economic life are: "Ye cannot serve God and mammon," and "Beware of covetousness."

It is not easy to move from this radical ethic of sacrificial love, of wholeness of commitment to God, of concern for *all* persons, to the kind of principles and attitudes that seem relevant to economic life in our American economy—or, for that

matter, in any viable modern economy. I believe we must admit at the outset that the ethical teachings of the New Testament are in the first instance most clearly applicable to the direct encounter of one person with another. Dr. Paul Ramsey has emphasized this aspect of Christian ethics most helpfully. He says: "We need to see clearly how we should be obliged to behave toward one neighbor (or how our own group should act toward one neighboring group) if there were no other claims upon us at all."[1] Only so can we see the depths and the height of the Christian life. But in the economic activities with which this study is concerned it is of the essence of the matter that there are many competing claims on us. So in what follows I shall attempt to show how we can move from the basic Christian ethic that is most clearly applicable to personal life, to our behavior as members of economic groups and to our responsibilities amid the economic institutions of the modern world. We have no chance of avoiding this step; for better or worse, in that world we live and in that world we must make our decisions. A decision amid the complexities of contemporary economic life is just as much a personal decision as one that involves only the relations between two persons. Love for most of our neighbors must be expressed within these economic institutions or not at all.

This radical ethic of love is subject to a vocational limitation on what is demanded of us at any given time. We are finite, and we have particular responsibilities that help to define what we should do. There is a special responsibility for those with whom we come in immediate contact, for our own families, our own communities, our own institutions. This does not mean a basic preference for the interests of those nearest to us as against those of people who are at a distance; it means merely that there is a division of labor, and our

[1] *Basic Christian Ethics*, New York, Charles Scribner's Sons, 1950, p. 43.

particular job lies here. I do not want to emphasize the geographical aspect too much, because our particular job might take us to some distant country; but there it would still be limited. We have a responsibility to concentrate on those tasks for which we are fitted by abilities and training, instead of trying to improve everyone else. A loose interpretation of Christian responsibility provides an excuse for going off in all directions, and for helping everyone except those who have the most right to expect our help. This vocational limitation on our responsibility is no excuse for narrow sympathies, for fencing ourselves in and becoming callous toward the suffering of people outside our own orbit. It is always provisional, and we can expect our comfortable vocational patterns to be broken up when new needs or emergencies arise.

CHRISTIAN LOVE AND ESSENTIAL SOCIAL VALUES

The Christian ethic has to be related to the problems of the economic order by way of several generally recognized values. I refer especially to four such values: justice, freedom, order, and what I shall call the material conditions of welfare. These values are not uniquely Christian. By *justice* I mean especially what is often called "distributive justice": what are the principles by which we determine who should get what? Much of our economic ethics depends on our answer to that question. *Freedom* in this context has to do with the freedom of persons in society. Here we have the question as to what economic institutions are most favorable to political and cultural freedom—to freedom from tyranny of any sort. By *order* I refer to the preservation of peace in society, the maintenance of stable government, the prevention of destructive conflicts and stalemates between various groups in the economy. It is hardly necessary to argue for the importance of these values.

What about the material conditions of *welfare*? First let me

say that I am not using "welfare" in the technical way in which it has been used by the representatives of "welfare economics," and which Professor Bowen has explained and criticized in the preceding chapter of this volume. I mean by it what is meant in common speech, though our conception of the content of welfare depends on what we believe to be good for man, and that is in turn much influenced by our Christian ethics. At this point it is sufficient to emphasize the material conditions necessary for physical health, for education, for opportunity to work, for many useful forms of participation in the life of the community, and for a reasonable security against the common hazards of life. I realize that each of these words is slippery, but I doubt that they will be seriously misunderstood. Welfare does depend on food and clothing and shelter, and on the possibility of developing one's own special gifts, and on various kinds of participation in the life of the community. These elements of welfare include opportunities for recreation, for some travel, and for various forms of cultural enjoyment; but it is very difficult to say how much of any of these is essential. It is even harder to say what our attitude should be toward all the extra things an American family now usually regards as essential to welfare!

As long as we remain within the range of the kind of welfare that can be universally shared under conditions of modern technology, we can say that there is a Christian obligation to produce and to produce efficiently for the sake of this welfare. It is clearly recognized in Christian ethics that the body has needs as well as the soul, that bread is important for life. There is a Christian emphasis on matter that furnishes a sure link with economic ethics. But whenever we move beyond material *necessities* to the innumerable *desires* to which our economy appeals—and which it often creates—the Christian becomes less sure of his ground.

As long as there is not enough produced to meet the needs

of the world's population, there must be great emphasis on efficiency in production. In volume five, in the discussion of the distribution of wealth in America, it is made clear that in spite of remarkable gains in this respect there are large segments of the population that have less than the minimum income necessary for a decent standard of living. When we consider the population of the world, the problem of poverty seems almost limitless.[2] I shall come back later to some of these issues; here it is enough to emphasize the point that efficiency in production is a primary moral demand on economic institutions. I believe that those who have been concerned chiefly with economic justice have often neglected this demand; no degree of justice in distribution can compensate for failure to produce enough material goods to go around. The economists in this study emphasize productivity and efficiency more than do the ethical critics of the economy, and it may well be their vocation to do so. I shall return to this issue again when I discuss the ethics of distribution.

Christian Ethics and Technical Issues

Those who represent Christian ethics must recognize the limits of any distinctively Christian guidance for economic institutions. There is no "Christian economics"; though there are Christian motives and Christian goals and Christian insights into human nature, which should guide Christian thinking about economic life.

Most judgments about economic questions involve technical issues that must be respected by those concerned about ethics. It is self-defeating to override in our ethical demands the kinds of wisdom about economic life possessed only by those who have the requisite technical training or intimate experience of the actual economic processes. We must know

[2] See Amer. Income, pp. 80–87.

the facts about the material resources on which our economy draws. We must know the regularities that may be thought of in terms of "cause and effect" and are characteristic of economic life. Most questions of means are laden with these technical issues. It is ethically imperative to prevent mass unemployment; but there is no Christian answer to the question as to what means will be effective in doing it. We may regard inflation as an unjust way of redistributing wealth; but there is no purely ethical and certainly no purely Christian wisdom as to what policies will encourage or hinder inflation.

There are issues also that are not technical in the narrowest sense but call for the wisdom that comes from inside knowledge of the way the economy works. Such an issue arises whenever we seek to preserve a delicate balance between government intervention in economic life and the free initiative of individuals and of various groups in the economy. Another example is the issue that is raised when we discuss methods of dealing with strikes in essential industries without destroying the right to strike on the one hand and without endangering the health and safety of the public on the other. Issues of this kind can be understood only by those who are themselves close to the activities involved. There is no Christian moral law that can determine for us what policy will best preserve the very delicate balance between the values to which we are committed.

In view of this situation I have described it is necessary to emphasize the corporate character of the judgments made in regard to the most concrete economic problems. Those who participate in these decisions should bring to them ethical sensitivity in regard to goals and to the effects of means upon persons; but they must learn from those who have expert knowledge, and from those who have had the most relevant practical experience. It is also important that the social experience of those occupational or regional groups that are affected

in different ways by any policy decision be represented. Christian ethics should be brought to such decisions by Christian laymen who have themselves sought guidance from their faith and from other members of the Christian community. The present study of the ethics of economic life is a good example of interaction among those who have their special contributions to make to such corporate wisdom about economic life.

The economic order is not autonomous, and the science of economics is not autonomous in relation to Christian ethics; but the way in which we relate Christian ethics to either must take account of these elements within them that can be understood only from within.

CHRISTIAN ETHICS AND ECONOMIC SYSTEMS

It is a natural inference from what has just been said about the elements of partial autonomy in the economic order, that there is no Christian economic system. Indeed, one of the most significant conclusions from this whole study is that no one of the economic systems associated with familiar labels and stereotypes is wholly adequate. All the writers take for granted—as far as America is concerned—a combination of economic institutions in which private ownership of the means of production is the dominant factor, and in which, over large areas of the economy, the free market continues to function. And yet they all admit great modifications of *laissez-faire* capitalism. They are willing to accept the present fluid type of capitalism, "present-day capitalism," and to set no permanent limits to experimentation in the direction of the social control of economic activities. Some of them are more ready to welcome these changes than others; but none of these changes would satisfy the doctrinaire individualist who now calls for a pure and consistent individualism.

Also none of these writers represents socialism; though some

of them have been influenced in the past by socialism—especially Christian rather than Marxist socialism. The main
reason why even those who have been most influenced reject
it is that they see the difficulty under socialism of avoiding too
close an identification of economic and political power. Capitalism does have the advantage that it preserves many centers
of power in society—that it encourages many different kinds
of initiative. I do not mean that a democratic socialism in a
country with a strong democratic tradition—like Britain—
may not be consistent with the essential types of freedom; but
I am sure that this should not be the American approach to
the problem. Americans, however, as they view the development of economies in other nations, should recognize that
where there is need for quick centralized action to solve
dangerous social problems that, as long as they remain unsolved, invite the deceptive communist remedy, a democratic
form of socialism may be the most viable form of economic
organization. That only goes to show that there is no one
Christian economic system.

In this country within the past twenty-five years there has
been a remarkable shift in thought among those Christians
who have been most interested in the problems of economic
justice. In the 1930s it appeared to many of them, including
this writer, that capitalism had reached a dead end, and that
it had to be replaced by a dominantly socialistic type of
economy. I no longer believe that; because I believe that an
experimental modification of capitalism to meet particular
needs is better than change of the system at its center. The
danger of losing the many centers of power to which I have
referred is my main consideration in this shift of conviction.
Without such a drastic change great progress can be made
toward giving the various groups in our nation a fairer share of
the national wealth; and we have made a great advance in our
general acceptance of the function of the national community

working through its government to maintain economic stability.

Christians in different countries will make different experiments. A thoroughgoing collectivism and a thoroughgoing individualism are two types of economic system the Christian can reject in advance. When we think of these experiments it is important to distinguish between even an extreme degree of socialization of economic institutions by democratic methods on the one hand, and Soviet communism as a political movement with its pretentious ideology and its conspiratorial tactics on the other. The confusion at this point in this country constantly darkens counsel and beclouds issues.

Before I leave this discussion of capitalism and socialism and economic systems, I wish to point to two factors that may undermine the kind of mixed economy we are developing in this country. The first is the tendency of great private centers of economic power to pervert political power to their own ends. We have many checks on this now in America, but there remains a danger here that must always be watched. Even the best formal checks can be neutralized by enforcement agencies that are easily influenced by those whom they are expected to regulate. This is the point at which the most destructive form of corruption is likely to enter our public life. Such indirect union of political and economic power may not necessarily be worse than a formal union of the two under a consistent socialism; but it is a threat that those who favor capitalism may have difficulty in counteracting on their own terms.

The second dangerous factor is the fact that historically there is a strong argument against the likelihood of our being able to preserve economic stability without more far-reaching social control than has yet been envisaged in this country. So far we have been spared the most severe test since the 1930s by a war economy or a cold-war economy. The economists who

have written for these volumes agree that it is technically possible for our society to solve the problems that will arise as we move to a peace economy. But a question remains that is political rather than technical: Will our people, and the forces that control our government, have the imagination, the intelligence, and the courage to do what will be necessary to effect that transition without falling into a catastrophic depression? There are strong grounds for answering "yes" to that question; but on that answer will depend the possibility of developing an alternative to a much greater measure of socialism in the next period.

Whether such a transition is possible is a technical question; and I bow to the economists who insist that the answer to that question is "yes." Whether the American people will find a way to do it is largely a political question, to which the wisest of us can only guess the answer. It is certainly true that neither the Republican nor the Democratic party can afford to permit a serious depression. Those who look at this problem from the standpoint of Christian ethics can emphasize what is at stake, and stimulate all Christian citizens to find new ways ahead.

All that I have said about economic systems is in line with a broad ecumenical tradition on this subject. Several times in these volumes there have been references to the Amsterdam report, which dealt with capitalism and communism. Its rejection of the extreme systems of *laissez-faire* capitalism and communism is well known. It contained criticisms of actual capitalistic tendencies that are worth repeating, because they suggest the kind of correctives for capitalism that we may support—whatever label we may give to the result. These criticisms are as follows:

1. Capitalism tends to subordinate what should be the primary task of any economy—the meeting of human needs—to the eco-

nomic advantages of those who have most power over its institutions.

2. Capitalism tends to produce serious inequalities.

3. Capitalism has developed a practical form of materialism in Western nations in spite of their Christian background, for it has placed the greatest emphasis upon success in making money.

4. Capitalism has kept the people of capitalistic countries subject to a kind of fate which has taken the form of such social catastrophes as mass unemployment.

Those criticisms constitute a good check list of the things to watch in our own country, as our own dominantly capitalistic economy develops during the years ahead.

I do not want to conclude this section about economic systems without emphasizing the creative nature of our American experiment with a modified capitalism—what is sometimes called in this study "present-day capitalism." We have shown that it is possible for the democratic impulses in our society to modify drastically the emphasis on profit and privilege for the few which rightly brought earlier capitalism under the strongest moral condemnation.

The logic of mass production, which requires mass consumption and therefore a wide distribution of purchasing power, was one factor underlying the economic changes of this century. The rise of the labor movement has altered the distribution of power in the economy; and it has been an essential element in the political coalition that brought about many of the legislative changes of recent decades. The experience of the depression of the 1930s did much to educate the American people, and seems to have produced one resolve that was new: the resolve to use the instruments of government to prevent the recurrence of such a depression. There has been a remarkable development of regulatory agencies, like the "Securities and Exchange Commission," and of provisions to establish a basic security for the people. These

developments have been piecemeal, and designed to deal with particular problems as they have arisen; but out of them has come a pattern of economic life that may well represent a better way for us than any of the systems so loudly defended in the ideological debates of our period. Already this pattern has had substantial results in overcoming poverty and in reducing economic inequalities.

CHRISTIAN ETHICS AND THE DISTRIBUTION OF WEALTH AND INCOME

As I have indicated, the economists in this study have brought to it an emphasis on the importance of production that was needed in Christian teaching. Too often Christian critics of economic life have concentrated on the problem of distributing the "pie" as it is, and have given insufficient attention to the enlarging of the pie. Professor Boulding can say that he is opposed to poverty, and he hopes to abolish poverty through the increase of production. He does not seem much concerned about inequality. Here I believe he not only corrects, but overcorrects, those who put their chief stress on distribution. What are we to say about the claims of equality?

We cannot deny the inequalities among men—inequalities of character, of ability, of stamina, of contribution. The only form of equality that is based on Christian faith is the conviction that all men are equally the objects of God's love and care. This is an ultimate equality before God that is at the forefront of Christian teaching on this subject. Perhaps the word "equality" hardly does justice to what we find in the New Testament. In the divine economy there is a reversal of the human ways of arranging people. We are told that the first shall be last; that the lost sheep will receive more attention than the ninety and nine that never went astray; that those who are accounted righteous will have a disadvantage

compared with harlots and "publicans." This is a drastic protest against the conventional inequalities, in the light of the ultimate status of men before God.

The Christian should be led to raise the following issues whenever he confronts serious forms of economic inequality:

1. If he is himself a beneficiary of inequality he should ask: Why should I have the chance to have a much higher standard of living than my neighbor? Why should I have better food for myself and my family, and why should I have forms of opportunity and security denied to him? Such a question, when put in concrete terms, should make us self-critical.

2. We should be warned about the ease with which in these matters we deceive ourselves. It is a universal expression of human sin to think up reasons why we and our group should have special privileges. It has never been difficult for privileged groups to convince themselves that the existence of their privileges was in the interest of society—perhaps even in the real interest of those who are on the lower social levels. Any Christian who becomes aware of this common tendency is likely to become very critical of existing inequalities. Today, when those who are less favored have become more articulate, he has their aid in debunking his own defenses.

There is also the recognition that, as a matter of common experience, economic inequalities tend to destroy fellowship; they tend to poison human relations; they encourage pride and resentment, snobbishness and envy. Those who are moved to any degree by Christian love should be aware of the extent to which economic inequalities can become obstacles to love.

We find nevertheless in the realities of human nature and human experience some justification for a degree of inequalities in distribution. The claims of inequality consistent with Christian ethics are discussed in a later paragraph.

So far, however, my conclusion from these aspects of Christian faith that favor equality is that the burden of proof is on

many forms of economic inequality to which we have become accustomed. To say this is to reverse the habit of thinking that has been characteristic of society during the whole of history. It has almost always been taken for granted that the few should live comfortably amid their great possessions, while the many remained doomed to poverty, drudgery, and hunger. The few were protected against the preventable evils of their time and culture, while the many had to take their chances without such security. There has been an enormous change in these respects within the past few generations. This has been brought about by the pressure of the ideas and the political instruments of democracy on economic institutions. Christian teachings about the significance of all men in the sight of God, and about the social responsibilities implicit in Christian love, have had a great part in preparing the way for this change; even though the decisive steps have often been taken by secular—sometimes anticlerical—political movements driven by ideals of justice mixed with the economic interests of the poor. This change has taken place in our own country; but, as Professor Reid's study shows, there is still a shocking contrast between the scale of living of important segments of our population and that of others who share more of our much-advertised prosperity.[3]

There is one type of equality we can aim for in this country with hope of considerable success. I refer to equality of opportunity. Most of the arguments in favor of permitting or encouraging inequalities of wealth and income cannot be used against the acceptance by society of equal opportunity for all children to develop their capacities. Children have not yet earned any privileges, nor have they shown what their contribution will be. A just society will try to counteract the disabilities children suffer because of the poverty of their parents; our system of public education is an embodiment of

[3] Amer. Income, pp. 125–128.

this purpose. We should realize, of course, that the best society can do will not provide parents or teachers who are equally good for all children. It is possible, nevertheless, to make a large-scale effort to neutralize the most obvious external disadvantages. Some nations, both near-socialist Britain and conservative Canada, have established allowances from the state to all families for their children. This is an extension of the principle embodied in public education. Whether this is the best method for neutralizing inequalities is much debated; the American labor movement, in fact, opposes it.

It is in this context, I believe, we can see most clearly the moral justification of the idea of a floor, or national minimum, below which no families should be allowed to sink. When we see the family as the social unit, we can understand that no considerations of discipline for shiftlessness that society might want to impose upon the employable father of a family should be allowed to penalize the whole family. The relation between such a minimum and the standard of living made possible by earned income must be considered in the light of the problems of incentive—to be discussed later.

Though the principle of equality should be an important criterion for the criticism of economic institutions, it should not lead us to advocate complete equality of income. The reasons for this are not specifically Christian, but they are consistent with Christian ethics if it can be shown that any such guaranteed equality of income would reduce the total product and threaten various forms of freedom. I find it impossible to disagree with the conclusions of the economists in this study, that incentives for production, for pioneering ventures, for efficiency, do depend on the existence of inequalities of income. How great these inequalities must be is not clear to me. Instead of putting all the emphasis on incentive, however, on the ground that as long as there is a sufficient production no one need suffer poverty, I believe that a careful balancing of

the values involved is important. Besides the consideration of incentives, we must also take into account that if the state assumed the task of rigidly limiting incomes in the interest of general equality it would tend to destroy freedom; and the suspicion that others were hiding wealth in various ways would corrupt personal relations.

There is no one principle that should govern our thought about the distribution of wealth and income. Because it is necessary to consider the claims of equality—especially the claims of equality of opportunity, together with the need for incentive and the importance of avoiding excessive regimentation—we must move in this area with our eyes on incommensurable values. Even in connection with the single problem of the suitable compensation for work done, we are in an area of the incommensurable.

There is the contrast between the compensation of business executives or entertainment stars on the one hand, and the compensation of many professions on the other. We have seen in dramatic form the difference in compensation between the President of General Motors and the Secretary of Defense of the United States. Does this difference measure a difference in incentive? There is also the contrast between the reward for capital without work and the reward for work. There is the problem of whether those who have work that is more than usually dull and unpleasant should not receive more compensation than those who can enjoy their work. In the main we are guided by the market value of the work, rather than by any estimate of what it costs the worker in distasteful effort or drudgery. It is in the line of least resistance to stress market value; but if we do so we must recognize that this is a matter of convenience rather than justice, and that society does have a responsibility to correct the result with these other considerations of justice in view. There is one over-all consideration that should have great bearing on social policy: the evil social

effects of having a nation divided by chasms between the rich and the poor. These chasms destroy fellowship, and encourage —as I have said—pride and bitterness. Society has a moral responsibility to level up and level down wealth and income to such an extent that people are not deeply divided from each other by this factor of economic inequality. This is in the interest of moral health and social stability.

This leads me to conclude this discussion of the distribution of wealth and income by calling attention to a decision of overwhelming importance that will face this country as we move from a war economy to a peace economy. Our great productivity and the remarkable national prosperity of this period have gone along with high taxation of incomes in the higher brackets. The generally accepted basis for this taxation policy has been the government's need of revenue for defense. Also it is of course true that this long-continued prosperity itself has been the result of large-scale defense spending; and this spending is made possible by taxation. If other ways were found to support this prosperity, would there be a tendency to have very high incomes without high taxation? If so, I can see the moral problem of our prosperity entering a new dimension, even if there continues to be a reduction of poverty. Is there not reason to fear that the accumulations of wealth would become so massive as to be antisocial in their effects? So far we have accepted the principle of a highly graduated income tax as a just method of apportioning the burden of taxation that is required for the national revenue. What will happen when revenue is no longer needed to the same extent? After we have made all necessary concessions to those who emphasize the need to reduce taxes in order to stimulate production, there may well be a moral problem beyond all present calculations, in the presence of greater accumulations of private wealth and even more showy spending than are now possible.

CHRISTIAN ETHICS AND MOTIVES
FOR ECONOMIC ACTIVITY

All the volumes in this study assume the complexity of human motives in economic life. The discussion of motives has often been controlled by a false psychology. Defenders of economic individualism and competition have often assumed that the only effective motive to be relied on is self-interest. The place of profit as the automatic regulator of a free and dynamic economy has created in the minds of many interpreters a one-sided psychology of profit. Professor Bowen, and Dr. Ernest Johnson in his criticism of Professor Bowen's book, both help to clear up this subject of the "profit system" and the "profit motive." Profit, as Professor Bowen defines it, is limited to the "total share of the national income paid to the equity owners of business after allowance for return at the market rate to all land and capital." It is this profit that in large measure determines the direction of economic activity, for it is the chief motive for choosing one form of activity for investment rather than another.[4]

There is a much broader economic incentive, which includes all efforts to gain an economic advantage for one's self or one's family. Anyone who works primarily for his wages or salary, or for an increase of wages or salary, is governed by the profit motive—in the looser use of the phrase. The desire for a reasonable profit, in an economy often described as a "profit-and-loss" economy by its defenders who are irked by the attacks on the profit motive, is entirely defensible. It is also defensible to work for wages and salaries in order to support one's self and one's family. The ethical problems become acute when we consider the relationship of any form of self-centered motive to other motives, and when the scale of economic advantage becomes disproportionate. When any group pushes

[4] *Soc. Res.*, pp. 147–8.

for its own economic advantage at the obvious expense of the community as a whole, the profit motive in the form that is rightly condemned is at work. When managers of corporations insist on salaries, bonuses, pensions, and expense accounts that add up to fabulous sums, they raise serious moral questions. It may be that their personal motives have not been primarily acquisitive, and that they are merely fitting into an accepted pattern; but at least they show a lack of moral sensitivity. That the salaries and expense accounts of some executives of labor unions are also in this class shows how far this insensitivity has permeated American society.

The profit system is defensible if it is the only available alternative to a system that completely unites economic and political power. The profit motive, interpreted broadly as a concern for financial rewards, is essential if an economy is to be efficient and productive. But, from the point of view of Christian ethics, both the system and the motive must be kept under scrutiny and criticism.

Those Christian idealists who have wholly condemned the incentive of economic advantage have been wrong; for they have failed to recognize that without this incentive less would be produced and in general the work of the world would be done less efficiently. One might raise the question whether we should not distinguish Christians from non-Christians in this connection. Should we say that in a mixed and largely secular society the motive of economic advantage needs to be used, but that in the case of those who are committed Christians we can disregard that motive and appeal only to their Christian vocation, to their desire to serve God by meeting human needs? I doubt that this, if made absolute, is a fair or viable distinction. For one thing, the degrees of Christian commitment vary indefinitely, and shade into a purely nominal relation to the Church. But even beyond that difficulty I believe that most of us at times need the prodding that comes from

having to work to support ourselves and our families—that is, we have to be made aware of that economic responsibility. This may not be our chief motive for work, but it does provide an external discipline that prevents slackness, and that makes us more likely to do justice to the less congenial aspects of our work. It may make us less likely to take time off when we have a cold! Moreover, there is a positive place among Christian motives for the "family motive" in economic life. To seek to improve the economic conditions of one's family, within limits, is a worthy motive, and a mark of responsible living.

After one has said these things in favor of the more self-regarding economic incentives, even in the Christian life, one must go on and emphasize how much they should be limited. Economic self-interest as a motive, except for the limited extent to which it is an expression of responsibility for supporting one's self and one's family, must be accepted as a result of a sinful tendency to see one's self as the center of one's world. It should always be kept subordinate to other motives, and especially to one's sense of Christian vocation.

There are motives which are intermediate between economic self-interest and what we may call a sense of Christian vocation. The one that is nearest to economic self-interest, but which has the advantage of being more easily harmonized with usefulness to the community, is the desire to be accepted by one's associates and by the community. This can be wholesome, or it can be an expression of pride and vanity that may actually corrupt the soul more than greed. Perhaps the worst form of this motive is where greed and vanity meet, and men work for high financial gains in order to be able to splurge and prove their success. In a society that is as controlled as ours by the emphasis on success, with wealth as the chief popular symbol of success, this desire for wealth may be a thoughtless and conventional following of a pattern rather than a mark of either unusual greed or vanity. It is important for those in

professions where success is marked in other ways to avoid self-righteous condemnation of those in occupations where wealth is the chief mark of success.

A motive that is closer to a distinctively Christian sense of vocation is the desire to do a good job. This is not the desire to be known as a success—though the two things are usually found together—but the love of creating. This exists at all levels, from the craftsmanship of the skilled artisan to the manager of a business empire. Professor Bowen has done a great service in his emphasis on the complexity of motive among managers. He shows that with them the profit motive is often subordinate to what may be called a professional motive; service to the company often becomes a compelling motive in itself. It involves loyalty to a cooperative enterprise with a distinctive tradition, workmanship in specific activities, and a sense of the social value of the company's products.

A Christian who sees all these motives at work in himself will want to keep them under examination, and seek to be so moved by divine grace that all of them become controlled by the vocation to seek God's will in serving man. When in hours of worship we see things together with minds and consciences illumined by exposure to God's revelation in Christ, we can be so changed that the more self-regarding motives are kept in a subordinate place. There is always a danger that the great words of the Christian faith may become slogans, used to deceive one's self and to provide an aura of sanctity to activities that are morally indefensible. Reinhold Niebuhr often calls attention to one major source of self-deception in the American tradition, the tendency to regard wealth as a sign of God's favor.[5] Probably few Americans would make such a claim explicitly today; yet there is still in our culture a hangover of that way of thinking. This is seen in a type of popular

[5] *The Irony of American History*, New York, Charles Scribner's Sons, 1952, Chapter 3.

preaching that makes much of those cases in which piety leads to business success. But the Christian confession of sin, which includes a rigorous examination of one's own most characteristic temptations in economic life and Christian commitment in the light of a real understanding of Christian love, should lead us away from any such misuse of the faith.

I have written at some length about the self-regarding economic motives, the place that should be allowed for them, and the limits that should be placed upon them. Now I should like to call attention to the great danger of the profit system. I have already said that I believe that the profit system is morally defensible, and that it may well be the best alternative to a system that runs the risk of uniting and abusing political and economic power. But we should be alert to the moral danger that is an inescapable aspect of it: that it tempts men to be acquisitive. It overstimulates the self-regarding motives, which are already too strong in most of us. It tempts men to take moral short cuts for the sake of profit. The more unlimited the possibility of accumulating wealth, the greater is this moral danger. Even though we may agree that the American profit system has proved to be a good instrument, it has certainly created a moral climate in which there is an overemphasis on money-making.

The judgment of the Oxford Conference (1937), which is considered by many Protestants to have produced the most significant body of Christian social teaching in the modern period, still stands: "When the necessary work of society is so organized as to make the acquisition of wealth the chief criterion of success it encourages a feverish scramble for money, and a false respect for the victors in the struggle, which is as fatal in its moral consequences as any other form of idolatry. In so far as the pursuit of monetary gain becomes a dominant factor in the lives of men, the quality of society undergoes a subtle disintegration." Therefore we should not

express a preference for the profit system without constantly reminding ourselves of the truth in this warning. I believe that it is an essential function of the churches in such a society as ours to keep the warning steadily before us all.

So far I have spoken of motives as they are related to one's specifically economic activity. We should have in mind also the motives that impel us as we form judgments as citizens about public policies. Here it is important to be realistic about the extent to which men tend to be influenced by narrow group interest. This is true of the larger segments of the population, such as labor, the business community, farmers, and the like; but it is also true of narrower groups within these larger classes. I refer to such groups as skilled workers versus unskilled workers, export industries versus those that rely on the domestic market, representatives of the interests of various regions, and farmers with differing crops. One of the most persistent conflicts is between people with fixed incomes and people whose incomes rise with inflation. Some of these conflicts have more effect on social and political judgment than others. One of the chief miscalculations of the Marxists was their assumption that there were only two classes whose conflict was important in social development. Actually we have the pattern of many economic groups with conflicting interests. Since these groups share many of the same cultural interests and social loyalties, and since the conflicts between them vary from time to time in intensity, we do not have ahead of us the prospect of a nation divided into two irreconcilable classes.

Marxist teaching, however, does help us to see how various economic groups do develop strong rationalizations of their interests. It is not difficult to predict how those who belong to a particular type of occupation, to a particular income bracket, or to a particular residential area will think about labor unions, taxation, or public housing; and to note how this interest

affects the choice between the major political parties. One of the gains of the past few years is that some issues, such as the desirability of the federal social security system, are less controversial than they were. There is perhaps greater feeling about such emotionally charged symbols as "Roosevelt," "Truman," "Taft-Hartley," "New Deal," "Socialism," than about the actual issues themselves. The relation of all of this to Christian ethics is that we need to be prepared to be self-critical when we find that the policies we advocate are in harmony with our own economic interest. The policies may not be wrong on this account; but to suspect our own motives is a useful corrective. It involves a simple application to ourselves of Christian teaching about the sinful weakness of all men—sinful weakness which it is not difficult to identify in others. Jesus' saying about the "mote" and the "beam" has great relevance to the attitudes of economic groups.

High Standards of Consumption and the Danger of Materialism

Several writers in this study have called attention to the moral dangers in our dynamic and increasingly productive economy. Miss Hoyt, Dr. Bowen, and Dean Muelder have all stressed the danger that we may suffer morally from the glut of material things. I believe that this is one of the most baffling problems the Christian faces in connection with our type of economy.

To stress this problem as one that can be distinguished from the problem of securing greater justice in distribution on a world scale may seem to be taking an unnecessary leap into the future. It is true that the two problems cannot be separated; but they can be distinguished. Even if we were to do all that can be done usefully to help raise the standards of living in other countries, we should still have in America the

problem of absorption in materialism, with perhaps too many things for our own good. Ours is an economy that must increase in productivity in order to remain stable. We must find ways of consuming the products of this expanding economy if we are to prevent mass unemployment and social catastrophe. We can give away part of our surplus; but there is a limit to such giving, unless we want other people to become too dependent on us and in the end resentful. The greatest tact and ingenuity are required of those who seek to be helpful to other peoples.

We can share the wealth at home more than we do; but there are limits to that, if we are to avoid hand-outs that self-respecting people do not desire. I have said that a system of graduated income taxes is a necessary corrective for the tendencies toward inequality in a free economy, and not merely an equitable method of raising revenue for the government. When defense spending tapers off we shall need to use our resources to improve the living conditions of all the people. But if, after that, our economy continues to increase in productivity, far too many of us will have more things than are good for us. Those segments of our population that chiefly influence our style of living and whose standards control our culture are likely to be most harmfully affected by these trends.

We need not identify Christian ethics with an ascetic attitude toward material things, or with a cheerless frugality in their use. In fact, the Christian teaching about creation should prepare us to take an affirmative attitude toward the material world, and toward the elaboration of all that is given in creation by human invention and technology. Our society for better or worse is already so far advanced in its technological equipment that many things that in a simpler society would be needless gadgets are for us necessities or near-necessities.

There is no reversing of this trend. The many labor-saving devices for the home come to be almost necessary if women

are to be able to fulfill all their responsibilties and keep their health at the same time. Abroad it is often assumed that an electric refrigerator is a symbol of the American love of creature comforts; but when once the methods of distributing food in a city have become tied to such refrigeration, it becomes important for health and efficiency to have access to a refrigerator. In our society the possession of an automobile may not be necessary, but it is far from being a foolish luxury for most families who possess one. I enlarge on this point because my criticism of the materialism that is encouraged by our rising standard of living should not be confused with a rejection of the things that greatly add to the comfort and convenience of life. All that I am calling for is a sense of proportion in the possession and use of these things.

I have been impressed by the balance in these matters in Miss Hoyt's discussion (Volume 4) of our habits of consumption. She sees clearly the real gains that have been made possible by technology (Chapter 2). She emphasizes three such gains: (1) the multiplication of the necessities of life; (2) the saving of human energy so that "human powers can be released from servile labor for more creative purposes"; (3) the service to many values through increase in the ease of human contact and communication. She says of that last gain that it "enables men to travel, to discover new sympathies and new truths, makes it possible for everyone to have easy access to stores of knowledge, to art, and to natural beauty." But she sees also that technology tends to monopolize interest; and that in doing so it appeals to "some of the least mature characteristics of the human being, especially the desire for the new and for something with which to show off." She emphasizes also the pressure on our culture of commercial advertising.

The combination of the momentum of technological change with the overemphasis on salesmanship is the root of much

that is cheap and false in our culture. Of all of the aspects of our economic life there is none that needs to be kept under more rigorous criticism than advertising. If there is to be mass production in a competitive economy it is necessary to have mass advertising of the product; but Christians who have responsibility for advertising ought to think some quite new thoughts about their vocation. What are we to make, for example, of the constant change of styles and models that creates a quite artificial dissatisfaction in people with what they already possess, and plays on the desire "to keep up" with others in the same social group?

Another moral problem connected with advertising is the tendency to deceive; not necessarily by making explicitly false claims, but by insinuation and exaggeration. The fact that advertising often involves concentration on one product, without the possibility of a fair comparison of it with its alternatives, prepares the way for deception. Much of this may be harmless, because the buyer soon learns by experience to discount the seller's comparative claims for his wares. But there is a falseness in this that cannot but be corrupting to a culture.

The Oxford Conference report to which I have referred speaks of the moral problem involved in salesmanship in the following words: "One other form of work which seems clearly to be in conflict with the Christian's vocation is salesmanship of a kind which involves deception—the deception which may be no more than insinuation and exaggeration, but which is a serious threat to the integrity of the worker."

There is another dimension of this problem which can only be mentioned here. It arises from the fact that the media for mass salesmanship are the same as those that have incalculable power over the culture, especially radio, television, and the press. The press is a less serious problem, because the reader has the privilege of skipping as much as he wants; but

radio and television bring into the home, in a way that is far more obtrusive, that advertising which constantly appeals to motives of envy, and which, for its effect, depends on the reiteration of half-truths.[6]

We cannot conclude this section on the ethics of consumption with any Christian laws that settle the difficult problems that have been mentioned. We cannot deny that gradually we shall come to accept most of the new things made available by our dynamic economy. But our emphasis should be on necessities for all, rather than on luxuries for the few. Christians who take the needs of others seriously will resist the temptation to spend nearly all that they have on themselves. They will guard against all expenditures for the sake of display, to make others feel inferior. There should be no place in the Christian life for "conspicuous consumption"— though few of us are without guilt in this respect. We shall all need a sense of proportion if we are to avoid being engulfed by new and somewhat glamorous possessions. The question may well be asked whether this kind of counsel would not, if common Christian practice were to conform to it, seriously cripple the economic system. I do not know the answer; but I believe that we may well believe that one of the criteria by which an economic system is to be judged is its compatibility with restrained and discriminating consumption.

Indeed, one of the most profound criticisms of capitalism—

[6] A prepublication reader has made the following comment, which I recognize is a useful corrective to what I have said: "This discussion of the ethics of advertising and salesmanship should not ignore a development that may be purely American. This is the increasing use of advertising by industrial, commercial, and financial corporations to serve such causes as Community Chest and Red Cross campaigns and to promote public health and safety. It may be balanced against other general advertising intended cleverly to create a political or economic bias by half-truths or other distortion. Mention should perhaps be made also of the instructive features of much of the advertising of processes and products. We need not minimize the values of advertising and its ethically defensible aspects in our rigorous criticism of its shortcomings."

even in its present-day form, which has overcome much that was unjust in the capitalism of the nineteenth century—is that it seems to be a structure in which particular habits of consumption are forced on a community and on the world by the requirements of the productive system itself. To some extent we may be in the position where we are forced to consume what we do not need in order to keep the system of production on an even keel. If this is the only way to preserve an economy favorable to political and cultural freedom, we may have to accept it. But it is well to recognize that if this means that the choices and the scale of values in our society are to be controlled in large part by the sheer momentum of this dynamic system of production, the price may be great.

14

Christian Ethics and Forms of Economic Power

by John C. Bennett

Other volumes of this study have emphasized the extent to which the ethical problems of contemporary economic life have to do with the behavior of groups that exercise power over the economy and over the destiny of the nation. Only on rare occasions in this country does the use of power result in overt violence, though the record of violence used by both management and labor during our earlier history was a grim one. The two forms of power most in evidence today are the economic power that comes from control over essential factors of production or resources, and the effort to win political power that enables various groups to control legislation and administration. Always in the background is the power that comes from the capacity to influence public opinion.

There is in the United States no trend toward a real and widespread monopoly of power by any of the major economic groups. There is always a tendency to complain that at a particular point such a monopoly exists; and this may be true for short periods, but there are usually balancing forces which correct this tendency. These balancing forces may be of the same kind as those they balance, as is the case when there is direct business competition or when there is a balance between organized labor and organized management. But

there is also the use of political power to check economic power. Sometimes in the period of the Roosevelt and Truman administrations the influence of the President and other top political leaders was able to counteract the dominant influences in the press and other opinion-forming agencies.

The fact of power is one of the primary realities to be accepted by the Church and by those who seek to interpret Christian ethics. There is a type of Christian idealism that attempts to bypass this primary reality by emphasizing standards that are applicable only to completely voluntary personal relationships. This is not surprising, since Christian love can be fully embodied only in such relationships. On the other hand, the Christian has responsibility to do his best in all relationships. As a member of an organized group that has power to defend its interests, power to influence national policy, power to make decisions that affect the welfare of other groups, his responsibility for the way in which his group uses its power is an essential aspect of his own moral life as a person.

Power is not itself evil; but it does bring with it great temptations. It should be kept under criticism from within, and it should be balanced by the power of other groups. This balance of power must itself be in a framework of law designed to regulate the actions of all groups in the public interest. Notice the emphasis here given to three kinds of check on power: an inner moral check, a natural check by other groups that can defend their interests, and a check by the larger community, partly through the influence of public opinion and partly through law.

There is nothing in the structure I am describing that is distinctively Christian; but it is in harmony with Christian teaching about human nature, which always emphasizes both the moral possibilities of men and their tendency to give undue weight to their own interests—with consequent need of

restraint. It also provides an opportunity for Christian action, for action that is inspired by love and undertaken for the general welfare. In this context we always have the responsibility to try to discover where justice lies in the conflict between interests.

It is a mistake to present the ethical problem as though it involved only conflicts of interest. It is true that in the short run these conflicts bulk large. There are ways in which many groups are tempted to gamble on being able to cash in on an immediate advantage for their own permanent benefit at the expense of others. Besides, any solution of a particular conflict is likely to involve real and often unfair losses to some of the parties to the conflict. But it is also true that in the long run there are great areas of common interest or mutual interest. It often requires both moral sensitivity and intellectual flexibility to discover them. In the long run all groups do depend on the economic well-being of the community as a whole. Employers and employees have a common interest in the solvency of a particular enterprise. The purchasing power among all groups that is necessary for the prosperity of any group is itself a mark of the economic well-being of the community as a whole. None of us are "economic men," and we do have a common interest in the moral health of the community, in its freedom from bitter social cleavages, in the stability of free political institutions, in the presence within the community of common loyalties and a sense of fellowship.

In a treatment of economic ethics from a Christian point of view the emphasis should be on the subordination of one's own economic interest to the welfare of the community as a whole—including, of course, these noneconomic aspects of its welfare. Yet it is important for the Christian to realize that there are limits to what he can expect of the economic behavior of large-scale groups that are morally mixed and that

must operate on the basis of common-denominator morality. This common-denominator morality may be above the morality of many individuals, but it will always be on a lower level than morality that is controlled by Christian sensitivity. The Christian has to recognize also that his membership in such groups involves moral responsibilities to the group that cannot be ignored, though they should be given a secondary place in his life as a whole.

The large-scale economic group to which the churches during the past half century have given most support is the labor movement. This may seem to many readers a surprising statement, since the lay leadership of most American Protestant denominations during that period has been closer to the business community than to labor. This interest in the labor movement has been characteristic of the national leaders of the denominations, of the Federal Council of Churches, and of others who have been most articulate in interpreting Christian social ethics. It has not necessarily represented attitudes that have been dominant within the membership of the Protestant churches. This situation reflects a persistent problem within Protestantism. Local churches do reflect the interests and the opinions of those economic groups that are dominant among their members. They do not often bring to their members a distinctively Christian social ethic that counteracts the influence of prevailing opinion in the community. Often the minister disagrees with this prevailing opinion; but his authority on social issues is limited. As one moves away from the local churches to the leadership of the larger units of the Church, one finds a different atmosphere, in which there is a definite effort to counteract the pressure of class interests, and to find distinctively Christian guidance concerning controversial social issues.

The story of the relation of the churches on this level to the labor movement during the first half of this century is

instructive. During the long period in which the labor movement was struggling for its existence it was considered the duty of those who sought to lead the mind of the Protestant churches to give labor as strong support as possible. When labor became a movement with great economic and political power, there had,to be less emphasis on support for labor and more emphasis on the health of the economy as a whole in the interest of all groups.

In the early days of the labor movement it was relatively easy to decide to give support to the cause of labor. In 1908 Walter Rauschenbusch, after discussing the moral limitations of the "business class" and the "professional class," wrote: "But there is another class to which that conception of organized fraternity is not only a moral ideal, but the hope of bread and butter; with which it enlists not only religious devotion, but involves salvation from poverty and insecurity and participating in the wealth and culture of modern life for themselves and their children" (*Christianity and the Social Crisis*, p. 403). He referred to the working class. Today we have to discount these words to some extent, because they reflect the optimism of the period; but the main point was valid. Labor, in its struggle to organize effective labor unions, was on the side of a greater justice to be embodied in the community as a whole. The individual worker was helpless in bargaining with a corporation, but the collective power of labor made it possible to balance in some measure the power of employers. The labor movement provided an alternative to exploitation on the one hand and to paternalism on the other. It made it possible for the workers to obtain a status of freedom and dignity denied them completely in the early period of capitalism.

Roman Catholic social ethics has, since the encyclicals of Pope Leo XIII, put more stress than Protestant teaching on the ethical significance of the labor movement. This has been

true especially in this country, because of the much greater proportion of the members of that Church in the ranks of the industrial workers. The Catholic clergy have encouraged Catholic workers to join unions, and have helped to train their members to become union leaders. Protestants have been far less active in following through on their basic teaching concerning the moral claims of organized labor. Yet it would be consistent for Protestants to insist on the moral responsibility of Protestant workers ordinarily to join labor unions and to work for their improvement from within.

One of the best examples of Protestant teaching about the responsibility of Protestant workers for labor unions is to be found in a report of a Presbyterian commission which was adopted as a resolution by the Presbyterian General Assembly (U.S.A.) in 1944.[1] This report was prepared by a representative group of churchmen after two years of study. It came from a denomination that is on the whole conservative, with a relatively small proportion of industrial workers among its members. We can regard this report as a remarkable example of the efforts some churches have made on the national level to see beyond the economic interests of their own constituencies. The report as a whole well expresses the reasons for regarding labor unions as indispensable for the welfare and the dignity of their members and as "a primary agent of democracy." The report then considers the question of the responsibility of a Christian to join a union. The answer given is as follows:

"We believe the Christian Church must confront its members who are employees with their obligation to consider their relationship to a labor union in the light of the Christian principle of social responsibility. We believe industrial relations generally stand a stronger possibility of improvement when management and labor are organized. The good that

[1] The Church and Industrial Relations, Board of Christian Education of the Presbyterian Church in the U.S.A., Philadelphia.

follows upon such organization works for the benefit of those who assume neither the obligations nor the responsibilities of union membership, which gives the labor movement social value and ethical validity." This statement lays down no law, but it does strongly suggest that refusal to join a labor union may be a refusal to accept an obligation.

Today the struggle of labor for the right to organize is won in most parts of this country. The labor movement has ceased to be a "cause" to be supported on all occasions because it represented those who were struggling for minimum rights, and has become one of several established groups with power in our economy. The issues at stake in strikes are often not so clear as they were in the earlier days of struggle. It is more difficult to determine what is just; for example, the issue of contributory versus noncontributory pension schemes is more difficult than the issue of the right to organize. Jurisdictional strikes are rightly condemned by the community. Christians in the labor movement need to be aware of the demands of the Christian ethic on themselves as well as on management. Christian responsibility within the labor movement calls for emphasis on democratic processes within unions, on faithful adherence to contracts, and on the concern by unions for the welfare of the public as a whole.

Those of us who do not belong to labor unions should not forget the great significance of their social contribution, which was emphasized so much when they were fighting for their existence. We should not forget the long and bitter struggle labor has had in this country to obtain elementary rights, and that this struggle still continues in parts of the South. We should always remember that whenever there is an industrial conflict the very nature of labor's power often seems to put labor in the wrong. The strike or the threat to strike is an essential element in its power, but a strike is easily made to seem an act directed against the community, while the employer can sit tight and appear to be on the side of the community.

Yet each side is exercising its strategic form of power. There is a bias against labor in the American press that makes the most of the situation. In any industrial dispute one of the most important contributions of the Church is the provision of opportunities by which the case for both sides can be fully and fairly expressed. Christians should not be uncritical advocates of labor; but they should be as clear as they ever were about the necessity of effective labor unions. The Christian employer should understand the tendency of all men to misuse power, and hence the unhealthy aspect of most situations that give employers power over others that is not checked by a labor union.

The strength of organized labor as one of the power elements in 1953 should be recognized; but the question needs to be raised of how secure this power is. What would a long period of unemployment do to the power of the labor unions? What would happen if those in centers of political power should at some future time desire to cripple the unions, and should take advantage of a falling off of employment to do so? Christians who belong to labor unions have a responsibility to keep them under criticism; but they also have a responsibility to defend them against those who seek to undermine them, and they should have the help of all their fellow Christians who recognize the truth of what has been said here about the moral claims of labor unions.

The volume in this series by Professor Bowen[2] deals admirably with the ethical problems involved in the way businessmen use their power. Much as their power is limited today by government and by labor and other organized groups, the power of businessmen to make decisions remains very great. They have power to affect public opinion, because of their influence over the press and the other media of communication. They are often able to exercise power through control

[2] *Soc. Resp.*

of government. Two less tangible controls are operative to limit their power. One such control arises from the fact that the public has come to be very sensitive to obvious abuses of power by the leaders of business; the other is that the structure of business has itself been so altered that, as Professor Bowen says, there is "broadened participation in decision making" (p. 99). He says that "the tyrannical individualist, 'the big boss,' is rapidly disappearing as an important figure in the American scene. In his place we have the 'business leader,' who functions as the coordinator of a complex network of boards, committees, conferences, reviewing agencies, and subordinate line officials, and who carries out his task with the advice of a host of specialized staff officers and outside consultants" (p. 100).

This concept of the corporation as a center of power with its own inner checks on arbitrariness and on antisocial behavior, because of the many persons involved in its decisions and because of the wide publicity given to its life, is something new, which those who interpret Christian ethics have not yet done much to evaluate. This taming of the American corporation has been in considerable measure the result of outside forces, of years of government regulation, of the pressure of labor's power, and of the influence of a public opinion made suspicious of business during the 1930s.

But something important has taken place in the attitudes and motives of business leaders themselves. Today they are managers rather than owners. They have an interest in the efficiency and in the welfare of the corporation with which they are identified, and that welfare includes both the morale of labor and the corporation's long-term reputation with the public. This "management motive" is distinctively different from the crude forms of the "profit motive," which in an earlier period was sometimes consistent with milking the corporation itself for private gain. Then, too, many leaders

of business have a deep concern for the public interest, and are open-minded concerning economic changes that would have shocked their predecessors. As Professor Bowen says, "the day of plunder, human exploitation, and financial chicanery by private businessmen has largely passed. And the day when profit maximization was the sole criterion of business success is rapidly fading. We are entering an era when private business will be judged solely in terms of its demonstrable contribution to the general welfare. Leading thinkers among businessmen understand this clearly. For them, therefore, the acceptance of obligations to workers, consumers, and the general public is a condition for survival of the free-enterprise system" (p. 52).

I do not doubt the essential truth of Professor Bowen's statement; but Christian businessmen need to recognize the importance of his final words. Leaders of business have learned a great deal under the threat of losing their power; but how long will they remember what they have learned under those conditions? The ethical responsibility of businessmen today should lead to a habit of self-criticism, which does not easily accompany the methods used to "sell" business to the public. We cannot assume that the present enlightenment among business leaders will persist without continued outside pressure. Furthermore, we cannot be sure that some of it is not a by-product of prosperity. The temptations may be greater if competition to survive becomes keener. Not even the many participants in decisions will necessarily guard corporations against antisocial conduct if government becomes lax, and if in a period of growing unemployment all but a few become afraid for their jobs. The economic power over those in the lower echelons of management can easily be a threat to their integrity. The churches should welcome the evidence of moral self-discipline in business; but they should not be less interested in the continued need of external checks. They

should be especially critical of the self-praise of business, when it is combined with an absolute identification of Christianity with the system of free enterprise.

I have said nothing about farm groups and others that exercise power in our economy. Farmers have learned how to use political pressure to defend themselves. Christians who seek to find their way as farmers in the power struggles are right in seeking justice for the farmer; but they are easily tempted to overlook the extent to which the farmer in America has been able to create vested interests of his own. There is a tendency among farmers to assume a degree of innocence in contrast to all who dwell in cities—both businessmen and industrial workers. This has led to a measure of moral unreality in the discussion of many issues.

One other aspect of this whole discussion of the ethics of power groups needs to be stressed: the responsibility of the members of these groups to the groups as well as to the community as a whole. This is particularly true of those who are chosen as leaders and representatives of the groups. The management of the corporation does have a responsibility to the stockholders that limits its right to do all it might choose to do for other groups and for the public; and the leaders of labor unions and of farm organizations have similar responsibilities. These responsibilities are morally subordinate in the life of an individual Christian, but they cannot be merged into an undifferentiated responsibility to all groups in general. The Christian subordination of this responsibility can be expressed in two ways. It should involve the effort to persuade those to whom one is responsible to accept a higher standard for the group. When that proves to be impossible, there may be occasions on which it is necessary to resign.

The situation in principle is not unlike that of a Christian statesman in his relation to foreign policy. He is a trustee for his own nation, and he cannot act only on the basis of his

own personal ideals. He has the responsibility to persuade his nation to accept a policy that is consistent with his own conscience; but if he fails, he may have to resign. Such a negative protest is of course a last resort. It may in the long run help to change public opinion, but it will leave the field free for those whose consciences are less sensitive.

As I have observed the attitudes of the representatives of the major segments of our economy—labor, business, and agriculture—I have noticed a very strong tendency for all three to be resentful of criticism from the outside. The representatives of agriculture are less articulate, but I remember an occasion when they refused to admit the degree of prosperity that has come to many farmers. Both labor and business are engaged in giving accounts of themselves that are too good to be true. Both are caught up in the practice of public relations that too often consist of a process of selection that makes things appear better than they are. Within the orbit of the Church there is no place for these pretty pictures of life. Though there is ample room for gratitude for every moral advance, there is also need for Christians in all social groups to begin by confessing their own sins rather than the sins of their neighbors, competitors, or opponents.

STATE INTERVENTION AND FREE ENTERPRISE

The most controversial ethical issues that arise in our economy usually lead at some point to the question as to where it is right for the state to intervene in economic life. The discussion of this subject has been anticipated in what has been said about economic systems. Those who are advocates of logical or consistent economic systems have ready answers to the questions that arise in this area. The emphasis of this chapter, and indeed of this whole study, is on the need to avoid the conventional stereotypes of a consistent capital-

ism or a consistent socialism, and to accept the principle of a mixed economy that will involve both private enterprise and intervention by the state. This is not in itself helpful, for every decision must depend on the way in which these two elements are mixed. Yet it does make a difference when we renounce all panaceas and doctrinaire ways of thinking that assume that the more planning by the state the better, or that unfettered private enterprise would provide its own sufficient automatic controls. To present the matter in this way does not mean that we are lost in a sea of complete relativism with no principles to guide us. I shall try to outline the chief considerations that may help us to find our way as Christians.

We have seen that there are sound reasons for giving large place to free enterprise in our economy. One is the fact that it has proved itself to be so productive. Still more important is the value of having many centers of initiative and economic power. Other forms of freedom in the culture are favored by this form of economic freedom. Both private enterprise governed by the profit incentive and cooperative enterprises which are also privately owned are favorable to pluralism and freedom.

These two reasons for giving an important place to free enterprise are based on modern economic and political experience, and are in no way inevitable Christian judgments; but, in so far as they are discovered to be true, Christians should take them into account. There may be situations in which emergency conditions, or the need of central planning to raise quickly a low living standard, may reduce to a minimum the areas of free enterprise in a nation. Tolerance of the economic experiments of other nations is much needed today in this country. But in the long run Christians in countries that have turned toward socialism will probably find themselves defending at least a limited place for free enterprise in economic life.

It is natural for us to be vividly aware of the threat to freedom from the totalitarian state that seeks to control the whole culture. Modern technology has provided such instruments of power as the worst tyrants in earlier periods did not possess. Centralized economic planning by the state has been a feature of totalitarianism on the right and on the left. But all totalitarian states have also been characterized by mass movements controlled by an emotionally charged ideology and a fanatical faith. This is one of the essential instruments of power in a totalitarian society. When this is absent, the gradual increase in the state's economic functions is unlikely to lead to totalitarianism. It is desirable in all this discussion of the functions of the state in this country to recognize that the greatest threat to freedom at present comes from demagogues who capitalize on the fears and frustrations of the American people growing out of the international situation, rather than from any particular experiments in government intervention in economic life.

Christians of necessity emphasize the limits of the state. The state is limited because it always stands under the purposes and the judgment of God. No form of idolatry is worse than the tendency to absolutize the state. The state is limited because it is not to be identified with the community—it is an instrument of the community. There are other associations and institutions in the community that have their own inner life, which the state must not seek to control. This can be seen most clearly in the case of the church and the university. These limits of the state's authority need to be coupled with distribution of power within the state itself, and the recognition of the desirability of giving many functions to local and regional political authorities. Division of powers within the structure of the national state is a final protection for the freedom of citizens from arbitrariness on the part of one department of government. A good state will zealously guard

the freedom of political minorities, of nonpolitical associations, and of the individual conscience. On this level of principle, issues are relatively clear; but when we seek to relate these principles to concrete policies we find ourselves beset by difficult dilemmas.

In the case of the church and the university it is usually easy to say in advance what the state should not do. It should never control in any way the worship or the teaching of the church—subject to the one reservation that there are some religious practices that conflict with a law to which the state cannot admit exceptions without apparently denying one of its essential responsibilities. The sanctioning of polygamy and the refusal of parents on religious grounds to allow their children to be immunized against disease are examples. These are marginal, but they raise tantalizing questions of principle.

The state should not interfere in the inner life of a university to determine what is true in the subjects taught. The stand made by most academic communities that they should discipline themselves in connection with subversive teaching also raises acute problems, especially when their administrations yield to public clamor; but the issue of subversion is an exceptional issue in the life of the university.

When we come to economic life I doubt that there is any type of economic activity that should never be undertaken by the state under any circumstances. For the state to decide what a university should teach about history is to impair or destroy the inner life of the university. But for the state to decide to undertake the manufacture and distribution of any particular products or to provide any particular services is not to destroy the values of those products or those services. The development and distribution of electric power, for example, by the state or any public agency, whether expedient or not, violates no principle. The argument against such action by the state has to do with degrees of efficiency and

with the danger of uniting or concentrating political and economic power at one point. This kind of argument does not involve an assumption of the inherent incompatibility of functions of the state and economic activities.

The state is the only agency that has the authority over a wide enough area, and the power to act effectively on a large enough scale, to cope with many of the problems that emerge in our complicated modern economy. Some problems have to be dealt with on a national basis or not at all. Also there must be authority to secure simultaneous action by the many parties involved. The development of technology has greatly broadened the area within which this kind of simultaneous action is required. Many problems call for action on a world scale; and these are today most difficult because economic nationalism is still the rule among nations—not least in our own when we come to deal with issues of trade and tariffs.

Another result of the development of technology is the growth of vast units of private economic power; and only the national state is strong enough to keep these great enterprises from abusing their power. Strict regulation by the state, or ownership by society through some agency created by the state, becomes the only alternative to a private monopoly so powerful that it is a threat to the economic welfare and to the freedom and opportunity of the people. It is interesting to note that in spite of the Roman Catholic opposition to socialism, Pope Pius XI took account of this factor of inordinate private economic power and admitted that some enterprises should be publicly owned. He said: "For it is rightly contended that certain forms of property must be reserved to the state, since they carry with them an opportunity of domination too great to be left to private individuals without injury to the community at large" (Quadragesimo Anno, par. 114).

There has developed in recent years a type of economic in-

dividualism that condemns almost all action by the state in economic life, and does so in the name of freedom. Several organizations provide much literature for the clergy defending this doctrine as the Christian understanding of society. It opposes state initiative in the promotion of economic stability. It rejects completely the effort of the state to secure for the whole population a minimum standard of living, through such measures as the present social security system. It emphasizes out of all proportion the coercive aspect of governmental action, and sees only evil in the use of the taxing power to correct inequalities in the distribution of wealth. Most of the economic functions assumed by the state during the past half-century are regarded as stepping stones to an oppressive socialism.

There are two positive assumptions that underlie this rejection of action by the state. The first is the assumption of the adequacy of the self-regulating elements in a totally free economy. The second is the assumption that voluntary action is always morally better than action that has the coercive power of the state behind it. The first assumption is strangely abstract, and has no relevance to the actual conditions under which we live. Under those conditions, if there is no coordinating action by the state, it is inconceivable that we can avoid socially disastrous swings of deflation and inflation. I believe all the writers in these volumes would agree on this point. The second assumption is ethically wrong, if it means in practice that we are to prefer voluntary action to action by the state even if the former proves to be totally inadequate to meet the situation.

There is a historic Christian doctrine concerning the state, which is often stated in a form that is repellent, but it has an element of truth in it when seen in this context. I refer to the doctrine that the state exists on account of man's sin. I believe that this is not the whole truth; but, as over against

this optimistic voluntarism, it emphasizes an important truth. Men are too sinful in their selfishness and greed, or in their complacency and indifference, to do enough voluntarily to meet the needs of those who are victims of defects or inadequacies in our institutions. The requirement that action be simultaneous by all parties concerned, if it is to be adequate, means that without coercion applied to recalcitrant minorities no effective results are possible.

The state is often an instrument of freedom for large sections of the population. There are times when it is the only means of rescuing them from the tyranny of circumstances. Provisions for social security suggest how through the state a community can plan in advance that all of its citizens may be comparatively free from or not reduced to misery by the purely external hazards of life. Most families cannot by their own efforts protect themselves at this point. The state through public education helps to provide opportunities that are the condition of freedom to children who would otherwise be tragically limited and lacking in freedom. The function of the state in helping society to control the business cycle, so as to prevent periods of large-scale unemployment and the impoverishment of great segments of the population through inflation, is a way of preserving real freedom. Freedom for those who are strong may be served by curtailing the activity of the state, but freedom for the great majority depends in part on what the state can do to provide opportunity for the development of their capacities and to defend them against economic forces beyond their control.

The totalitarian developments of our time have come not because people have decided to strengthen the state in order to have its help in solving social problems. In many countries they have come because such problems have gone unsolved for too long, because governments were too weak to meet the crises thrust on them. Such situations of governmental weak-

ness have led to the development of mass movements like national socialism and communism, which through false promises and well-timed violence have established their tyrannical systems. Those who oppose all significant action by the state in economic life have much responsibility for the existence of the neglected problems that are the real invitation to an oppressive "statism."

In this discussion of the role of the state in economic life it is occasionally necessary to shift one's emphasis. Christian ethics knows no universal formula by which to draw the line between state action and private initiative. The churches will have to be sensitive to the values that are neglected or threatened by the prevailing tendency at any given time. It may seem that Christian teaching is too often negative—a "no" to this extreme and a "no" to its opposite. That is often true. The Christian purpose for society is positive, but it does not lead to a discovery in advance of exactly the right way of serving or reconciling all the many values involved in it. But whenever a particular wrong is done, whenever there are human victims, whenever the spiritual freedom of persons is threatened, Christian minds should become especially alert to the damage that is being done.

If in this country during the past few years there has been too great readiness to call on the federal government to assume responsibility, a shift in emphasis is called for. But this shift will be constructive only if those who guide it care for all the values that are involved and for all groups of the people who are affected. We can expect little from those guides who put all their emphasis on freedom and who seem to care only for the freedom of the economically strong.

I shall have accomplished what I intended to do in these pages if both the extreme individualists and the extreme collectivists who read them feel that I have yielded too much to their opponents.

OUR USE OF PERSONAL WEALTH AND INCOME

There is one final ethical problem that every Christian faces in his own life: his use of whatever property or income he has. One basic principle that has always governed Christian thinking about property is that nothing we possess is ours to use as we choose without qualification. One way of saying this has been to affirm that God alone is the owner of all property. This of itself does not give us much guidance, but it does destroy that hard sense of ownership that so easily becomes an obstacle to any ethical sensitivity in relation to property. The only absolute Christian law that stems from this basic conviction concerning God as the ultimate owner of all things is that each one of us is responsible to God for the use of wealth. This doctrine of stewardship has become conventional in the churches; but in practice it is usually so diluted that, if the Christian gives a tenth of his income to the church, he becomes in effect the absolute owner of the nine tenths that remain. The high income taxes to which we are accustomed probably increase our tendency to assume that all we have left is unconditionally ours. The idea of stewardship must mean that even what we keep for ourselves is still to be used with a sense of responsibility to God.

One indirect effect of conventional Protestant teaching, especially in the Calvinist and Puritan tradition, has been to emphasize the virtue of thrift, and along with that the moral responsibility to accumulate capital for productive purposes. One of the elements in the theory that Calvinism has given special moral support to capitalism is the recognition of this tendency; which is indeed important, even though the theory based on it has often been pushed too far.

Far deeper in the Christian tradition than the Protestant sanctions of capitalism has been the distrust of all wealth. The Gospel record is full of this distrust, even though it does not

encourage us to establish for ourselves any universal law of poverty. We cannot brush off Jesus' teaching about the "eye of a needle," about the "rich fool," or about Dives and Lazarus. In this tradition wealth is regarded as a handicap to the soul, and associated with callous living in the face of the needs of others.

It is a mistake to attempt to lay down rules in this area. There is a place for corporate Christian guidance as a source of suggestion to the individual conscience, but each of us will have to find his own way. Careful budget-making by individuals or families is an ethical obligation, as well as a matter of financial prudence. It is obviously wrong to follow the line of least resistance and assume that we have a right to all we can get; or that we should spend all of it on ourselves, except for a small percentage that decency requires us to give to various philanthropies. The decision as to how we use what we are pleased to call our own is an ethical question; it is one of the ways in which we *act*. Sensitivity to the needs of others, self-criticism concerning any special privilege we possess, resistance to the tendency to multiply our own needs with increased income and with the conventional pressures to "keep up" with our neighbors—these are all important guides to decision. If there is one common use of wealth and income that needs to be morally rejected more completely than any other, it is the use of wealth and income for purposes of proud display at the expense of the feelings of others.

There is a Christian group in Scotland that has established for itself the rule that its members should never spend on themselves and their families more than the national average. This is suggested here as only an illustration of the kind of drastic thinking that is needed on this issue. There is no distinctively Christian reason for choosing the national average rather than the average income among the people of all nations; it was chosen because it represents a standard that is

within the range of practicality. Any effort to apply it should take account of distinctive needs and responsibilities. It does establish a point above which all that we spend on ourselves should be watched with special care.

Christian love does not mean a sentimental dispensing of charity; nor does it mean a disregard for all considerations of self-development or a willingness to sacrifice the welfare of one's family. It does involve a willingness to scale down our living standard; to give to causes and institutions that depend on private support; to welcome the justice that is often embodied in public taxation; to support economic changes that may be costly to us if they are in the public interest; to share and share again wisely and generously.

What I have written inevitably reflects the situation in America. It is important to say again what has been suggested at various points in this discussion: that a Christian writing in different circumstances would place his emphasis differently. In some countries the major economic fact is that the people depend on foreign trade, and as a result their well-being depends in considerable measure on policies of our government. In some countries the tasks of postwar reconstruction and the sharing of goods that are in scarce supply necessitate greater governmental initiative than in this country. In still other countries there is a demand for national planning that will enable them to do in a few years what it has taken generations to do in the older industrialized countries in order to lift the vast majority of the people out of ancient conditions of poverty that can no longer be accepted in a spirit of fatalism. In the long run it may be seen to be the terribly costly contribution of communism that it has forced those who oppose it to find solutions in our time for this ancient problem. American Christians, as they view these different situations, should avoid hasty judgments concern-

ing what economic institutions are right for other countries. They are called to two definite responsibilities of their own: to support in American foreign relations those economic policies that express a concern for the welfare of other peoples; and to press for a continuance in our own country of the movement toward an economy that benefits all segments of the population.

Appendix

by HOWARD R. BOWEN

The range of ethical issues involved in economic life is as broad as the range of economic behavior itself. Yet most of these varied decisions and actions are relevant to eight basic questions. Some of these questions are concerned with the choices of individuals, others with the choices of groups. The questions are:

1. How should the economic system be organized and controlled?
2. How much should people work?
3. How should the product be divided among households?
4. What arrangements should be made for personal security?
5. What provision should be made for future generations?
6. What should be the content of current consumption?
7. What kinds of working conditions should be provided?
8. What should be our economic relationships with other countries?

Every society—regardless of its location, its place in history, the degree of its civilization, or the nature of its political institutions—must work out its own answers to these questions. Usually these answers become imbedded in culture patterns. The kinds of answers reached determine the degree to which the goals of economic life can be realized in that society.

In the remainder of this section we shall list a few of the specific issues underlying each of these eight main questions. These are the kinds of issues—many of them highly controversial—which involve ethical as well as technical considerations.

1. HOW SHOULD THE ECONOMIC SYSTEM BE ORGANIZED AND CONTROLLED?

What should be the fundamental structure of the economy? Should it be organized along lines of socialism, *laissez-faire* capitalism, or some intermediate "ism"? To what extent should in-

259

dividuals have property rights in wealth and in their own labor power, and under what limitations (if any) should these rights be exercised? What should be the scope of individual freedom with reference to consumer choice, enterprise, choice of occupations, geographic mobility, etc.? To what extent should freedom be constrained by competition, by voluntary assumption of social responsibility, by custom and informal social pressure, and by formal governmental control?

Should individuals be permitted or encouraged to organize into economic groups, such as giant corporations, labor unions, trade associations, and farm organizations? What tactics may these groups employ, and what limits should be placed on their activities? What should be the relationships between these organized groups and their individual members? What efforts should be made to achieve common understanding and mutual accommodation of these groups? What should be the relationships of owners, managers, workers, consumers, and the public in the management of enterprises? Who should have the power to control or influence the agencies of mass communication, and what limits, if any, should be placed on the exercise of this power? What principles should underlie the use of propaganda and political pressure by those who desire or oppose social change?

2. How Much Should People Work?

How large should be the real national income, and how much should people strive to increase social productivity? What percentage of the population should be gainfully employed? At what age should young people enter the labor force and old people retire? Under what conditions should women be employed outside the home? Should everyone have the right to work—even if this sometimes means that the government must supply jobs, or even that people must be given unnecessary work? Do all able-bodied persons (within certain age limits) have a duty to work? What should be the hours of labor at various times and for various classes of workers? How much time should be given over to vacations and holidays? How intensively should people work? What is the content of an "honest day's work"? How keen should be

our pursuit of efficiency? Are we overly preoccupied with high productivity, and should we be better off if we devoted less of our talent and energies to the production of goods and services?

3. How Should the Product Be Divided among Households?

Should income derived from inheritance, luck, and monopoly be reduced? Should difference in earning power due to differences in opportunity, education, home environment, health, race, and other personal characteristics be reduced? Should some minimal amount of income be available to every person? Should limitations be placed on profits or on executive compensation? Are taxes at steeply graduated rates desirable? Should the government subsidize lower-income groups through housing, school lunches, relief, family allowances, etc.? To what extent should private individuals give for charitable purposes? How much inequality of incomes is justified as a source of incentive? To what extent should each individual be responsible for his own economic status?

4. What Arrangements Should Be Made for Personal Security?

What and how much should be done to achieve greater economic stability? Does the government have an obligation to prevent fluctuations in the general level of prices, or production beyond given magnitudes? What are the responsibilities of business, labor, agriculture, investors, and consumers toward economic stability? To what extent should individuals be responsible to provide for their own contingencies? Should personal thrift be encouraged for this purpose? Should the family take greater responsibility for its members? To what extent should voluntary insurance be provided? To what extent should compulsory social insurance be provided? What should be the function of relief and charity? What are the obligations of individuals to help others? Should individuals be protected from their own mistakes? Should the risks of competition be mitigated? Should special provisions be made to protect the farmer?

5. WHAT PROVISION SHOULD BE MADE FOR FUTURE GENERATIONS?

How much of current productive effort should be devoted to building up the stock of capital goods, i.e., what should be the rate of saving? How much effort should be devoted to research and technological advancement? At what rate should natural resources be used up, and what efforts should be made to reclaim and develop natural resources? What should be the rate of population growth? What amount of resources should be devoted to public health and education? Should a given generation in a poor country be asked to make supreme sacrifices (e.g., as in prewar Russia) in order to achieve greater productivity for later generations? To what extent should these matters be determined by the free choices of individuals, or by group decision?

6. WHAT SHOULD BE THE CONTENT OF CURRENT CONSUMPTION?

Would welfare be increased if the content of our consumption were changed? Does preoccupation with material things interfere with the attainment of higher values? Should individuals be formally free to buy whatever they want, and should production be guided by these choices? Should producers or the government attempt to guide consumer choices by advertising and propaganda? Should the government control consumer choices, and if so to what extent? Should the government insure that each person has the minimal requirements for good nutrition, housing, etc.?

7. WHAT KINDS OF WORKING CONDITIONS SHOULD BE PROVIDED?

What are acceptable conditions of work with reference to physical and nervous strain, health, safety, comfort, and physical surroundings? Should work provide opportunities for creativity, aesthetic satisfaction, enlightenment, personal development, self-expression, new experience? What are acceptable human relations in the work place, including face-to-face relationships and relationships among organized groups? Should work provide fellow-

ship, sense of belonging, sense of serving one's fellow man? Should workers participate in decisions affecting them, and if so to what extent? What degree of discipline is required in the work place, and how should it be enforced? What might be done to mitigate adverse effects of some kinds of work upon family and community life? What might be done to prevent some kinds of work from degrading personality by employing base motives, deadening finer sensibilities, or requiring violations of conscience? What are acceptable human relations between business employees and customers or between businessmen and government officials?

8. What Should Be Our Economic Relationships with Other Countries?

What are the duties and responsibilities of a rich nation vis-á-vis poorer nations? Should we export capital and technical assistance, and if so under what terms? Should we provide international relief? What should be our immigration policy? Should we lower barriers to imports and encourage free trade throughout the world? Should we discriminate in our relationships with other nations according to their race, religion, and internal policies?

The foregoing is indeed a long list of questions, but it is by no means exhaustive. It is intended only to illustrate the enormous range of economic issues in which ethical considerations are important. Each of these questions must be answered partly in terms of the goals of economic life—such goals as were suggested in Chapter 4 of this book.

Index of Names

Index of Subjects

of, 103-5, 235 ff.; control of, 29,
31, 33, 53; dispersal of, 29, 31, 33,
213, 216, 247; as goal, 51, 53; in
international relations, 103, 104,
120, 130, 157-161; responsibility
of, 29, 103-5, 107, 109, 178-90,
236-240, 245
Press, the, influences on, 242; responsibility of, 9, 33, 232
Pressures, group, vii, xiv, 3, 7, 11-2,
30-1, 33, 69, 178, 179, 190, 228,
238, 245, 260
Production, conditions of, 9-10, 52,
72, 88-9, 114, 189-191; export,
100; as goal, 10, 23, 29, 52, 185,
210, 261; incentives to, 20, 220-1,
222, 223-9; mass, 216; quality of,
76-80; requiring cooperation, 50,
107; responsibility for, 9, 209, 210;
surplus, 50, 78, 230
Productivity, 69; affected by economic
policies, xiv, 20, 72; future, 125;
incentives to, 23, 39, 62, 69, 114,
262; relation to welfare, 36, 50-53,
75, 80, 187, 210, 228, 230, 260-1,
262
Profit, as motive, 19, 20, 24-5, 26,
30, 48, 73, 223-9; relation to production, 26, 73, 185, 223-5, 227;
subordination of, 26, 226, 261
Property, acquisition of, 6, 20, 185-7,
227; distribution of, 5, 20, 210-1,
213, 217-222; ownership of, 12,
26, 212; regulation of, 18, 19, 24,
25, 216, 260; taxation of, 99, 222,
230; use of, 6, 7, 18, 24, 59, 216-
217, 254-6
Prosperity, insufficiency of, 5, 48, 60

Resources, natural, 19, 59, 75, 100,
162, 211
Responsibility, of churches, see
Churches; ethical, xiv, 6, 26, 27,
29-31, 45-50, 65-7, 70-4, 77-80, 86,
97-8, 102, 104-5, 107-110, 121,
127, 129, 132-6, 145, 154, 155,
169-170, 172-9, 183-5, 191, 201-
234, 235-257; international, xiii,
99-102, 103-5, 121, 130, 179-80,

228, 230, 263; press, 9, 33, 242;
social, xii, xiii, 6, 10, 17, 18, 20,
28-9, 39, 49, 70-4, 241. See also
Ethics, Government, Individual,
Management
Revolution, Industrial, 17
Risk, 31, 32, 55, 56

Scarcity, as economic factor, 185-7
Security, as goal, 56-7, 62, 64, 65,
90, 91, 99, 113, 209, 218, 239;
old-age, 6, 85-6, 90; problems of,
74, 85-6, 87, 90, 92, 100, 188;
social, 6, 85-6, 90, 99, 117, 209,
229, 261
Self-interest, 17, 59, 185, 206; as
incentive, 20, 24, 48, 49, 223-9;
group, 228-9, 236; national, 105,
109-116, 257
Service, as motive, 11, 20, 23, 25
Socialism, 16, 21, 22, 31-2, 201, 212-
214, 259
Sociology, ix, xii, 4, 197, 199, 201
Specialization, 69, 71, 187, 192, 194
Stabilization, economic, 57, 99, 105,
114, 119, 120, 121, 127, 130,
132, 134-6, 139, 214, 222, 261
Standard of living, compared, 165-7;
material, 5, 9, 20, 102, 113, 114,
117, 129, 137, 210, 218, 219, 220,
229, 231, 248, 251; spiritual, 5
Status, social, as goal, 17, 51, 53-4,
62, 69, 77, 93, 186, 188, 225,
231, 232, 233, 261
Stewardship, 20, 27, 49, 254
Strikes, 7, 8-12, 211, 241
Systems, economic, 212; dynamic, 98,
233; international, 98; mixed,
98-9, 212-5, 246; static, 101. See
also Capitalism, Communism, Socialism

Tariffs, foreign, 126, 129, 136, 139,
141, 142, 158-9, 263; United
States, 136, 141, 143-6, 159
Taxation, attitudes toward, 65, 228,
256; for redistribution of income,
99, 168, 222, 230, 261; injustice
in, 40